LIVING FREE!

ENJOYING FREEDOM AND VICTORY IN CHRIST

A Life-transforming manual for Christian Discipleship

Revised Edition

Colin Dye

First Edition copyright © Colin Dye 2005
Revised Edition copyright © Colin Dye 2010

Kensington Temple
PO Box 54108
London
W5 9AE

All rights reserved. No part of this publication may be
reproduced, stored in a retrieval system or transmitted,
in any form or by any means electronic, mechanical
photocopying, recording or otherwise, without the written
consent of the author.

Scriptural quotations, unless otherwise stated, are from the
New King James Version. Thomas Nelson Inc. 1991

Contents

Introduction

Enjoying Freedom and Victory in Christ — Part 1

Your Devotional Life	19
The Family of God	27
Your Testimony	37
Real Change	45
The Fruit of the Spirit	57
Inner Healing	67
Handling Your Emotions	83
Walking in Freedom	97
The Spirit-filled Life	123
Serving God	131
A Word of Encouragement	139

Transformation Track — Part 2

Why Change?	147
The Dynamics of Change	151
Sharing Your Testimony	155
Renewing Your Mind	159
God Meets All Your Needs	163
Discovering Your Idolatrous Beliefs	167
Walking in Freedom	171
Choosing to Change	175
Putting-off and Putting-on	179
Making Change Stick	183

Life Issues — Part 3

Handling Emotional Problems	191
Sexual Problems	207
Marriage and Family Problems	221
Freedom from Occult Bondage	235
Developing a Healthy Self-image	243
Forgiveness and Inner Healing	251
Dealing with Drug and Alcohol Problems	261
Financial Problems	275

Appendices

(1) Breaking Strongholds of the Mind	283
(2) Emotional Problems and Mental Health	293

INTRODUCTION

An Invitation

The gospel is the power of God for your complete deliverance from sin and the total transformation of your life.

The gospel is good news. It tells of the unmerited favour of God found in his one and only Son, Jesus Christ who died on the cross that we might be forgiven all our sins and receive his gift of righteousness. Salvation is free. It comes to us by divine grace and not by human effort or religious deeds. If you are reading this book, it is probably because you have already met Jesus and believed in him for your salvation[1]. Always keep in mind, the gospel is the power of God for your complete deliverance from sin and the total transformation of your life.

For I am not ashamed of the gospel of Christ, for it is the power of God to salvation for everyone who believes, for the Jew first and also for the Greek. For in it the righteousness of God is revealed from faith to faith; as it is written, "The just shall live by faith."

Romans 1:16-17

Through a simple act of faith, you receive the righteousness of God. This guarantees your place in heaven, which can never be taken from you.

Nothing… shall be able to separate us from the love of God which is in Christ Jesus our Lord.

Romans 8:39

You receive God's free gift of salvation by faith, and by faith alone. No other condition is attached to God's promise of new life in Christ.

---

[1] If you have never put your trust in Christ personally for your salvation turn to page 13 where there is an explanation of what it means to know Christ and a prayer to help you do so.

Romans 10:9-10

...if you confess with your mouth the Lord Jesus and believe in your heart that God has raised Him from the dead, you will be saved. For with the heart one believes unto righteousness, and with the mouth confession is made unto salvation. by faith.

If you have genuinely trusted Christ for your salvation and confessed this faith before others, it means you are now in Christ and your life is totally acceptable to God. This is not of your doing, or a position you have earned. It has nothing to do with anything you have ever done, or ever could do. Only God can save you, assure you of his eternal love and bring you finally to heaven. Salvation, from start to finish, is all about the *pure grace* of God, and you receive it by *simple faith* – nothing more.

The process of change

You may have had a powerful encounter with Christ, on your own, in a church service or on an Encounter Weekend[2]. Such experiences are vitally important as you go on in your Christian life. They help you realise that Jesus Christ is real and that he is alive today.

An encounter with the Lord will always bring an experience of real freedom and deliverance in your life. You come to realise that what Jesus said is true:

Matthew 28:18-20

If the Son makes you free, you shall be free indeed.

You also begin to see for yourself the truth of these words of the apostle Paul:

2 Corinthians 5:17

Therefore, if anyone is in Christ, he is a new creation; old things have passed away; behold, all things have become new.

New creation living

Salvation is all about the pure grace of God, and you receive it by simple faith

But this truth is not just to be experienced in special moments with Christ. It applies to you every day as long as you live. Because you are a new creation in Christ, God wants you to live out that new creation life. He calls you to put off the old patterns of thinking and living and to put on the new life Christ gave you. He expects you to exchange your old ways for new ways of thinking and behaving consistent with who you are now – a new creation. He wants you to become in your daily life more like the new person you really are through your faith in Christ.

---

2 Encounter Weekends are special times of seeking God for his freedom and building strong foundations for your life in Christ.

INTRODUCTION

As you fix your focus on Christ, the Holy Spirit keeps on transforming you from the inside out, bringing real and lasting change into your life. You were completely set free from your sin and old life the moment you believed in Christ, but the practical process of becoming like Jesus takes longer. God by his grace leads you to become more and more like Jesus, from the moment you believe to the moment you finally enter heaven, where you will be with him forever. The Bible calls this process 'sanctification'.

God's plan for you

The Christian life is more than getting your 'ticket to heaven'. It is about how you live here on the earth walking as a disciple of Jesus Christ and serving him according to his plan for your life. True discipleship is 'the life that springs from grace'. The apostle Paul shows that we have been saved freely by God's grace which we receive as a gift from God, not as a reward for our own works or efforts (see *Ephesians 2:8-9*). He also shows us the life that flows from this grace and the salvation we have received: the life of good works God has prepared in advance for us to do.

For by grace you have been saved through faith, and that not of yourselves; it is the gift of God, not of works, lest anyone should boast. For we are his workmanship, created in Christ Jesus for good works, which God prepared beforehand that we should walk in them.

Ephesians 2:8-10

Living Free! is an invitation for you to join in God's plan for life transformation. It will lead you through the process of getting to know God, learning how to draw from his Word and his Spirit the power and help you need to receive deep healing for your life, to find real freedom and victory in Christ and to see his process of change happen to you from the inside out.

As you fix your focus on Christ, the Holy Spirit keeps on transforming you, bringing real and lasting change into your life.

LIFE TRANSFORMATION COURSE

Living Free! is the textbook for the LIFE TRANSFORMATION COURSE at Kensington Temple, London City Church, although it will also be of great value for you to work through on your own. The 10-week course is designed to:

- Lead you into true discipleship
- Establish real transformation of your life
- Prepare you for leadership training.

The course consists of 3 main elements:

- Weekly Teaching on topics relevant to discipleship, establishing the new lifestyle of Christ
- Life Transformation Groups led by a facilitator who will lead the group through the practical process of change

- Daily Devotionals which the person does at home keeping a journal of their fellowship with the Lord[3].

Let's see these 3 elements in more detail:

PART ONE: 10 TOPICS – presented each week by a Bible teacher and included in this book:

1. YOUR DEVOTIONAL LIFE
   - Worship
   - Prayer
   - Bible reading
   - Your daily walk

2. THE FAMILY OF GOD
   - Repentance
   - Faith
   - Baptism in water
   - Receiving the Holy Spirit
   - Belonging to the family of God

3. YOUR TESTIMONY
   - Being a witness
   - Sharing your testimony
   - The Evangelism of 3

4. REAL CHANGE
   - Who you are in Christ
   - The Lordship of Christ
   - How God brings about change in your life

5. THE FRUIT OF THE SPIRIT
   - Faith not works
   - Fruit not effort
   - The character of Christ

6. INNER HEALING

   - Acknowledging your hurt

---

[3] The *LIVING FREE! Daily Devotional* is a separate book designed to accompany the Life Transformation Course.

INTRODUCTION

- Healing for your inner pain
- Freedom through forgiving

7. HANDLING YOUR EMOTIONS
   - Understanding your emotions
   - Beneath the surface of your life
   - Thoughts, feelings and intentions
   - Identifying negative beliefs
8. FREE INDEED
   - Christ's victory
   - Freedom from evil powers
   - Freedom from soul ties
   - Freedom from curses
   - Freedom from hereditary bondage

9. THE SPIRIT-FILLED LIFE
   - Power from on high
   - The enabling of the Holy Spirit
   - Proof producing power
   - Being filled with the Holy Spirit

10. SERVING GOD
    - Fruitfulness
    - Faithfulness
    - Obedience
    - Leadership

PART TWO: THE TRANSFORMATION TRACK – small group work led by a facilitator working from notes found in the second part of this book.

Be transformed by the renewing of the mind   *Romans 12:2*

The 'transformation track' will lead you through three areas of change in the course of a 10-week programme. This will then equip you to continue the process of change as you go on in your life of discipleship in Christ.

Areas of change:

1. Developing an enjoyable and fulfilling daily devotional life
2. Discovering and changing the negative patterns of thinking which are the source of your negative patterns of living
3. Walking in freedom as you experience one major change in your life. You will be choosing a specific area you need to change from the *Life Issues* list.

LIFE ISSUES:

1. Handling Emotional Problems
   - Fear and Anxiety
   - Bitterness and Anger
   - Depression and Loss of Hope

2. Sexual Problems
   - Learning to Handle Your Sexuality
   - Freedom from Homosexual Sin

3. Marriage and Family Problems

4. Freedom from Occult Bondage

5. Developing a Healthy Self-image

6. Forgiveness and Inner Healing

7. Dealing with Drug and Alcohol Problems

8. Financial Problems

Eternal life comes from knowing Jesus Christ as God the Son and Lord of all.

PART THREE: YOUR SPIRITUAL JOURNAL – to be undertaken at home but shared each week in the groups.

The *LIVING FREE! Daily Devotional* (available as a separate publication[4]) enables you to record your spiritual journey over a period of 4 months. Each day there is:

- A Scripture passage to read
- A brief explanation of the passage
- A key thought to meditate on
- A prayer to pray
- An important discipleship step to take
- A place for you to record your thoughts and the things God is saying to you.
- A place for questions, your thoughts and action points to follow up.

The 120 days is divided into 4 sections dealing with the following issues:

1. Assurance and Blessing
2. Guidance and Security
3. Power and Authority
4. Obedience and Surrender

---

[4] To receive a copy of the *LIVING FREE! Daily Devotional*, please ask you facilitator or contact the KT Bookshop at KTshop.com

INTRODUCTION

FINDING JESUS

Getting to know Jesus Christ as your Saviour and Lord is the most significant thing you can ever do in life. This is how your eternal destiny is settled. Jesus made it clear what eternal life is and how we may obtain it.

This is eternal life, that they may know you, the only true God, and Jesus Christ whom you have sent. — John 17:3

It is clear that Jesus is talking about a personal relationship with Abba God, our Father. This comes from knowing Jesus Christ as God the Son and Lord of all.

Jesus also made clear that the Father had sent him into the world so that the world could be saved and that he was the only way back to the Father.

Jesus said to him, "I am the way, the truth, and the life. No one comes to the Father except through me." — John 14:6

This could only mean one of three things: Jesus was highly arrogant, deeply deluded or he was speaking the truth. The way Jesus dealt with people shows that he was humble, compassionate and sound in mind. So, he must have been speaking the truth – truth he was prepared to lay down his life to demonstrate. The Father sent his Son to save the world by dying on the cross and Jesus accepted this purpose gladly. He refused to save himself so that we could be saved.

Now my soul is troubled, and what shall I say? 'Father, save me from this hour'? But for this purpose I came to this hour. — John 12:27

The Bible teaches that when Jesus died on the cross he didn't die for his own sins, but he became the substitute sacrifice for the sins of the world.

For he made him who knew no sin to be sin for us, that we might become the righteousness of God in Him. — 2 Corinthians 5:21

Isaiah the prophet spoke about this 700 years before Christ was born:

But he was wounded for our transgressions, he was bruised for our iniquities; the chastisement for our peace was upon him, and by his stripes we are healed. All we like sheep have gone astray; we have turned, every one, to his own way; and the LORD has laid on him the iniquity of us all. — Isaiah 53:5-6

By the sacrifice of his life, Jesus opened up God's way of salvation and all we have to do is to turn to him and accept his offer of salvation.

John 3:16

For God so loved the world that he gave his only begotten Son, that whoever believes in him should not perish but have everlasting life.

Your sin was dealt with at the cross. Now you trust Christ alone for your salvation.

God's judgement on your sin was dealt with at the cross and when you accept what God has done for you, you trust Christ alone for your salvation.

If you want to receive God's free gift of salvation and forgiveness, pray this prayer of salvation and then immediately tell someone that you have done it:

"Dear Lord Jesus, thank you for dying for me on the cross for my sins and for being raised again from the dead so that I might be saved. I acknowledge that I am a sinner and that I need to be saved. I turn away from my sin and my past life and turn to you now. I accept you now as my Saviour and my Lord and I receive the gift of eternal life. Thank you for becoming my Saviour today. Help me live the rest of my life for you. Amen."

Walking With Jesus

Walking with Jesus is real freedom! He brings freedom from despair, bondage and negative thinking. His presence in your life is the antidote to all the poisons that life brings. He leads you out of darkness to walk in the glorious light of his freedom.

This is the freedom and liberty of the children of God who know Christ. It is not just the promise of freedom to come, but a real taste of that freedom now. Jesus explained that mere intellectual knowledge of the gospel doesn't bring freedom. Rather, it comes by knowing him personally and experiencing his freedom in your daily life and living.

John 8:32

And you shall know the truth, and the truth shall make you free.

This freedom in Christ has to do with finding Christ's power to be effective in your life. And your mind is the primary battleground.

Free thinking

A humanist philosophy originated in Western Europe around 300 years ago called, 'enlightenment thinking'. The world, through this idea, is proclaiming 'freedom' to the captives. But what kind of freedom is it? Are they showing us how to be free from the bondages of sin and guilt? Do they offer freedom from the enslavement of addiction, hopelessness, anger or injustice? No! They are proclaiming a freedom *from* God, not the freedom *of* God. They insist that we must be freed from his values, his life and his purposes.

Think how incredible this is. People actually believe that to be 'released' from the loving embrace of the Father's unconditional love is freedom! This reminds us of Jesus' story about the son who ran away from home. He rejected what he thought was the boring life of bondage at home on the farm only to find that life in 'Sin City' was not so good after all.

Fresh from the stench and humiliation of the pigpen, he found what he had missed all along – freedom at home. Ironically, he was willing to come home as a hired servant – the very thing he thought he had run away from. But he became a son set free, not a slave in chains.

Now is the time for lost sons and daughters to return home and find freedom in the Father's house – to experience the loving embrace and acceptance of God who paid a high price for our reconciliation to him. The Father wants to restore us so that we can live in true freedom.

The Father wants to restore us to himself so that we can live in true freedom.

Real freedom

Walking in wholeness and real freedom begins by rejecting all God-diminishing thoughts from our minds. It means reversing the curse of the tragic deception we, by nature, have all bought into – that life without God works.

This deception is at the root of sin's existence in the world. Eve bought into it wholesale. Tricked by the cunning serpent-like nature of Satan she believed that rejecting God's way would bring her the 'wisdom' she was lacking. Adam too rejected God's truth and went his own way and so the entire human race fell into sin.

Sin gripped the entire human race and brought its bitter fruit: shame, rejection, loneliness and isolation. Its violence soon became clear as hatred, murder and bloodshed took their hold on humanity. The same deception is with us today. We are all heirs of that same lie. At the root of our rebellion is the belief that we can find fulfilment and satisfaction apart from God. Satan's poison still flows in the human bloodline. Rather than the freedom it guaranteed, sin brought bondage, decay and death. What happened to the promised utopia? It didn't come. In fact, paradise was lost and could never be regained until Jesus came to deal with the sin problem.

At the root of our rebellion is the belief that we can find fulfilment and satisfaction apart from God.

That's why we need to be washed and purified by the blood of Jesus. He was the only human who, being God as well as man, lived against the lie. When Jesus came, he broke this spiral of despair by conquering sin, death, hell and the grave!

Shaking off the broken chains

The freedom we have in Christ is freedom from the damage that sin does to us. Jesus came to undo what the devil had done to us. This means freedom from the negative emotions of fear, anger and hopelessness. We are set free from the binding habits and dehumanising bondages of sexual addiction, mental torment, anger, hatred and every other self-destructive way of thinking and living.

Jesus has started a process in our lives that will only be fully completed in heaven; nevertheless, this process brings us freedom now.

By faith we are born into the freedom that comes from God's grace. This freedom is your birthright as a believer in Jesus, but you don't automatically experience it. You first have to understand that it is yours and then actively choose to walk in it.

There is a famous illustration of a man in prison looking out through the bars of his tiny prison window longing for freedom. But what he doesn't see is that behind him the prison doors are open. He is free! All he has to do is to change his perspective and understand that he only has to get up, turn around and walk right out of the prison. But he is ignorant of his true position and state.

This is like so many Christians today. We long to be free from the things that bind us, but we don't know how to deal with them. We don't know that all we have to do is to shake off the chains that appear to be binding us, turn around and walk out of bondage unshackled and free! Just one tug at those chains and we discover they are already broken. Christ has delivered us and we can walk free. We can live free!

Spiritual and emotional wholeness

God's will for us is spiritual and emotional wholeness. This freedom is ours in Christ. Some think it is only a future freedom – that we have our sins forgiven on earth but wholeness has to wait for heaven. Jesus has started a process in our lives that will only be fully completed in heaven; nevertheless, this process brings us freedom now.

You can step onto the path of victory and march on the road to freedom. The goal of the Holy Spirit is for you to meet with him in a powerful, life-transforming way and discover this freedom every step you take on your journey with Christ. As you receive the Father's love, repent from sin in your life and experience his deliverance from every bondage, you will find the joy of living in the real freedom that is rightfully yours as a child of God.

That way you can grow and mature as a disciple of Christ and become equipped and ready to serve him in his Great Commission today and for the rest of your life on earth

TOPIC 1

YOUR DEVOTIONAL LIFE

God has called you to an intimate and personal relationship with him. He is ready to reveal himself to you, fill you with his life and love and satisfy the deepest longings of your heart.

We learn from Jesus' example to live for God's glory by worshipping him in spirit and truth.

One leader prominent in church history said, "Our hearts are restless until they find their rest in you." Worship is about knowing God deeply and recognising who he is, and this knowledge brings with it the ultimate experience of life.

Jesus spoke these words, lifted up his eyes to heaven, and said: "Father, the hour has come. Glorify your Son, that your Son also may glorify you, as you have given him authority over all flesh, that he should give eternal life to as many as you have given him. And this is eternal life, that they may know you, the only true God, and Jesus Christ whom you have sent."

John 17:1-3

Knowing and enjoying God

Jesus lived only for the glory of Abba, God the Father. This was the motivation of his life. That's why he came, that's why he lived and that's why he died. Jesus, being the Son of God, is worthy of receiving glory equal to the Father. But he came to this earth, and lived a humble life. We learn from Jesus' example to live for God's glory by worshipping him in spirit and truth as we experience his eternal life.

This life brings deep joy and all the fullness God created us to know. Some Bible teachers once put it like this. They asked the question,

In worship, we recognise God for who he is.

We see his real worth, which is associated with his glory, the 'weight' of his value, and the reality of his presence.

'What is our chief purpose in life?' They gave the following answer. The ultimate purpose of our lives is to 'know God and to enjoy him forever.'

The word 'worship' means to acknowledge the worth of someone or something. We can appreciate many good things in life – our friends and family or the gifts and talents we have ourselves or see in others. But these things are the precious and gracious gifts of God, 'who gives us all things richly to enjoy' *(1 Timothy 6:17)*. When we understand that these things come from God, the source and giver of all good things, it is natural to return thanks and appreciation to him. That way we acknowledge what is right and true and line ourselves up with the real purpose of our humanity – to live in loving, grateful relationship with God.

The Father is seeking worshippers

Jesus spoke about true worship. In worship, we recognise God for who he is. We see his real worth, which is associated with God's glory, the 'weight' of his value, and the reality of his presence. When we recognise God for who he is we give him glory or, in other words, we line ourselves up with the ultimate reality of the universe – the living, loving, giving and forgiving God who is the creator, sustainer, lord, ruler and righteous judge of all things, both visible (the physical world) and invisible (the spiritual world).

This is why God is seeking worshippers and requires us to worship him in spirit and truth.

John 4:23-24

But the hour is coming, and now is, when the true worshippers will worship the Father in spirit and truth; for the Father is seeking such to worship him. God is Spirit, and those who worship him must worship in spirit and truth.

Worship in spirit and truth

The word 'seek' means 'actively pursue' or 'desire', but it also means 'require'. God expects our worship, not for his sake, but for ours. He is not insecure about who he is, as if he needed people to praise him all the time! We owe him worship because he is God and worship aligns us with him – the ultimate reality of the universe. The ultimate reality is not matter or energy or natural law, but the personal God, who has revealed himself in creation, the Bible (the written Word) and supremely through Christ (the Personal Word).

Jesus also explains that God is not looking for worship on its own, but he is seeking worshippers – those who worship him in spirit and truth. It is all about having a deep and meaningful relationship with God. This kind of worship is spiritual, that is, a function of our human spirit as it is activated, filled and motivated by the Holy Spirit. At heart, spirituality is not about moral values, aesthetics or mystical experiences. It has nothing to do with empty religious practices or human ideas of the divine. Spirituality means worshipping God with the whole of our lives according to his revealed will (the Bible) and by the power of the Holy Spirit in us.

But true worship is also about being real. Time and again in the Bible, God speaks about those whose worship is nothing more than religious pretence. True worship comes from our heart, not like the worship spoken against in the following scriptures.

...these people draw near with their mouths and honour me with their lips, but have removed their hearts far from me, and their fear toward me is taught by the commandment of men... — Isaiah 29:13

"Now, therefore," says the LORD, "Turn to me with all your heart, With fasting, with weeping, and with mourning." So rend your heart, and not your garments; return to the LORD your God, for He is gracious and merciful, slow to anger, and of great kindness; and he relents from doing harm. — Joel 2:12-13

And you will seek me and find me, when you search for me with all your heart. — Jeremiah 29:12-14

Jesus said to him, "'You shall love the LORD your God with all your heart, with all your soul, and with all your mind.' This is the first and great commandment. And the second is like it: 'You shall love your neighbour as yourself.' On these two commandments hang all the Law and the Prophets." — Matthew 22:37-40

Talking to God in Prayer

An important aspect of your devotional life is prayer to God. This is not a complex matter – as if you have to put on a special religious voice or use religious vocabulary in order to get his attention. Prayer is simply talking to God, having a conversation with him. Remember, a conversation is two-way, so be prepared to listen to what God is saying to you as well as tell him what is on your heart.

Don't worry about anything; instead, pray about everything. Tell God what you need, and thank him for all that he has done. — Philippians 4:6 (NLT)

There are many things you will want to talk to God about. You can share with him your joys, your sorrows, your hopes and your dreams. You will want to talk to him about your failures and your weaknesses, asking him for his help and thanking him for the forgiveness he has given you in Christ. And you must also be ready to share with him your needs. It is OK to ask God. He wants you to ask him.

John 16:24

Until now you have asked nothing in My name. Ask, and you will receive, that your joy may be full.

Intercession

There are many ways of praying, but intercession is particularly important. It means that you stand before God and plead the cause of someone else. You become like an advocate in the court of heaven. You ask God to intervene on behalf of others.

Intercessors plead for the needs of:
- *The nations of the world*
- *Family and friends*
- *The lost.*

God is looking for intercessors who will care about the needs of the world, of nations and localities. God wants you to bring to him the needs of your family, your friends and your colleagues. It is particularly important to pray regularly for your spiritual leaders that God will keep them and use them powerfully.

It is also vitally important to pray for those who don't yet know Jesus as Saviour and Lord. Often, it is the prayers of loved ones and close associates that help bring people to the Lord. Begin to pray now for a list of friends, family and other contacts close to you. Ask God to reveal himself to them and for them to come to faith in Christ.

The Bible

The Bible is an amazing book. It is in fact a library of 66 books written over a period of more than 1,600 years by over 40 different authors. And yet all these writings speak with one voice – the voice of God. The ultimate author of the Bible is not men but God. That's why we call it the Word of God. The people who wrote the Bible were so divinely inspired that what they wrote was exactly what God intended for them to write as a complete and full record of his Word to us. See how the Bible describes itself in the following verses.

2 Peter 1:20-21

…knowing this first, that no prophecy of Scripture is of any private interpretation, for prophecy never came by the will of man, but holy men of God spoke as they were moved by the Holy Spirit.

2 Timothy 3:15-16

…and that from childhood you have known the Holy Scriptures, which are able to make you wise for salvation through faith which is in Christ Jesus. All Scripture is given by inspiration of God, and is profitable for doctrine, for reproof, for correction, for instruction in righteousness…

Ultimately, belief in the Bible as the Word of God is an act of faith. But this is not blind faith. There are many reasons to believe that

TOPIC 1   YOUR DEVOTIONAL LIFE

what the Bible says about itself is true. It speaks with historical and archaeological accuracy, it contains thousands of prophecies which have been perfectly fulfilled, and it carries a ring of authority and unity of thought that is absent from other books claiming to be sacred or divine.

The Bible's ultimate test is whether its teaching is true and effective in people's lives. Throughout history the lives of countless people, small and great, rich and poor, educated or uneducated – people from all nationalities, cultures and conditions, have had their lives changed by reading the Bible and applying its teaching.

The Bible reveals to us God's words of life. Speaking of God's word to him, the prophet Isaiah says, "Lord, by such things men live; and my spirit finds life in them too. You restored me to health and let me live" *(Isaiah 38:16)*. Learn to feed on God's Word and draw from it life-giving nourishment to your soul.

The Bible is also God's manual for life and living. It tells us everything we need to know about how to find God, get saved and live a life that's holy and effective for God. *2 Timothy 3:15-16* gives you 4 steps for change in your life so that you can put its teaching into practice.

The Bible gives you:

- Teaching – God's standards, or his instruction concerning what is right and wrong
- Reproof – where we are going wrong, the things that we have to change, beginning with trusting Christ alone for our salvation and holiness
- Correction – how we can put these things right in every practical detail of life and living
- Training or instruction in righteousness – how we can build good habits and right ways of thinking and behaving so that God's way becomes our lifestyle.

The Bible speaks with historical and archialogical accuracy.

It contains thousands of fulfilled prophecies.

It speaks with a single voice of authority.

It changes lives.

Daily walk

Therefore, the Bible is not just literature for us to read, or nice ideas to think about. It is spiritual food and instruction in life and living, which is both practical and powerful. In it, you find wisdom to deal with any situation you may come across. Biblical principles can govern your whole life, including the things that are not specifically mentioned in the Bible. For example, the Bible does not specifically mention abortion or eating disorders. But the underlying principles of the Bible give us the guidance we need to make informed and Bible-based decisions about these and other issues concerning life in the modern world.

The Bible is spiritual food and instruction in life and living, which is both practical and powerful.

This means that the Bible is our guidebook for daily life and we are called to live according to its insights and obey its commands. God's Word gives us wisdom and authority to make clear-cut decisions about how to live and bring glory to God in the world.

Most important of all, remember the Bible is not a book of rules or an ethical code. It carries the life of God and imparts that life to you. God speaks deep into your heart and breathes into you his life-giving Spirit. Jesus said, "The words I have spoken to you are spirit and they are life" *(John 6:63)*.

Your daily devotional life

It is important to develop the joy of a daily devotional life. Try to begin and end each day in communion with God. Learn to worship God by living the whole of your life for him. Worship God regularly, along with other believers. Enter deeply into the corporate times of worship in your cell meeting and church services. It is also vitally important to develop your own practice of daily worship, prayer and Bible reading. Make sure that this grows out of a genuine delight in the Lord. Your worship and love to him is a response to his love and grace.

The Bible is God's message of life - not a book of rules or an ethical code.

- Set aside a regular time, each day for God. It doesn't have to be long but make sure that it is quality time. In other words, keep this time fresh, vibrant and enjoyable. God hates religious practices!

- Begin with a time of worship in which you focus on his goodness and love. Receive a fresh revelation of his grace every time you approach him. You can put on a praise and worship CD or think about something special you can thank God for, or something for which to give him praise. Remember, worship is any expression of appreciation of God's worth, praise is a declaration of who God is and what he has done, and thanksgiving is an expression of your gratitude to him for specific things.

- Then spend time talking to God in prayer. Be specific about your needs and the needs of others. Believe that he hears your prayers and thank him in advance for his answers. God always hears and answers prayer made in the name of Jesus according to his will, so don't try to persuade him to do your will. Rather, pray according to God's will as revealed in the Bible and as the Holy Spirit leads you.

- The Lord's Prayer gives us helpful framework for daily prayer and it is all about praying for the things that accord with his will: "May your kingdom come; may your will be done on earth

TOPIC 1   YOUR DEVOTIONAL LIFE

as it is in heaven." You can ask him for your daily needs to be met, for strength to overcome the enemy, for grace to live in the forgiveness of God. As you pray, you depend on him and trust him to govern your circumstances by his power and glory.

- You can then spend time reading the Bible. It is important to choose a Bible version that suits you. The Old Testament was originally written in Hebrew and the New Testament in Greek, but there are many excellent translations to choose from. The New King James Version is in fairly modern English and has much of the dignity of the old King James Version without the 'thees' and the 'thous'. The New International Version has more modern and free-flowing English, whereas the New Living Translation is written in clear, simple and even more modern English. The choice is yours!

- As you read the Bible and pray each day it is good to note down what God says to you – the words of life he gives to you through prayer and the Scriptures. You can begin to keep a daily spiritual journal by using the *LIVING FREE! Daily Devotional*

Set aside a regular time with God.

Begin with worship.

Talk to God in prayer.

Follow a Bible reading plan.

Keep a spiritual journal.

25

TOPIC 2

THE FAMILY OF GOD

Christians are called to be committed to a particular expression of Christ's body and live and serve Christ together as part of the family of God.

You do not live in isolation as a Christian. God has called you to be part of his family, which is the community of God's people who are spiritually-connected in Christ. This is the family of Abba God, our Father.

For this reason I bow my knees to the Father of our Lord Jesus Christ, from whom the whole family in heaven and earth is named…

Ephesians 3:14-15

As we believe in Jesus Christ, so we are included into the family of God. Abba God is the Father of all who believe in Jesus, and that makes us all one family. All believers are our brothers and sisters no matter what their race, age, social standing or nationality. The family of God is the Church of Jesus Christ, which also is his body, the Body of Christ.

And he put all things under his feet, and gave him to be head over all things to the church, which is his body, the fullness of him who fills all in all.

Ephesians 1:22-23

We are told that there are over 6,000 different church denominations in the world, but despite that, there is only one Church of Jesus Christ, and that is the body of all true believers made up of every different church tradition, denomination or stream with Jesus Christ as the head.

Although the Body of Christ is universal, it has many expressions. We call these 'churches' or 'fellowships'. Christians are called to become a committed part of a particular expression of Christ's body and live and serve Christ together as part of the family of God in that specific gathering or fellowship.

For a church to be a real church and to function properly as the body of Christ it must have all of the following:

- Membership
- Leadership
- Stewardship
- Partnership.

Membership

This means that every church consists of a committed membership – those called to be part of that body. The members commit themselves to love God and to build each other up in Christ. It is a life calling to serve God *together*. In Bible understanding, the members are the true ministers of the Church. Each member is called to reach out to the lost, win them to Christ and disciple them as new believers in the community of the church.

Leadership

God has set in the body those with gifts of leadership. The main gifts are: apostles, prophets, evangelists, pastors and teachers *(Ephesians 4:11)*. These gifts are organised into the body of elders assisted by what the Bible calls deacons who are appointed to special areas of practical service in the church. The leaders are called to train and equip the members of the body of Christ so that the members can do the work of the ministry of Jesus *(Ephesians 4:12)*.

Stewardship

This is the role or job description that Jesus, the head of the church, has left us to fulfil. The fullest description is found at the end of Matthew's Gospel:

Matthew 28:18-20

And Jesus came and spoke to them, saying, "All authority has been given to me in heaven and on earth. Go therefore and make disciples of all the nations, baptizing them in the name of the Father and of the Son and of the Holy Spirit, teaching them to observe all things that I have commanded you; and lo, I am with you always, even to the end of the age." Amen.

This Great Commission must become the ultimate purpose of our personal lives and the principal priority and focus of our church.

Partnership

A mistake that churches often make is to isolate themselves from other groups of believers as if they are trying to 'go it alone'. But you cannot have an independent church any more than you can have an independent hand or foot. Cut off from other expressions of the body of Christ, churches become isolated, narrow and inward-looking. We can never achieve all that Christ calls us to achieve as long as churches are divided and fragmented from other expressions of the Body of Christ.

All believers share in the life of Christ together. Therefore, we must extend the hand of fellowship to all the 'branches' of the true vine, who is Christ.

I am the vine, you are the branches. He who abides in me, and I in him, bears much fruit; for without me you can do nothing. — John 15:5

For example, our church, Kensington Temple, is not an isolated or unconnected group. We are part of the Elim Pentecostal Churches of the UK. Elim is part of the Pentecostal movement, which is part of the wider Evangelical movement. In fact, we are one with every other church expression or denomination that accepts and walks in the testimony of Jesus Christ.

London City Church

As a church, we are also organised into a citywide grouping called London City Church. This is an apostolic expression of church, touching London and the nations for Christ.

The London City Church consists of congregations, fellowships and cells networking across London, uniting as one body to fulfil the vision God has given us.

Expressing our church fellowship

There are many ways in which we express our fellowship in Kensington Temple, London City Church.

Cells

These are small groups of people committed to working together to build one another up in Christian discipleship as well as working together to reach the lost for Christ. We make it our goal for every member to become an active part of a cell group.

All expressions of the body of Christ share in the life of Christ together.

The cells are a blessing because this is where *companionship* develops, deep fellowship is forged and where we train and equip believers to fulfil their life calling to serve Christ.

Congregations

These are larger groups of believers who gather regularly for stronger expressions of witness and service in the community. They often consist of a group of cells, called together by a primary cell leader for training, prayer, fellowship or evangelism. We have also planted city congregations who gather across London for weekly expressions of this level of church. We call these 'satellite churches'.

Celebrations

We regularly gather the members of London City Church in a large venue. The purpose of this is to witness to Christ on a large scale, to celebrate his victory, to engage in spiritual warfare and to experience a powerful outpouring of the Holy Spirit. Sometimes these celebrations take the form of convocation, which is a calling together of the whole London City Church in order to receive some special message or empowering from the Lord as well as to exercise a strong influence on the wider society.

Becoming a part of the family of God

This process leads us through the door of salvation into the life of the kingdom of God – his rule over our hearts. We identify with the community of the kingdom (the church) and discover a life of freedom and victory. It is a narrow path of self-denial that can bring with it rejection and persecution from the world, but it also leads to abundant life and boundless joy.

There are 5 aspects to the process of becoming part of the family of God:

- Repentance
- Faith

- Baptism in water
- Baptism in Holy Spirit
- Joining the family of God.

Obviously, the moment you are saved, you belong to Jesus and to his body, the church. But this must be outworked in practical and meaningful ways by living and sharing your life with God's people. The process begins with a change in attitude and leads to a complete surrender to the purposes of God for your life.

Repentance

To 'repent' means to change your mind, but not just intellectually. It is a refocusing of your entire life. It means you have experienced a total change of heart. This radical turnabout of heart and mind, leads to a total turnabout of life. You realise that you have been going in the wrong direction – *away* from God. Now you see that error and you turn around and run *towards* the Lord.

Repentance doesn't mean, in the first instance, a change of behaviour, although we are required to do that as Christians. God commands us to stop going our own way and to begin to go his way. But repentance is, in essence, a change of *heart*.

This is where the Christian life begins. To please God means to obey him from your heart. God is not interested in outward conformity or mere good behaviour. He wants our hearts. All true God-honouring change is from the heart. The true response to the gospel is turning to the Lord in total dependence on him for our complete salvation. This is the real obedience of the gospel.

Repentance involves a total change of heart and leads to a radical turnabout of life.

Without repentance, there can be no salvation. We must accept that we are far from God and that we need to return to him or we are lost forever. That is why repentance is not, in the first instance, a change of behaviour. God doesn't say to us, 'First change your behaviour, and then I'll accept you.' No. God accepts us just as we are, the moment we turn to him. We change our lives because we have been accepted by God, not in order to be accepted by him.

The woman caught in the act of adultery was accepted by Christ the moment she looked to him *(John 8:1-8)*. He said, "I don't condemn you." But, immediately he called her to a new life of holiness, saying, "Go, and sin no more."

We begin by understanding that Jesus loves us and accepts us exactly as we are. This love transforms us from within, and we begin to follow

God's ways, obeying him from the heart. He is not looking for mere behaviour modification, but for true heart transformation.

Jesus loves us so much that he releases us from the power of sin at work in our hearts. We discover how much he hates sin and how offensive it is to Abba God. We begin to feel deep pain for having sinned against him, especially for keeping him out of our lives for so long. We also get to see what Jesus endured for us in his Passion. His sufferings and death on the cross were the price he gladly paid to become our sin bearer and to set us free. The cross shows us the deep sinfulness and offensiveness of sin, but most of all, it shows us the love and grace of God. This turns our sorrow into joy.

The cross shows us the deep sinfulness and offensiveness of sin, but most of all, it shows us the love and grace of God. This turns our sorrow into joy.

Jesus willingly took up our sins and our offenses and bore them all on the cross. We see all our sins nailed to the cross and realise we carry them no longer. We leave everything behind at the cross and begin to follow Christ with joy, full of loving gratitude knowing he has forgiven all our sins. This leads to a radical change of living. Once we have been to the cross and seen the grace of God we will not wish to tolerate sin in our lives, but live in a way that truly pleases him. The Holy Spirit helps us by showing us the Father's love and teaches us to love him because he first loved us. We do not depend on our obedience or our efforts to please him. Rather, we trust in his unfailing love and are changed from glory to glory, by the Holy Spirit at work in our hearts.

2 Corinthians 3:18

But we all, with unveiled face, beholding as in a mirror the glory of the Lord, are being transformed into the same image from glory to glory, just as by the Spirit of the Lord.

Faith

The other side of the coin of repentance is 'faith' or believing in Jesus. The two are always linked, as Jesus showed in the first recorded words of his public ministry in Galilee.

Mark 1:14-15

Now after John was put in prison, Jesus came to Galilee, preaching the gospel of the kingdom of God, and saying, "The time is fulfilled, and the kingdom of God is at hand. Repent, and believe in the gospel."

Faith is about putting your trust in Jesus Christ. It means trusting him alone for your salvation. The only possible response to the *pure grace* of the gospel is *simple faith*. It is like opening our hands to receive a free gift. Faith recognises who Jesus is. He is the Christ, the Son of the Living God *(Matthew 16:16)*. It also means depending on him to be your Saviour. In that way, the benefits of the salvation Jesus accomplished on the cross become yours. They become real to you and part of your personal experience, bringing a revelation of your unassailable position in Christ. This is how you are saved.

TOPIC 2   THE FAMILY OF GOD

Paul, the apostle, explains what it means to believe from your heart:

...that if you confess with your mouth the Lord Jesus and believe in your heart that God has raised him from the dead, you will be saved. For with the heart one believes unto righteousness and with the mouth confession is made unto salvation.

Romans 10:9-10

When Jesus died on the cross he cried out in triumphant victory, "It is finished!" *(John 19:30)*. At that moment, Jesus accomplished your total and complete salvation. He also paid the price for every promise of God to be fulfilled in your life. The moment you put your trust in Jesus Christ as your Saviour, he became for you everything you will ever need.

God provided for all your needs at the cross:

- Forgiveness
- Healing
- Material needs
- Assurance
- Acceptance
- Protection
- Victory
- Deliverance
- Holiness
- Preservation.

The moment you put your trust in Jesus Christ as your Saviour, he became for you everything you will ever need.

Every one of these promises of God is yours as you walk in faith believing in the goodness of Abba God.

...without faith it is impossible to please him, for he who comes to God must believe that he is, and that he is a rewarder of those who diligently seek him.

Hebrews 11:6

Baptism in Water

This is an important step as you begin your spiritual journey. In New Testament times, baptism was a mark of initiation into discipleship. It meant that you were following Jesus Christ as your Lord and Master, your teacher and model for life.

Jesus himself was baptised and when John the Baptist questioned him, he said, "It is right to fulfil this act of righteousness" *(Matthew 3:15)*. If Jesus did it, then who are we to say it isn't relevant for us?

But many people ask, 'What is baptism really?' They have heard about church ceremonies in which infants have been christened and wonder about baptism by full immersion. In my view 'christening' babies as a religious practice, has damaged the spiritual life of Britain and other

Baptism is a powerful reminder that you have died and been raised with Christ. It is an effective spiritual burial of your old life

nations of the world, almost more than anything else. Many people put their trust in this religious ceremony as if it gave them a place in heaven. But that is not so. We are not saved by religious deeds, but by faith in Jesus Christ alone – without the mediation of clergy, religious ceremonies or church traditions.

Water baptism, as taught in the New Testament is the full immersion of believers as a sign and a seal of their commitment to Christ. It is the act of Christian initiation and an outward expression or confession of their faith in Christ.

Baptism in water is the first step of obedience in the life of a disciple and it means the person is committing their life to follow Jesus Christ totally. It signifies our death and burial with Christ by which we leave behind the old life and embrace our new life in Christ. It means we are taking up our place in the Church of Jesus Christ and identifying with the people of God.

Baptism is symbolic, but it is also a powerful occasion in which the Holy Spirit acts to bring you into a deeper experience of all you have in Christ. It is a powerful identification with the grace of God in lifting you out of your former way of life and bringing you into union with Christ. His death becomes your death and his life becomes your life. By dying and rising with Christ through faith, you were also lifted up with him to be seated in heavenly places. Baptism is a powerful reminder of this fact and it is an effective spiritual burial of your old life and a testimony to who you are in him.

Baptism in the Holy Spirit

We will be looking more closely at the Holy Spirit later on this book. The Bible reveals him as the third member of the Trinity. The Holy Spirit is a person, like Jesus and the Father. Jesus promised to send us the Holy Spirit after his death and resurrection.

John 14:16

I will pray the Father, and he will give you another Helper, that he may abide with you forever…

Jesus fulfilled his promise and he sent the Holy Spirit on the Day of Pentecost *(Acts 2:1-4)*. But before that day, he gave some specific instructions to his disciples so that they would know exactly why the Spirit was going to come upon them.

Acts 1:4-5

And being assembled together with them, he commanded them not to depart from Jerusalem, but to wait for the Promise of the Father, "which," he said, "you have heard from me; for John truly baptised with water, but you shall be baptised with the Holy Spirit not many days from now."

TOPIC 2   THE FAMILY OF GOD

John's baptism had been in water, but he announced that Jesus would be the Baptiser in the Holy Spirit. This means that when we receive the Spirit of God into our lives, we are baptised or immersed into the Holy Spirit. It is a definite experience in which we are conscious of being filled with the Holy Spirit. When we put a sponge in water, the water begins to fill the sponge. We can say the sponge is in the water and the water is in the sponge.

So it is with the Holy Spirit. Being baptised in the Holy Spirit means we are filled as we are immersed into God's presence. Just as water baptism initiated us into the life of the Church, so Holy Spirit baptism is God's way of initiating us into the life of the Spirit. But the big difference is this: in water baptism we get out of the water, but we stay in the presence of God through Spirit baptism. We continue to be immersed and filled with the Holy Spirit as a lifestyle.

Jesus made it clear that a primary purpose of Spirit baptism is that we might receive power to witness to him.

But you shall receive power when the Holy Spirit has come upon you; and you shall be witnesses to me in Jerusalem, and in all Judea and Samaria, and to the end of the earth." Acts 1:8

When we become filled with the Holy Spirit, he naturally overflows out of our life and this means we are equipped to reach out to others with the power and enabling of the Spirit. First of all, this means receiving the gift of tongues just as on the Day of Pentecost.

And they were all filled with the Holy Spirit and began to speak with other tongues, as the Spirit gave them utterance. Acts 2:4

There is a God-given connection between the heart and the mouth. That's how he made us. Jesus said, "Out of the overflow of the heart the mouth speaks" *(Matthew 12:34)*.

When you are filled with the Holy Spirit, new words will flow out of your mouth. We receive a new 'prayer language' or the 'gift of tongues'.

> *When you are filled with the Holy Spirit you receive a new 'prayer language' or the 'gift of tongues'.*

But it doesn't end there. The coming of the Holy Spirit in our lives is like opening a deep river on the inside. That river bursts its banks and begins to flow out of our lives into the barren world of human hurt and need.

He who believes in me, as the Scripture has said, out of his heart will flow rivers of living water. John 7:38

Joining the Family of God

This is the climax of all the aspects of new life in Christ we have mentioned. We begin with repentance and faith and become baptised in water and in the Holy Spirit, but all this is so that we can take up our place in the Church, the Body of Christ.

Christ lives in his body, and we cannot fully enjoy his presence or experience his life apart from his body. God has ordained the Body of Christ to be his agent on the earth and the vehicle through which he brings glory to his name.

Ephesians 3:20-21

Now to him who is able to do exceedingly abundantly above all that we ask or think, according to the power that works in us, to him be glory in the church by Christ Jesus to all generations, forever and ever. Amen.

The Church of Jesus Christ is the only hope for the world. It is the only body on earth that can make a real difference by bringing the message of life. Only we can demonstrate the life of Christ to a world in desperate need of him.

Taking up your place in the body of Christ is part of being a Christian. It means you become an integral part of his body and begin to function in a unique role. The body only grows, matures and becomes effective in the world *as each part* takes its share in the work of God.

Ephesians 4:15-16

… speaking the truth in love, [we] may grow up in all things into him who is the head – Christ – from whom the whole body, joined and knit together by what every joint supplies, according to the effective working by which every part does its share, causes growth of the body for the edifying of itself in love.

The *Living Free* course will set you on the road to your ministry in Christ's church. It prepares you for the next step, which is *Mastering Leadership* – the training programme for cell leaders. Begin to anticipate how God wants to use you. Get ready to pass on to others all that you receive from this course.

TOPIC 3

YOUR TESTIMONY

Your personal experience can touch many lives.

When we testify to Jesus, the Holy Spirit takes over and brings people to Christ, if they are willing to respond to his love and grace.

Jesus Christ has called you to be a witness for him. One of the most significant things you can ever do in your life is to direct people to Christ.

The gospel begins with the witness of John the Baptist pointing to Christ, "Behold the Lamb of God who takes away the sins of the world" *(John 1:29)*. And it ends with Jesus' statement, "You shall be my witnesses, beginning in Jerusalem… and to the ends of the earth" *(Acts 1:8)*.

A witness testifies to what he or she knows from personal experience. That is the most powerful testimony in the world. Your personal experience can touch many lives. Witnesses cannot force people to accept their testimony. Their job is simply to present their experience as proof. When we testify to Jesus, the Holy Spirit takes over and brings people to Christ, if they are willing to respond to his love and grace.

Effective witnesses

The world is longing for credible witnesses to Christ and, as his disciples, we must rise to this challenge. Jesus called us to be 'salt and light' in the world *(Matthew 5:13-16)*. This means actively engaging in the world around us, and not withdrawing into our own little 'Christian ghetto'. It means that we take the light and life of Christ into every sphere of our influence as people in our society: our home, our school, our work, our recreation and our social life.

God wants us to witness for Christ everywhere and actively influence every part of society: the world of art, media, politics, education, industry, retail, medicine, sport, thought, philosophy, finance, business, law, police, film, television, and so on. In order for this to happen, we must adopt a certain disposition.

We must determine to influence our society rather than conforming to its values and attitudes. Paul says, "Do not be conformed to this world, but be transformed by the renewing of your mind" *(Romans 12:2)*. Jesus asked the question, "How can salt act as salt if it loses its saltiness?" *(Matthew 5:13)*.

In the world but not of the world

This means getting the 'world' out of us, but it never means withdrawing from it. Jesus taught that we are "in the world, but not of the world" *(John 17:15-18)*. It is vital that we break from our past habits and sins and sometimes that means disassociating from certain company we once kept. After all, "bad company corrupts good character" *(1 Corinthians 15:33)*. But we must also build new relationships with those who don't yet know Christ. However, this time we do so with the love and compassion of Christ seeking to win the lost just as Jesus did.

If you really want to be an effective witness of Jesus, you will begin to shape the whole of your life around this calling.

Jesus spent so much time with sinners that he offended the religious leaders who despised them. Scandalised by his actions, they said, "He associates with sinners!" Jesus loved the poor and the needy. He spent much of his time with the prostitutes, the tax collectors (who were notorious villains), the immoral, the drunks, and with all those who needed him the most. He rebuked the religiously minded people who ignored the deep needs around them, "Those who are well don't need a doctor," he said, "I have not come to call the righteous, but sinners to repentance" *(Mark 2:17)*.

The 'Evangelism of 3'

If you really want to be an effective witness of Jesus, you will begin to shape the whole of your life around this calling. You don't have to give up your regular employment to become a preacher! For nearly everyone, that is *not* the way forward. Determine to flourish where you are. Make sure that you become the best witness that you can be, right where you are – in your home, with your family and among your friends. Seek, through the help and wisdom of the Holy Spirit, to win to Christ your schoolmates, your acquaintances and your colleagues at work.

TOPIC 3   YOUR TESTIMONY

The 'Evangelism of 3' strategy is a good way to start witnessing. Begin by listing 10 people whom you know and meet regularly, people like you, with whom you can develop a close relationship and who will begin to show interest in your Christian testimony. It is important that the people on this list are the kind of people you can invite to your cell, or to a church event, so that they can have an opportunity to commit their lives to Christ. It is important also to be genuine in your friendship with these people and not treat them as mere fodder for your evangelism.

Choose three people to become part of your 'Evangelism of 3'.

Then pray over this list of 10 people and ask the Holy Spirit to help you choose 3 of them to become part of your 'Evangelism of 3'. Begin to pray daily for them to get saved. Join with 2 or 3 others from your cell and pray also for the names on their lists. Then come together once a week to pray very earnestly and specifically for these people to be saved.

Begin to pray daily for them to get saved.

Join with 2 or 3 others from your cell and pray also for the names on their lists.

But, remember, prayer alone is never enough. You must meet regularly with the people you are seeking to win to Christ. Meet socially out of genuine friendship and let your Christian faith shine through your life even more than your words, as Jesus said,

Let your light so shine before men, that they may see your good works and glorify your Father in heaven.   *Matthew 5:16*

Begin to share your testimony with them. Let them see what has happened to you and the difference Christ has made in your life. Do all this in the context of friendship and work with others from your cell. Organise frequent social events like meeting up in a coffee house, a film, a meal at a restaurant or at home. Parties, sporting events, clubs, courses and special interests – all these are great contexts for friendship evangelism.

Then at the right time invite your friends to a service or a special event in the church where there will be an opportunity for them to respond to the gospel. Don't wait until they 'go to church' to lead them to Christ. Pray the prayer of salvation right where they are, in their work place or at school or in the cell meeting. However, it is important that they also make a public confession of Christ in a formal church service. Then they will understand that to come to Christ is more than a decision they make in private. They will also understand that they are called to follow Christ publicly and to do so as part of the Church of Jesus Christ.

Sharing your testimony

All this may seem challenging, and it is. But remember the joy of discovering the love of God for you – you cannot keep that to yourself. It is too much to hold in. We've got to share this good news. We must also be prepared to experience some resistance, some insults or even rejection. When this happens, don't be alarmed, Jesus said, "They loved darkness rather than light" *(John 3:19)*. But remember that the God who revealed Jesus to us can do the same for them.

2 Corinthians 4:6

For it is the God who commanded light to shine out of darkness, who has shone in our hearts to give the light of the knowledge of the glory of God in the face of Jesus Christ.

Also, remember, you are not alone. Your brothers and sisters in Christ are standing with you. The church is there to help train you to become an effective witness. The Holy Spirit will give you his supernatural ability to be a witness producing 'proof' that Jesus Christ is alive. We cover that in Topic 9 later in this book.

We've got to share the good news. The Holy Spirit will give you his supernatural ability to be a witness.

When sharing the gospel with others, remember to tell your story. People love a good story. This is not only true in drama, television, film or novels. In business and education also, story is being rediscovered as an effective way of communicating a message. Personal experience is valued highly in today's world. Your testimony can make a real difference. What has touched you will touch them. Your personal story can connect with others who will identify with your experience. At root level, we all have very similar needs, desires, concerns and interests.

When you share what Christ has done in your life, it will encourage others to believe he can do the same for them.

How to give your testimony

Giving your testimony is very simple. You can do in one or two sentences or in a much longer format. Simple statements such as, 'I have never had so much peace' or, 'Jesus has helped me break the drink habit!' or, 'Our marriage has been transformed since we came to Christ!' are all powerful testimonies to the living Christ.

A good testimony will have three basic parts relating to the past, the present and the future. You can think of it in this way:

1. *"Before I came to Christ my life was…"* Here you describe:

    - what life was like for you before you came to know Christ

- what your felt needs were and the reason why you needed Christ (for example, your sins and their consequences in you)
- how you came to hear about Christ and the gospel
- how you responded to the gospel and got saved.

2. *"Since I came to Christ…"* This is where you describe the changes that have come to you since committing your life to Christ. It will be how your needs are being met by Christ and the peace that comes from the knowledge that your sins have been forgiven. Remember to:

- emphasise that Christ came to save us from sin
- point out that Jesus gives us 'new life' or the 'new birth' and that we must be 'born again' and live a new life
- show how your needs are being met, without exaggerating or glossing over the challenges you face in seeking to follow Christ today.

3. *"When I look forward to the future, I know…"* Finally, you draw attention to your hope for the future. You will want to include things like:

- your assurance of heaven – not through your own efforts but by the free gift of God
- your confidence of God's future protection and care
- your knowledge that in all circumstances of life God is working out his plan
- your purpose in life is to live for him and serve him forever.

A good testimony will have three basic parts:

1. Before I came to Christ my life was…

2. Since I came to Christ…

3. When I look forward to the future, I know…

All this may seem a little complicated, but you will soon discover how much you have to share with others. You can practice writing out your testimony and sharing it in your cell meeting so that you can have confidence when you speak to others about what God has done for you.

To help you understand how to make your testimony effective, here are some real life sample testimonies to look at. As you read them, notice how each person uses the principles we have looked at in this chapter.

My testimony: Andrew

I gave my life to Christ when I was 6 years old. However, I was living as if I didn't have Christ at all and started drinking at the age of 11. This was the start to a downward spiral that lasted for 12 years of my life.

My Dad is a Baptist Minister so I was brought up in a church environment. At the age of 11 I started to hear about sex and alcohol at school which was new to me as I was very naive. I knew that deep down I wanted to be accepted, and this need in me was made greater by the fact that I thought my Dad had more time for people who were in the church than he had for me.

By the time I was 20, I was on the verge of becoming an alcoholic and had tried nearly all the drugs that are available and was heavily enticed by pornography. My language was filthy and I had no respect for my Dad. These things brought me a lot of worldly success (friends respected me, several intimate relationships, fulfilling my desires of wanting to be heard, generally acting in whatever way I wanted), but I could not run away from the fact that deep down I felt empty. I knew that there was so much more to life and that I was missing something.

I was always aware of who Christ was but I chose to completely dismiss him which eventually led to an experience where I almost died. I was close to death but somehow was brought back to reality, which made me really start to consider that God is real and that he was the answer I was looking for. I ended up dragging myself to a youth meeting at Kensington Temple.

It was a communion service and Christ radically met with me. At that moment, I knew that he is very much alive and I was being cleansed from the inside out. I had heard that he could give you a new life which was what I had just experienced. I was 'born again' and I left that meeting a completely different person, radically transformed from the heart. I had life.

My need for acceptance was fully met and I now had purpose to my life, which had only just begun. All my past desires were being worked through and, with the help from my cell leader. I have been able to get rid of all past hurts and desires. I am free in my life now without a heaviness that I seemed to be carrying about with me and I know that my sins have been washed away. I am cleansed in every way and my friends and family are amazed at the transformation.

Every day is a new day with life struggles and battles with thoughts and desires, but I know that I am secure in Christ. He is my everything and I know that he has a plan for my life. I have such a hunger to live for him and to serve in his kingdom as Christ came to give us life and to set us free. My whole life is different now – for the better, with so many amazing experiences. This is the best journey I could ever be a part of with challenges, rewards, excitement, pain and freedom from the world's clutches and freedom from sin. Through Christ my life is complete and I know he only wants the best for me.

My testimony: Jane

My parents separated when I was little, but although my mother was a strong Christian she could not really look after us so I lived with my aunt and her kids. When I was 13 I ran away. I was frightened and scared and met a man. I lived with him and his family and eventually became pregnant when I was 15. I moved to the UK when I was 19 and thought I would become a model – but it was a different sort of modelling than I thought, and I became involved in the lifestyle that goes with 'glamour' modelling. I would go to clubs and meet men, and basically just lived my life for myself. Eventually I met a boyfriend, he took care of me and I gave up everything for him, so when we split up I was left with nothing, no money, no job and no home. It was really tough and I was tired of the whole thing. So one day I decided to end it all.

I had made the decision to kill myself and remembered what my mum had said about the Book of Life – thinking that if my name was not in the book I would go to hell. I decided to find a church and tell God what I was going to do and that maybe if I said sorry, my name would then be in the book.

The preacher that night was talking about how God does not condemn us but loves us and wants to clean us up. I remember him saying, "There is room for everyone in the father's arms, even if you think that there is no way out – God is opening his arms to you." Almost before I knew what I was doing I was giving my life to Christ and felt a powerful thing happen inside me. After the service I was given a Bible – I had never owned a Bible before. I was introduced to my cell group leader and she prayed for me. From that moment I fell in love with Christ. I gave up my old life, and God helped me get a fantastic new job. I have started to deal with my issues and now I just want to work for Jesus – I want to know everything about him. I am a new person and I have Jesus to thank that I am here today.

My testimony: Joel

I was fortunate enough to have been born into a Christian family. I had learned about and gave my life to Christ at the age of ten. I did not really question my beliefs as I just trusted what my parents and teachers at Sunday school taught me – I basically just had an answer to the question "What is your religion?" As I grew older, I stuck to the same routine of going to church every Sunday but I did not really experience fulfilment. I wasn't able to commit to God fully and I just did not understand how people could have that desire to go to church and be enthusiastic about meetings.

I was a typical 'submarine Christian'. It felt so tedious and even though I would pray for repentance, I seemed to always end up committing the same sins again. I began to realise that I desperately needed to change my spiritual life. My mother continued to talk about joining a cell and how this would be good for me. I eventually gave in and decided that was the step I had to take.

I went on an Encounter Weekend and it proved to be the biggest turning point in my life. I met with Jesus and truly felt the presence of the Holy Spirit and for the first time I felt completely free from all sin. I had never experienced such freedom before. It was as though I had been reborn with a new, clean and fresh soul with the need to know more about Christ. For the first time, I would hold onto every word preached. I began to understand that God was not just about religion but I was to walk with him in every area of my life. He has become the priority in my life and I have a great desire to be the best person for Christ, which is leading me to get involved with the church. My goals in life have become much more orientated towards God's vision, realising that there is so much more to the Christian life than Sunday services!

I know that no good works that I have done earned me the gift of eternal life. I have full confidence in God's plan for me and no matter what happens, I know it will all be a part of his plan. My life is in his hands and I am excited about the future with him.

TOPIC 4

REAL CHANGE

The more we focus on Jesus, the more we release the Holy Spirit to work in us.

All that we have been looking at so far in this book has been about Jesus Christ and the difference he makes in our lives. We have seen that,

...if anyone is in Christ, he is a new creation; old things have passed away; behold, all things have become new.

2 Corinthians 5:17

We have also seen that God calls us to a new lifestyle – the outworking of the new creation life of Christ in us. True holiness and transformation of life comes when we see Jesus and all he has done for us. The more we focus on Jesus, the more we release the Holy Spirit to work in us. By the power of the Holy Spirit, we learn to put off our old thoughts, habits and patterns of behaviour and replace them with the thoughts, habits and behaviour patterns of the new life. All this depends on understanding one of the most important principles of Christian life and living.

Become what you are

Many people think that the Christian life involves the impossible task of trying to be what they are not. They think it's about making an effort to behave in a way that's totally different from who they really are, so they struggle with lack of motivation and ultimately live defeated lives riddled with guilt and failure.

But this is not the triumphant life of victory God has called you to. You have been totally set free in Christ and he has totally delivered

You are no longer who you once were. You are a brand new creation in him - and God wants you to become in your daily, practical experience the person who you really are through your relationship with Christ.

you from the past. You are no longer who you once were. You are a brand new creation in him. Every New Testament call or command to holiness of life is a call to be who you are, not a call to be what you are not! It's about learning to become in your daily life on earth that person whom God has already made you to be in Christ. Quite simply, God wants you to become in your daily, practical experience the person who you really are through your relationship with Christ.

God says to you, 'You are born again. Live the new life you have received. You are a new creation. Live that new creation life. I have set you free and delivered you from sin. Live that new life of freedom. Become in your daily walk who you are in your spiritual position before me.'

In *Ephesians 2:1-10*, the apostle Paul puts it this way. He says we are, "seated with Christ in heavenly places." This means that we have died with Christ to our old ways, which dominated and controlled us before we came to Christ. He made us alive in Christ through his resurrection power and seated us with Christ in a place of authority and accomplishment.

We have nothing to do with the old life – it is gone forever! We now follow Christ, turning our back on that old life with its sinful desires. We live according to the new ways of the Spirit of God. This is about putting off the old and putting on the new. We put behind us the attitudes and actions of the old way of life and follow the new ways of Christ.

Ephesians 4:20-24

But you have not so learned Christ, if indeed you have heard Him and have been taught by him, as the truth is in Jesus: that you put off, concerning your former conduct, the old man which grows corrupt according to the deceitful lusts, and be renewed in the spirit of your mind, and that you put on the new man which was created according to God, in true righteousness and holiness.

Changing from the inside out

Real change, change that honours God, happens from the inside out. It must come from the heart. The heart carries all our hidden motives, our presuppositions and our beliefs. These explain why we do what we do, the way we feel and how we live our life. The book of Proverbs shows that our behaviour is the outflow of what is in our heart.

Proverbs 4:23

Keep your heart with all diligence, for out of it spring the issues of life.

As the Holy Spirit gives us a revelation of Christ and his love for us, we begin to see him as he really is. We glimpse his glory and realise that he alone can fulfil our deepest desires, our highest aspirations and our most profound longings for joy and fullness. The Psalmist got it right when he said,

You will show me the path of life. In your presence is fullness of joy. At your right hand are pleasures forevermore. — Psalm 16:11

Once we see that, we will be willing for the Lord to search out the hidden things of our heart and transform us from within. The Word of God is like a sword cutting deep into our hearts and exposing our inner thoughts and intentions. This is where true change must take place. All meaningful change begins in the heart as God's Word exposes these hidden thoughts, intentions and attitudes directing us towards the fullness we have in Christ.

For the word of God is living and powerful, and sharper than any two-edged sword, piercing even to the division of soul and spirit, and of joints and marrow, and is a discerner of the thoughts and intents of the heart. — Hebrews 4:12

Right motivation of the heart

We cannot afford to ignore our motivation, or the reason why we do things, when we are living for the Lord. He is not interested in mere outward conformity to his commandments. He wants us to serve him with a willing heart.

If you are willing and obedient, you shall eat the good of the land — Isaiah 1:19

We understand this principle from daily life. A child who breaks the vase deliberately in an act of rage, and the child who does the same thing accidentally in the course of playing, should be treated differently. The offence is not equal in both cases. In the same way, a child who sits still all day, never saying a word out of place in order to avoid being beaten by an angry parent, is living a life of fear not loving obedience. God sees the motives of our heart behind our actions. He is not looking for mere outward acts of obedience, but calls us to respond to him with willing, loving and trusting hearts.

A willing heart

God is looking for willing hearts that are open and responsive to him. A dead sacrifice involves a once for all commitment, but a living sacrifice must continually yield to God's will. In other words, we must choose to go God's way, and this is a constant, on-going experience.

The way to a willing heart is through the love of Christ. People will do almost anything for love. Love lifts the burden of obedience and makes

When we have tasted and seen that God is good, we will be passionate about going his way, even if it costs us personally.

it a delight. Jesus said, "The one who is forgiven much loves much" *(Luke 7:47)*. John says, "We love him because he first loved us" *(1 John 4:19)* and, "This is the love of God, that we keep his commandments. And his commandments are not burdensome" *(1 John 5:2-3)*.

Once we see how much Christ loves us and that he has freely forgiven all our sins, our hearts will be filled with his love. The Holy Spirit will manifest that love in our hearts. This love makes us willing to follow him and to delight in him at all times. That willingness leads to practical acts of obedience and loving service.

A loving response

Paul reminds us of God's mercy and calls for a response that is consistent with the love God has shown to us. Our 'reasonable service' is loving gratitude to God for all he has done for us. God has blessed us in every way, but most important of all, he has accepted us in the Beloved through his mercy and grace. The only right and reasonable response to this is to love God from the heart and to live for him in all things. Faith works through love.

Romans 12:1-2

I beseech you therefore, brethren, by the mercies of God, that you present your bodies a living sacrifice, holy, acceptable to God, which is your reasonable service. And do not be conformed to this world, but be transformed by the renewing of your mind, that you may prove what is that good and acceptable and perfect will of God.

Living by trust

Because we are conditioned by our past way of thinking and living, it takes an act of real faith to go God's way. To deny our own desires and abandon those things that we once believed gave us fulfilment is an act of trust. But when we do, we begin to prove in our personal experience that God's way really works. We find his way is best after all. When we have tasted and seen that God is good, we will be passionate about Christ and willing to go God's way, even if it costs us personally.

1 Peter 2:2-3

As newborn babies, desire the pure milk of the word, that you may grow thereby, if indeed you have tasted that the Lord is gracious.

This means that we depend on what Jesus as done for us and not what we can do for him. God is looking for heart transformation and not behaviour modification. Jesus saves us and Jesus makes us holy. Walking with Jesus means that we trust him daily to work in our hearts and to shape our lives by the Holy Spirit at work in us.

TOPIC 4 REAL CHANGE

Transformed by looking at Jesus

One very important verse that shows how we can be changed to be like Jesus is found in 2 Corinthians 3:18.

But we all, with unveiled face, beholding as in a mirror the glory of the Lord, are being transformed into the same image from glory to glory, just as by the Spirit of the Lord.

2 Corinthians 3:18

This verse is the climax to a wonderful passage in which the apostle Paul shows the difference between trying to please God through our own fleshy efforts and depending on the power of the Holy Spirit in us. Only the Holy Spirit can change us and make us like Jesus.

First of all, notice that in Christ the veil of separation between us and God has been removed. The way is open for us to approach God, not in our own merits but through the blood of Jesus who died to reconcile us to God. Next, see how real change happens. It begins in our heart. As we gaze lovingly on Jesus and appreciate him for all he has done for us, we are transformed from within. Finally, understand that all lasting and meaningful change is initiated by the Holy Spirit. He is the agent of change in our lives – not our own efforts to live godly lives.

In Christ the veil of separation has been removed.

As we look at Jesus we are transformed to be like him.

There are only two possible ways of attainting to a righteous life: by trying to do it ourselves, or by letting God work in our hearts the changes he wants. The first way is the way of the flesh. We try to obey God's law and to qualify ourselves for God's favour. This always ends in disaster. We can never live the godly life God requires through our own efforts. That is why Christ came to establish a better way – the way of the cross. On the cross, Jesus carried all our sins and our law-breaking setting us free from the penalty and the power of sin. We cannot mix these two ways – it is either the one or the other. Either we come the way of grace (unmerited favour) and succeed, or we struggle and fail under the bondage of the law (self-effort).

We walk in the new way of the Spirit.

From now on, we walk in the new way of the Spirit and reject the old way of the law. God's laws are now written on our heart and we no longer follow the external dictates of the law or the rules legalistic Christians try to impose on us. Instead, we look at Jesus and revel in the forgiveness and freedom he has given us. When you look at yourself, you see sin, but when you look at Christ, you see righteousness – the righteousness he has given to you. As we look away from ourselves to the finished work of the cross, the Holy Spirit fashions us into the image of Christ.

Always focus on Christ and never on yourself

The best advice I can give to you if you really want to go God's way, is to stop trying to change yourself – trying to be different, trying to become what you are not. This is fleshly, human self-effort. It is totally useless and absolutely unnecessary! You are not what you were because you are now in Christ. This has nothing to do with your efforts or your actions. It is one hundred per cent the work of God. He has totally re-created you in Christ. Now, you are a new creation and he is transforming you from within by the Holy Spirit.

Stop trying to change yourself - you are a new creation in Christ and God is transforming you from within by the Holy Spirit.

The secret lies in learning to be conscious of Jesus and his glory in you. Everything Jesus has accomplished belongs to you. In him you have 'wisdom, righteousness, holiness and redemption'. Christ is your life because 'your life in now hidden with Christ in God'. That means you are acceptable to God at all times, no matter what is going on in your life. You do not fall in and out of favour with God depending on how well you are doing as a Christian each day.

Always focus on Christ and his righteousness, never on yourself. You are complete in him. You are righteous in him. You are perfect in him. Stop trying to add to the perfection of Christ's work on the cross. It is a completed work and does not have to be supplemented by your own efforts. The more you see who you are in Christ and the more you meditate on all that he has done for you and in you, the more you will be transformed into his image. Understanding who you are in him will lead you into breathtaking levels of conformity to Christ in your daily life.

Transformed by the renewing of the mind

But none of this is possible without a profound change of mind and understanding. We must deal with our deceitful thoughts, some of which are natural to our fallen human nature, while others are the habits we acquire from early childhood. This means that true and genuine transformation of heart and life can only happen when we deal with these thoughts and motives of our heart.

The way God calls us to follow him shows that he has a profound understanding of human nature and psychology. This is hardly surprising seeing he is the One who created us in the first place!

God knows how we tick and deals with us accordingly. As we surrender to the transforming influences of the Holy Spirit, it is particularly important to grasp one significant biblical principle of human nature.

The principle is this:

We are motivated to go in the direction in which we believe our needs will be met.

Paul shows he understands this principle when he invites us to prove that God's will is good, acceptable, pleasing and fulfilling. You are never more fulfilled as a human being than when you are drawing your spiritual life and sustenance from Christ.

This means you must abandon your old beliefs that drove you away from God who is the only real fountain of life and fulfilment. Because your beliefs determine your intentions you will always be motivated in the direction set by these beliefs. In order to be delivered from negative patterns of life and living, you must challenge your false beliefs. You must deal with the deceptive patterns of thought that lead you in the direction of sin.

The truth of Christ brings freedom

The Bible shows us that the deception we hold in our hearts generates evil desires. Equally, the truth found in Christ produces godly desires. We begin to desire to go God's way when believe he, and he alone, can truly satisfy the deepest longings of our heart. The fundamental point we must grasp is that life cannot truly work apart from Christ. This is the truth that sets us free.

But you have not so learned Christ, if indeed you have heard him and have been taught by him, as the truth is in Jesus: that you put off, concerning your former conduct, the old man which grows corrupt according to the deceitful lusts [lusts of deceit], and be renewed in the spirit of your mind, and that you put on the new man which was created according to God, in true righteousness and holiness [righteousness and holiness of truth]. — Ephesians 4:20-24

Being renewed in the 'spirit' or 'attitude' of the mind is the key to change. We combat desires fuelled by the deception in our hearts with the truth that motivates us towards righteousness and holiness. This renewing of our mind destroys the lies at the root of our evil desires and releases new desires empowered by the revelation of the truth of Christ. The solution is to focus on Christ – his love, his redemption and power in our lives. He sets us free to reject the age-old lies that sin satisfies and that life without God works. These lies lead us into idolatry. We reject God's way and seek fulfilment in the pleasures of the flesh, which operate according to the false wisdom of the world.

Eve was the first to be deceived in this way. She believed the subtle lies of the devil that the forbidden fruit "was good for food, that it was pleasant to the eyes, and a tree desirable to make one wise" *(Genesis 3:6)*.

The so-called 'wisdom' she opted for was the deception that sin works and satisfaction comes from going your own way.

But Eve's deception brought tragic consequences. Sin, rather than bringing life, freedom and fulfilment, brought the exact opposite. *Genesis 2:25* and *Genesis 3:10* show the true consequences of sin to be everything relating to death and the opposite of life:

- Shame
- Alienation
- Cover up
- Fear
- Suspicion
- Expulsion
- Negative thoughts, feelings and intentions.

Real change comes into our lives when we reject the deception of sin and begin look to Christ alone to give us the fullness of life we long for. This is exactly what Peter realised when the Lord challenged his disciples. After a particularly testing sermon, many on the fringe of discipleship left him and Jesus asked his twelve,

John 6:67-68

"Do you also want to go away?" But Simon Peter answered Him, "Lord, to whom shall we go? you have the words of eternal life."

Peter understood that pursuing Christ meant pursuing the one who gives eternal life. Once we realise that Jesus offers us the only life that can truly satisfy we will pursue him passionately with all our heart. Jesus fulfils the deepest longings and needs of the human heart. He brings us back to the Father who is the source of all life and goodness.

Fundamentally, as human beings we have basic needs for:

Security – *to be safe in the presence of unconditional love and acceptance*

Significance – *to have impact and meaning, knowing we can make a difference and our being here matters*

Self-worth – *to know that we are people of infinite value and esteem.*

The question that reveals the deep motivation of our lives is, 'where do we think these needs will be met?' As fallen human beings, we have developed idolatrous beliefs that are deeply rooted in our experience. Often we learn from our childhood experiences what to do or avoid doing in order to have our needs met. Bad experiences bringing pain or dissatisfaction show us what to avoid if we want to escape bad feelings. In the same way, experiences resulting in positive emotions of fulfilment or satisfaction, teach us what to pursue in order to keep these good feelings alive.

One childhood recollection illustrates this point. I was about 5 years old and living with my family in East Africa. My father dreamed about having a boat even though we were many miles from the sea. He spent every weekend in the garage making his dream come true, as my brother and I watched him build the boat. Finally, when the project was completed, we all set out for a local dam to give the little boat its maiden voyage. We named the little rowboat 'Pot Luck' because my dad wasn't sure it would float!

Reluctantly, my father agreed to let us all get into the boat at the same time. I can remember the sense of joy and satisfaction I felt at being included, even though I was the younger brother and had the least to do with the building of the boat. But my father decided that the boat was too overloaded and asked me to get out while he and my brother set out into the deeper waters.

Even though I was left behind for my own safety and protection, I felt bad that I had been excluded. I can remember the feelings associated with rejection and loneliness as I saw my father, together with my brother, float out and return some time later exhilarated after a successful maiden voyage.

It is surprising to learn that experiences like that, particularly if they are part of a pattern in early childhood, can affect you later on in life. I gained from this and many other similar experiences, a false understanding of how to get my needs met. I learned that in order to feel that I was a person of worth I had to be accepted by people who were significant to me. I had to be included in their group. If I didn't want to end up feeling bad about myself, I had to adopt patterns of behaviour that would prevent me from being rejected or excluded. Many years later, I was still fighting feelings of low self-worth and rejection when faced with any situation in which I judged I was being unfairly excluded.

Many of us have learned patterns of avoidance or other behaviours which are based on our perceptions of how to have our needs met. Over time, these perceptions become deeply held and firmly fixed beliefs, often built into our very personality and unconscious way of seeing things. They tend towards idolatry because they lead us to believe that *fundamental fulfilment* lies outside of God and his gracious provision for our lives. But these false beliefs never work. They always lead us in the wrong direction – towards superficial and short-term satisfaction.

The answer lies in experiencing a profound repentance, or change of mind. Renewing our mind means exchanging those old idolatrous

Many of us have learned patterns of avoidance or other behaviours which are based on our perceptions of how to have our needs met. But these false beliefs never work. They always lead us in the wrong direction.

beliefs for new beliefs based on the deep, experiential knowledge that it is good to be near God and to follow his will. When we see God's goodness and grace and understand that he is a giver and not a withholder, we begin to draw near to him, trusting that his ways are good, perfect and pleasing. Then we begin to depend on him for power to overcome the past. Psalm 73 speaks about all this, especially verse 28:

Psalm 73:28

But it is good for me to draw near to God; I have put my trust in the Lord GOD, that I may declare all your works.

The dynamic of change

Once you truly believe that going God's way and submitting to the Lordship of Jesus Christ will bring you into fullness of life, you will be ready to change. Your motivation will be different. You will now want to go God's way. You will begin to reject the old, idolatrous ways of thinking and replace them with new thinking that directs you towards the Father's pure heart of love and grace.

Having been renewed in your mind, you will be ready to be transformed in your life. You will begin to put off the old and put on the new. You will replace old thoughts and intentions with new ones and you will develop new patterns of behaviour in your life.

How you can change

We are now ready to outline the steps towards real change in your life.

1. Look to Jesus and ask for a revelation of who you are in Christ. For a glimpse of this, see the list at the end of this chapter.

2. Keep your eyes on Jesus as you turn away from every thought of having your needs met in anything other than him and his gracious provisions for your life.

3. As the Holy Spirit prompts you, put off the old patterns of thinking and behaving, and put on thoughts and actions that are appropriate to your new life in Christ.

4. Persist in the new, replacing old habits with new habits in Christ through the power and energy of the Holy Spirit living in you.

TOPIC 4   REAL CHANGE

Who I am in Christ

The following list is taken from *Ephesians chapters 1 & 2*:

1. I am blessed with every spiritual blessing *(1:3)*
2. I am chosen before the foundation of the world *(1:4)*
3. I am holy and without blame before God *(1:4)*
4. I am loved by the Father *(1:4)*
5. I am predestined for a relationship with God *(1:5)*
6. I am adopted as a son by Jesus Christ *(1:5)*
7. I am pleasing to Christ *(1:5)*
8. I am a demonstration of the praise, glory and grace of God *(1:6)*
9. I am accepted and highly favoured in the well-loved Son of God *(1:6)*
10. I am redeemed and set free by the blood of Jesus *(1:7)*
11. I am forgiven of all my sin *(1:7)*
12. I am an inheritor of God *(1:11)*
13. I am secure in Christ *(1:13-14)*
14. I am enlightened with spiritual revelation knowledge and wisdom *(1:17-18)*
15. I am empowered and enabled by God *(1:19-20)*
16. I am seated with Christ in heavenly places at the right hand of the Father *(1:20)*
17. I am a victorious member of the body of Christ *(1:22-23)*
18. I am made alive in Christ *(2:1)*
19. I am delivered from Satan's control *(2:2)*
20. I am a child of his mercy *(2:3-4)*
21. I am saved by grace through faith *(2:8-9)*
22. I am the Father's creative workmanship *(2:10)*
23. I am made ready for God's prepared purpose *(2:10)*
24. I am part of the commonwealth of Israel *(2:12)*
25. I am included in the covenants of promise *(2:12)*
26. I am brought near by the blood of Christ *(2:13)*
27. I am a person who has immediate and permanent access to God by the Holy Spirit *(2:18)*
28. I am a fellow citizen with the saints of God *(2:19)*
29. I am a member of God's household *(2:19)*
30. I am built on the foundation of Christ *(2:20)*
31. I am part of the holy temple of the Lord *(2:21)*
32. I am a habitation of God by the Holy Spirit *(2:22)*.

TOPIC 5

THE FRUIT OF THE SPIRIT

When you were born again through faith in Jesus Christ an amazing miracle took place in your life. You received a new nature, the nature of Jesus Christ himself. This nature is spiritual, because the Holy Spirit gave it to you. Therefore, your new life in Christ is also the new life of the Spirit.

When you were born again through faith in Jesus Christ you received a new nature - the nature of Jesus Christ himself.

As we saw in Topic 4, the call to the new lifestyle in Christ is God's call for us to become what we are. Because we are no longer dominated by our fleshly desires we can live a life of surrender and obedience to the Holy Spirit. That way Christ's forms his character in us, and we become more and more like him as the days go by.

Paul gives us God's command in Galatians, 'Walk in the Spirit and you will not fulfil the desires of the flesh' *(Galatians 5:16)*. This shows both the problem and the solution, both the diagnosis and the cure.

First of all, it's important to recognise that we all still have the desires of the flesh. These negative influences of our own heart pull us away from God. Temptation comes through our evil desires that draw us away and entice us to give in to the negative patterns of our former life.

This pull towards sin can be very strong and for that reason, we must know how to deal with it effectively. In this book, we see how the flesh operates in our lives and how such things as damaged emotions, past hurts, demonic powers and bloodline bondages can all have a negative effect on us as we seek to follow Christ. We also see that in Christ we have been totally delivered from all these things and that he has given us the power to live free with Abba Father. It all comes down to this: walking in the strength and enablement of the Holy Spirit.

The Lordship of Jesus Christ

Our spiritual walk begins when we acknowledge that Jesus Christ is Lord of our lives. This is not just confessing him as Lord with our mouths, but actually submitting to his Lordship in our hearts. This is the only way to enter into the joys, privileges and the rewards of the kingdom of God.

Matthew 7:21

Not everyone who says to me, 'Lord, Lord,' shall enter the kingdom of heaven, but he who does the will of my Father in heaven.

An important part of acknowledging the Lordship of Jesus involves following him as his modern day disciples. Discipleship is 'the life that springs from grace'. Jesus draws us by his grace to the sacrificial, yet rewarding life of becoming like him in everything – our attitudes, our character, our behaviour and our ministry. But this not the automatic experience of every believer. We must choose it daily, and choose it because we really want it. As we saw in Topic 4, it's all about where we believe abundant life can be truly found.

Spiritual desire

If we have discovered that Jesus Christ is the abundant life we are looking for, we will be willing to lose our life to gain his. But if we don't really believe that true life is in him, we will always be half-hearted in spiritual matters, living on the periphery of God's kingdom and never entering right into the fullness of what he has for us. That's why Jesus was very careful to preface his call to discipleship with the issue of spiritual desire:

Luke 9:23-25

Then he said to them all, "If anyone desires to come after me, let him deny himself, and take up his cross daily, and follow me. For whoever desires to save his life will lose it, but whoever loses his life for my sake will save it. For what profit is it to a man if he gains the whole world, and is himself destroyed or lost?"

It's all about what you desire in your heart. Jesus first wins our hearts through the revelation of his love and grace. Then he shows us how to enjoy his deep satisfaction and fullness. Basically this mans taking up your cross daily and following him. If you want to save your life, and live according to your own wisdom, you will lose it. You will miss the abundant life he offers you. But if you truly desire what Christ has for you, you must be willing to lose your own life – your old way of thinking, believing and living, centred on yourself. In particular, it means dropping all self-effort to live for God. The wonderful surprise is that this new lifestyle centred on Christ releases the very life of Christ who lives in you. You lose your life and gain his!

Just as Christ carried his cross and was crucified, so we must also carry our cross and die daily to 'the self' in us – the things that displease him and the things belonging to our former way of life, including trying to live for God through our own efforts. The good news is, resurrection follows crucifixion! We discover that taking the way of the cross brings resurrection life and the fulfilment of our deepest longings and desires. God's way works!

Taking the way of the cross brings resurrection life and the fulfilment of our deepest longings and desires.

Paul put it like this:

I have been crucified with Christ; it is no longer I who live, but Christ lives in me; and the life which I now live in the flesh I live by faith in (or, the faith of) the Son of God, who loved me and gave himself for me.

Galatians 2:20

Here we see important principles of life in the Spirit:

- It begins with being crucified with Christ and dying to self
- This death leads to resurrection life, the very life of Christ in you
- The new life comes through the faith of Jesus Christ working both for you and in you.

The faith of Christ

We know that we could never be saved apart from Christ's death and resurrection. But very few understand this phrase, 'the faith of Christ'. What does Christ's faith have to do with our being saved and living a holy life before God? Jesus did two main things for us while he was on this earth: he *lived* for us and he *died* for us. In everything, Jesus was the pattern for obedience, but he is more to us than a mere example. He makes his very life available to us as we live by faith.

We know that Jesus died for us so that we could receive the righteousness of God and be saved, as Paul explains.

For he made him who knew no sin to be sin for us, that we might become the righteousness of God in him.

2 Corinthians 5:21

When he lived on the earth, Jesus perfectly fulfilled the Law of Moses for us, which was God's measurement of a holy life. Jesus perfectly matched the Father's will. He never committed a single sin but lived a life of perfect righteousness.

When Jesus died on the cross, he paid the penalty of our sin, taking away our unrighteousness and replacing it with his righteousness. We are saved by this righteousness, the righteousness of Jesus Christ, not our own. That's why our salvation is secure and we, who truly believe, can never be lost. We are saved by the righteousness of Christ and not through our own actions. This is Jesus' *work on our behalf*. He has now ascended to heaven to present himself before the Father as our intercessor, our advocate and our High Priest. He "ever lives to make intercession for us" *(Hebrews 7:25)*. He speaks to the Father in our defence, constantly applying the benefits of his sacrificial death to our lives *(1 John 2:1-2)*. This means that as Jesus is now before the Father, clothed in glory and holiness, so are we in the world *(1 John 4:17)*.

On the cross, Jesus paid the penalty of our sin, taking away our unrighteousness and replacing it with his righteousness.

But that is not all Jesus does for us. When Jesus rose again he made available his resurrection life by the Holy Spirit. Now we live by the faith of Christ *working in us*. The faith of Christ is both the free gift of righteousness by which we are saved, and the power of Christ in us by which we now walk in the ways of righteousness. We have been crucified with Christ, and Christ now lives in us. We live the life of Christ through the strength and enablement of the Holy Spirit who forms the character of Christ in us. All we have to do is step out of the way, cease from our striving and allow the new nature to take over. That's what it means to live by the faith of the Son of God. As Paul says, "I have been crucified with Christ, nevertheless I live – yet, not I, but *Christ* lives in me."

When Jesus rose again he made available his resurrection life by the Holy Spirit. Now we live by the faith of Christ working in us.

Another way of putting this is that the Holy Spirit reproduces the nature of Christ in us. As this new nature begins to take effect, we are changed to be like Christ. This is the *fruit* of the Spirit's work in our lives.

2 Corinthians 3:17-18

Now the Lord is the Spirit; and where the Spirit of the Lord is, there is liberty. But we all, with unveiled face, beholding as in a mirror the glory of the Lord, are being transformed into the same image from glory to glory, just as by the Spirit of the Lord.

Life in the Spirit

It is important to understand the significance of the life we are called to live in the Spirit. This means that we are made holy by what the Holy Spirit produces in us and not by our human effort. Holiness does not come from ourselves, but from Christ's nature in us. We must co-operate with the Holy Spirit and surrender to his leading, but we can never initiate holiness or live up to it in our own strength.

Some people wrongly argue that if we kept the right rules and regulations we would become holy. But rules and regulations can never make us holy. Only the Holy Spirit can do that. If it is

TOPIC 5   THE FRUIT OF THE SPIRIT

impossible to be saved by keeping the Law of Moses, then it is equally impossible to be made holy by trying to keep that same law. In fact, we have been gloriously set free from the law in all its forms and applications. We have been joined to Christ by the Holy Spirit. We are now under the law of Christ, or 'in-lawed to him' *(1 Corinthians 9:21)*. He now directs our lives by the Holy Spirit. This is where the inclination and the power to change come from. Just as we are saved by faith and not by works, so we are motivated and enabled to live a holy life by the Holy Spirit. We follow his promptings in our hearts. It has nothing to do with our self effort.

Rules and regulations can never make us holy. Only the Holy Spirit can do that.

Just as we are saved by faith and not by works, so we are motivated and enabled to live a holy life by the Holy Spirit.

However, it is important to avoid some wrong conclusions that people can mistakenly draw from these facts.

Holiness requires our active co-operation

First, there is the wrong conclusion that because the Holy Spirit produces the fruit of the new life in us, we don't have to do anything at all to become holy. That is not the case. We must believe and act on our faith by putting off the old and putting on the new. We *trust* and *obey* the Holy Spirit.

We must actively cooperate with the Spirit as we walk in holiness. God is not going to do it for you, nor is he going to do it through you. Rather, he will enable *you* to do it. You must choose to live for God and walk in his ways. But you can only be successful as you rely on the Holy Spirit to enable you to do it.

Next, there is the wrong view that because we are not under the Law of Moses it means we don't have to live a holy life. Some even teach that because God's grace covers all our sin we can live as we like!

Paul had to deal with this error, but look closely at his reply:

What shall we say then? Shall we continue in sin that grace may abound? Certainly not! How shall we who died to sin live any longer in it?   Romans 6:1-2

Sin cannot keep you from grace, but grace will keep you from sin. Grace is not a license to sin. It is *how* we conquer sin.

Sin shall not have dominion over you, for you are not under law but under grace.   Romans 6:14

Grace covers all our sin and deals with it completely, but we must never use this fact to cover up our sin or justify our sinful actions. The apostle Peter teaches strongly on this point.

1 Peter 2:16 — *Live as free men, but do not use your freedom as a cover-up for evil; live as servants of God.*

Holiness is necessary

Can you see how totally inconsistent people are when they say that because we have received God's grace it doesn't matter if we keep on sinning. We have died to sin and continuing in sin after we are saved is unthinkable! The very opposite is the case. As John Newton writes in his hymn *Amazing Grace*, 'It was grace that taught my heart to fear and grace my fears relieved!'

Newton knew that God's grace saves us but that also those who have truly been saved will want to deal with every sin in their lives out of awesome respect and love for God.

This is how Paul described it to Titus:

Titus 2:11-12 — *For the grace of God that brings salvation has appeared to all men, teaching us that, denying ungodliness and worldly lusts, we should live soberly, righteously, and godly in the present age…*

The Psalm writer put it like this:

Psalm 130:3-4 — *If you, LORD, should mark iniquities, O Lord, who could stand? But there is forgiveness with you that you may be feared.*

Holiness can be instructed

Another important misunderstanding needs to be corrected when we explain that Christians are not under the law. Some people wrongly take this to mean that there are no instructions that we need to obey as Christians. All we have to do is follow the leading of the Spirit. Yes, this last point is true, all we have to do is obey the Holy Spirit, but his leadings and promptings can be turned into godly instruction.

The New Testament describes in detail what life in the Spirit looks like and this is our authoritative pattern for living.

In fact, that is exactly why much of the New Testament was written. It records the Holy Spirit's instructions concerning the new life. But the New Testament is neither a new law nor a Christian code of ethics. Rather, it describes in detail what life in the Spirit looks like and this is our authoritative pattern for living. Christian discipleship is all about learning what the will of God is and abstaining from the things that displease him. The Spirit reveals these things to us, both from the Scriptures and to our hearts directly.

TOPIC 5   THE FRUIT OF THE SPIRIT

Anything that is not in line with the Golden Rule or Principle of Love is to be avoided. Jesus told us to, "Do unto others what you would have them do unto you" *(Matthew 7:12)*.

The Holy Spirit makes it clear to us what God's will is. What the flesh produces is obvious when you really think about it, and so are the consequences of yielding to it. How can we inherit the good things of Abba God while we are preoccupied or dominated by these works of the flesh?

Now the works of the flesh are evident, which are: adultery, fornication, uncleanness, lewdness, idolatry, sorcery, hatred, contentions, jealousies, outbursts of wrath, selfish ambitions, dissensions, heresies, envy, murders, drunkenness, revelries, and the like; of which I tell you beforehand, just as I also told you in time past, that those who practice such things will not inherit the kingdom of God.

Galatians 5:19-21

We have a simple choice to make. Do we want to submit to the works of the flesh or be liberated into the life of the Spirit? Our focus makes all the difference. If we focus on the flesh and try to overcome it through our own efforts, we will fail. But if we surrender to the Spirit we will overcome the works of the flesh.

Works or fruit?

Notice Paul speaks of the 'works' of the flesh and the 'fruit' of the Spirit. His choice of words is deliberate. Human effort, trying to please God by what we do, is just the same as trying to gain his favour by our works. Those who live by the law, or seek to be influenced by it, are easily dominated by the flesh. All the law can do is to show us our weakness and failure. Paul writes, "by the law we become conscious of sin" *(Romans 3:20)*. The Holy Spirit does not want us to live under the consciousness of sin, he wants us to live conscious of the righteousness we have in Christ.

Do we want to submit to the works of the flesh or be liberated into the life of the Spirit?

Those who are continually languishing under the guilt of having failed God, continually reminding themselves that they are sinful, will never break out of the cycle of trying and failing. We were not saved by our works. Neither are we made holy by our own efforts. Paul reveals that the real power behind sin is the law *(1 Corinthians 15:56)*. We must be delivered from our own efforts, from trying to please God under the law. But the good news is that Jesus has set us free from the vice-like grip and the stranglehold of the law. Remember, we are set free from sin because we are not under the law but under grace *(Romans 6:14)*.

If we focus on the flesh and try to overcome it through our own efforts, we will fail. But if we surrender to the Spirit we will overcome the works of the flesh.

We escape the power of the law in order to reap the fruit of righteousness, the fruit of the Spirit. When we stop trying to please God through our fleshly efforts to keep the law we can surrender to the

Holy Spirit who produces his fruit in us. In other words, once we give up our self-effort we release the Spirit to do his work in us.

Sowing to the Spirit

Surrendering to the Holy Spirit is like sowing seeds that produce the fruit of righteousness in us. Sowing and reaping is a principle of nature – whatever you sow, you reap. If you sow apple seed you will have a harvest of apples, grape seed will produce a harvest of grapes – and so on. This is also a spiritual principle. If you sow to the flesh, you will reap things in your life that are fleshly and unprofitable. But if you sow according to the Spirit you will reap the rich, refreshing and fulfilling fruit of the Spirit. In other words, if we submit to the flesh we will reap accordingly, but if we sow to the Spirit and surrender to his influences we will reap everything good that flows from God's kingdom and his rule in our lives.

Galatians 6:7-8

Do not be deceived, God is not mocked; for whatever a man sows, that he will also reap. For he who sows to his flesh will of the flesh reap corruption, but he who sows to the Spirit will of the Spirit reap everlasting life.

The context of this passage is giving our financial resources into the kingdom of God. Paul shows that our finances are like seed that can be sown wrongly or rightly. Right use of your money can bring much blessing to others and to yourself. But if you abuse your finance by sowing it into your fleshly pleasures you will end up with rotten fruit in your life!

How do you stop sowing to the flesh and start sowing the the Spirit?

First, you choose to believe that you are righteous in Christ and that you do not have to do anything to come under his favour.

Second, you live under God's favour, pursuing Christ and his goodness and leaving behind the false promises of the flesh.

Applied to your spiritual life, the principle of sowing and reaping means you must stop sowing into the unproductive soil of the flesh. Instead, you live according to the Spirit who produces his fruit in you. But how do you stop sowing to the flesh? You do this in two ways. First, you *choose to believe* that you are righteous in Christ and that you do not have to do anything to come under his favour. You acknowledge that you are greatly blessed, highly favoured and deeply loved in Christ *(Ephesians 1:6)*. Second, you *live* under God's favour, pursuing Christ and his goodness and leaving behind the false promises of the flesh. You stop trying to find life under the law and you stop trying to find fulfilment through your own efforts and wisdom. Instead, you trust in Christ's righteousness finding your joy and fulfilment in him.

As you yield to the Spirit, you overcome the desires of the flesh. The Holy Spirit shapes you into the character of Christ. The new nature of the Spirit produces the fruit of Christ's life in you. This fruit of the Spirit is also easy to recognise.

TOPIC 5   THE FRUIT OF THE SPIRIT

But the fruit of the Spirit is love, joy, peace, longsuffering, kindness, goodness, faithfulness, gentleness, self-control. Against such there is no law.   Galatians 5:22-23

When we live like this, we are living a higher level of righteousness than if we were simply obeying the Law of Moses. Because we are pleasing God through the internalised operation of the Holy Spirit, our righteousness comes from within. The Holy Spirit gives us the road map of life, but he also is our living guide who accompanies us on the way, and he is our motivating and empowering influence who enables us to walk in the paths of holiness.

Total surrender

Recognising the Lordship of Jesus leads to total surrender. You learn how to place the whole of your life under his control and rule of love. Your time, your talents, your possessions and your finances are now no longer your own. All that you have comes from him and has been entrusted to you as God's steward, to manage and use on his behalf. This is how the kingdom of God works. We have no right to hold anything back. Total commitment is not be feared but welcomed. Honouring God in everything never means that you lose out. Even suffering rejection and persecution for the sake of Christ have their reward.

So Jesus answered and said, "Assuredly, I say to you, there is no one who has left house or brothers or sisters or father or mother or wife or children or lands, for my sake and the gospel's, who shall not receive a hundredfold now in this time – houses and brothers and sisters and mothers and children and lands, with persecutions – and in the age to come, eternal life."   Mark 10:29-30

What an amazing salvation Jesus has given us! Not only are we saved by his grace, but we are also made holy by his grace. That is the power of his unmerited favour over our lives. He sets us free from sin and the law and he releases us into the life of the Spirit. Jesus gives us his righteousness as a free gift and then works in us that very righteousness so that our lives carry the fruit of his character. And after all that, he rewards us still more by blessing us with his abundant provision in every area of our lives.

TOPIC 6

INNER HEALING

God's salvation is total and complete. It touches every part of your personality: spirit, soul and body. This means Jesus' finished work on the cross has made full provision for every part of your life.

Now may the God of peace himself sanctify you completely; and may your whole spirit, soul, and body be preserved blameless at the coming of our Lord Jesus Christ. — 1 Thessalonians 5:23

The New International Version says,

May God... preserve blameless your entire spirit and soul and body.

Look at how God's salvation works:

Physically – *healing for your body now and resurrection to come*
Emotionally – *healing for your inner life, your soul, your mind and your emotions*
Spiritually – *your spirit is made alive and whole.*

> *Jesus' finished work on the cross has made full provision for every part of your life.*

The restoration of the whole person will not be complete until the coming of Jesus. In the meantime, there will always be more of him to experience, more opportunity to grow in grace and in the knowledge of the Lord. The pressures of daily life will always be there – coming from people, circumstances and situations that negatively affect our lives. Christian maturity does not bring a problem-free existence but is measured by how we handle these things.

Notice the order in which God restores the various aspects of our humanity: first the spirit, then the soul, and finally the body, which will be redeemed on the Day of Resurrection. God begins with the greatest healing of all by dealing with the root of all problems, which is sin. The forgiveness of God is the greatest miracle you will ever experience. Even Jesus' miracles of physical healing were signs pointing to his authority to forgive sins. This is clear from the story of the healing of the paralysed man.

Mark 2:10-11

"But that you may know that the Son of Man has power on earth to forgive sins" – he said to the paralytic, "I say to you, arise, take up your bed, and go your way to your house."

But there is another dimension to healing that is not just physical or spiritual. This is the healing of our emotions, which we call 'inner healing'. God wants to heal our 'inner person', as the following verses show.

2 Corinthians 4:16

Therefore we do not lose heart. Even though our outward man is perishing, yet the inward man is being renewed day by day.

Proverbs 18:14

The spirit of a man will sustain him in sickness, but who can bear a broken spirit?

Proverbs 4:23

Keep your heart with all diligence, for out of it spring the issues of life.

God wants to heal you of:

- A wounded spirit
- A broken spirit
- A grieving spirit
- Inner pain
- Inner conflict
- Damaged emotions.

These inner problems are not visible from the outside. Many Christians look happy enough, but this does not mean they are free from inner pain. You can praise and worship every Sunday but still be hurting inside. You can be free from physical pain, but still be suffering emotional pain.

The presence of pain

There is dangerous traffic on life's highway and much that can harm us, leaving us by the side of the road broken, bleeding and hurting. We are all casualties in something, whether broken relationships, abuse in our childhood, parental failures, personal sins or tragic happenings.

TOPIC 6   INNER HEALING

Pain caused by other people

God has made us dependent on other people. We need companionship, acceptance, approval, recognition and many other things that God provides through relationships with people. Whenever these needs are violated in some way, we can suffer great personal pain.

Bad relationships in marriage and the family can result in the most severe forms of emotional damage. Pain caused in childhood by bad parenting can leave behind a lifetime of misery. Divorce is notoriously painful, no matter what circumstances surround it.

There are so many people who suffer the pain of loneliness or rejection. They open up to another person, get rejected and then recoil behind a hard protective barrier, hurting and afraid to ever come out again.

Separation can come through the death or unfaithfulness of another. Intense pain can be the result of some gross sin committed against you, such as verbal, physical or sexual abuse.

Casualties lie fallen everywhere. Selfish ambition and greed lead to all kinds of hurts inflicted upon people who are trampled down by others in their clamour for personal advantage. Violence overtakes a society of individuals who deny others their value or worth, seeing them either as obstacles to be removed or objects to be used and then discarded.

We need companionship, acceptance, approval, recognition and many other things that God provides through relationships with people. Whenever these needs are violated in some way, we can suffer great personal pain.

Pain caused by events that happen to you

Life is full of uncertainties and we are surrounded by many tragic circumstances. Traumatic experiences can leave you shattered and in deep shock. Slowly the true extent of the painful damage becomes apparent, making way for fear, mistrust, loneliness and depression. Somehow the pieces never seem to come back together.

At other times, the events are just as tragic but not so sudden or dramatic. Your boyfriend marries another woman. Your brother excels leaving you to bear the pain of your parents' disappointment and their constant negative comparisons between you and him. You miss the opportunity of a lifetime in your career. You fail an exam, which alters the course of your life. Your teenage son walks out on you and your Christian faith. You make a wrong choice in a major area of your life and deep disappointment sets in.

Pain caused by your own personal sin

It is unhelpful to suppose that all suffering is due to personal sin.

Some of our pain, however, is our own fault.

It is unhelpful to suppose that all suffering is due to personal sin. It is not that simple. The Bible gives us many examples of righteous people suffering. The best-known example is Job who suffered the accusation of his friends, adding to his already extremely painful circumstances. They could not understand Job's sufferings apart from the narrow view that said he was suffering because he was a sinner.

Biblical writers also record the fact that many unrighteous people seem to flourish. Psalm 73 records what Asaph observed on this matter and how he came to terms with the whole question. God showed him that he would never forsake the righteous and, even though the wicked may appear to flourish for a season, their time is short.

Psalm 73:26-27

My flesh and my heart fail; but God is the strength of my heart and my portion forever. For indeed, those who are far from you shall perish; you have destroyed all those who desert you for harlotry.

Some of our pain, however, is our own fault. We disobey God's word and refuse the things that bring wellbeing into our life. The consequences can be both physical and emotional.

Proverbs 6:27-28

Can a man take fire to his bosom and his clothes not be burned? Can one walk on hot coals and his feet not be seared?

Psalm 7:14-16

Behold, the wicked brings forth iniquity. Yes, he conceives trouble and brings forth falsehood. He made a pit and dug it out, and has fallen into the ditch which he made. His trouble shall return upon his own head, and his violent dealing shall come down on his own crown.

Psalms 32 and 38 describe the physical, emotional and spiritual pain caused by sin. But the answer is always near: forgiveness and restoration through Christ.

The place of forgiveness

Forgiveness is the standard for the Christian. God has forgiven us and he calls us likewise to forgive others. No matter what the sin or hurt committed against us, God always calls us to forgive. His forgiveness sets the standard for our lives.

Ephesians 4:32

Be kind and compassionate to one another, forgiving each other, just as in Christ God forgave you.

In the parable of the unmerciful servant Jesus showed the total inconsistency of those in God's kingdom who refuse to forgive. We have been forgiven a very large and unpayable debt. How can we now withhold forgiveness from others? The king in the parable says to the unmerciful servant,

Should you not also have had compassion on your fellow servant, just as I had pity on you? — Matthew 18:33

The dangers of unforgiveness

Unforgiveness is totally negative and destructive and nothing good ever comes from it.

- *Unforgiveness brings distress*

The unmerciful servant was thrown into prison and put into the hands of debt collectors (torturers), until he paid up in full. This means as long as we refuse to forgive others we will lack peace of heart and be vulnerable to distress in the form of anxiety, stress, sorrow and other kinds of emotional pain.

And his master was angry, and delivered him to the torturers until he should pay all that was due to him. So my heavenly Father also will do to you if each of you, from his heart, does not forgive his brother his trespasses. — Matthew 18:34-35

- *Unforgiveness blocks the parental forgiveness of God*

In the Lord's Prayer, Jesus teaches us to forgive daily all those who sin against us. He warns us that our heavenly Father will withhold his parental forgiveness from us, if we withhold forgiveness from others.

For if you forgive men when they sin against you, your heavenly Father will also forgive you. But if you do not forgive men their sins, your Father will not forgive your sins. — Matthew 6:14-15

When God withholds his *parental* forgiveness, he does not put us back under condemnation. Our sins can never count against us again because God has totally forgiven and forgotten them. He cancelled our debt and credited us with the righteousness of Christ. We received this *judicial* forgiveness once for all by faith in the blood of Jesus. God, the righteous judge, judged all our sins on the cross and removed condemnation from our lives forever!

Now we can understand that our heavenly Father will never reject or abandon his children, even when we let him down. But when we sin, it hinders our fellowship with him, especially when we withhold forgiveness from others. The only way God blesses us is by grace, and when we move away from this principle, God cannot pour into our lives all the blessings he has for us. Therefore, the Father always calls us back to his grace. A person who is truly walking in grace will also walk in the light of God's total forgiveness and will have no problem forgiving others.

Every day we come before our heavenly Father and thank him for his forgiveness – the forgiveness that makes us his sons and daughters. Every day we show him that we are walking in grace by forgiving others the wrongs they have done against us. And the blessings of the Father flow freely into our lives.

Every day we come before our heavenly Father and thank him for his forgiveness – the forgiveness that makes us his sons and daughters.

- *Unforgiveness gives the devil a foothold*

There is nothing the devil likes more than when people remain bitter and unforgiving. It gives him a foothold into that situation and if it is not dealt with, the foothold can become a stronghold. Unforgiveness provides the devil with an open door to bring his division and destruction into a situation or a relationship.

Ephesians 4:26-27 (NIV) *In your anger do not sin: Do not let the sun go down while you are still angry, and do not give the devil a foothold.*

- *Unforgiveness hinders effective prayer*

Our prayer life can be severely hindered by unforgiveness. Withholding forgiveness from others prevents our faith from operating freely, and that can rob us of God's blessings and block the release of his promises into our lives. Grace is our only confidence that God will answer our prayers. We never get answers because we deserve them. That's why God brings us back to the principle of grace every time we pray. We are not walking in grace when we hold unforgiveness in our heart. When we pray we must remember the grace God has shown to us and extend that same grace to others. That's how prayer works.

We are not walking in grace when we hold unforgiveness in our heart.

Mark 11:25 *And when you stand praying, if you hold anything against anyone, forgive him, so that your heavenly Father may forgive you your sins.*

Consequences of judgmentalism

Closely related to unforgiveness is the sin of judgementalism. The harsh and negative judgements you make against others will always rebound on you.

Proverbs 26:27 *If a man digs a pit, he will fall into it; if a man rolls a stone it will roll back on him.*

Many bring suffering on themselves as a result of the bitter judgements they make against others. Jesus sternly warned against allowing ourselves to fall into this trap.

Matthew 7:1-2 *Judge not, that you be not judged. For with what judgment you judge, you will be judged; and with the measure you use, it will be measured back to you.*

The judgements we use against others bounce back on us and this can bring tragic results in our lives. When we judge others, we close our own hearts to God's merciful provision for us and this can block the flow of God's blessing.

For example, one reason why parental sins can reappear in their children is due to this principle. Bitterness held against parents for such things as violence, abuse, divorce and alcoholism can provide Satan with an opportunity to reproduce the parents' problems in the children. This is one way the sins of the parents can be visited on the children for many generations.

When we judge others, we close our own hearts to God's merciful provision for us and this can block the flow of God's blessing.

...you shall not bow down to them nor serve them. For I, the LORD your God, am a jealous God, visiting the iniquity of the fathers on the children to the third and fourth generations of those who hate me, but showing mercy to thousands, to those who love me and keep my commandments.

Exodus 20:5-6

We are set free from all generational sins when we come to Christ. The blood of Jesus has dealt with them *(1 Peter 1:18-19)*. But we will find it hard to experience full freedom if we refuse to forgive our parents or any other parental figures who have sinned against us.

The sins of the parents

Parental relationships are crucial in a person's development. Your relationship with your parents is of utmost importance to the whole of your life as the Scripture says, "Honour your father and mother which is the first commandment with a promise, that it may go well with you and that you may enjoy long life on the earth" *(Ephesians 6:1-2)*. The value God places upon parents cannot be overstated *(Leviticus 19:3; 20:9; Proverbs 17:6)*.

God designed the parent-child relationship to be both a model and preparation for our relationship with God.

God designed the parent-child relationship to be both a model and preparation for our relationship with God. Any rebellion or lack of respect towards parents is a serious sin against a primary provision of the Lord. Any abuse of authority or failure to fulfil parental obligations before the Lord is also a serious offence in the eyes of the Lord *(Ephesians 6:4)*.

Resentment of the children

It is particularly important that you examine your heart and see if you are holding any resentment towards your parents. No parent has ever completely fulfilled God's requirements in parenting and some parents make serious mistakes that are in reality serious sins against their children. Negative reactions to these can linger in the heart of the young person, and soon turn to destructive resentment. Jesus warned about the principle of our harsh judgements and bitter resentments having a harmful effect upon ourselves *(Matthew 7:1)*. Experience shows the devastating effects resentment can bring within such significant relationships.

Walking in forgiveness

We have seen that anger, resentment and bitterness are at the root of much that is negative and destructive in our lives and in our relationship with others. This means we must learn to walk in forgiveness – *first* the forgiveness of God to us, and *second* the forgiveness he calls us to extend to others.

When we walk in God's grace and his forgiveness, we are able to reject the slanderous and unjust accusations the enemy uses against us in the spiritual realm.

When we walk in God's grace and his forgiveness, we are able to reject the slanderous and unjust accusations the enemy uses against us in the spiritual realm. Satan tells us that we are sinners worthy of God's condemnation and totally unqualified to receive his blessings and favour. That was true once. But it is not true now. We are sinners no longer. Jesus' blood has made us righteous before God. We are not even 'sinners saved by grace'. We are the righteousness of God in Christ as Paul makes abundantly clear.

2 Corinthians 5:21

For he [God] made him [Jesus] who knew no sin to be sin for us, that we might become the righteousness of God in him.

In the Lord's Prayer, Jesus taught us principles to govern our daily life of prayer. For example, he taught us to depend on him for physical provision: "Give us this day our daily bread."

We reject the kind of morbid introspection some religious teachers demand.

He also taught that we are to walk in the light of his forgiveness: "Forgive us our trespasses as we forgive those who trespass against us." Many people misunderstand Jesus' meaning here. They think he is teaching that *no* sin can be forgiven until we specifically confess it to God. But remember God has already forgiven all our sins at the cross! We have received *judicial* forgiveness once for all.

They tell us to search within ourselves for every imperfection and confess every single new sin we discover, because until we do that, these sins remain unforgiven.

Jesus is not going back on his word. In fact, the Lord's Prayer calls us to remind ourselves daily that God is our heavenly Father – that we live under his *judicial* forgiveness and cleansing. This means we reject the kind of morbid introspection some religious teachers demand. They tell us to 'keep short accounts with the Lord' searching within ourselves for every imperfection and confessing every single new sin we discover, because until we do that, these sins remain unforgiven. Nothing could be further from the truth. Jesus took *all* our sins and nailed them to the cross. This means that the judgment of God has now been completely lifted from us. God has totally forgiven and forgotten all our sins – past, present and future.

Some people ask how God can forgive the sins we have not even committed yet! When Jesus died, you were yet to be born. You had not yet committed one single sin – all your sins were in the future. Jesus became your substitute sacrifice for sin more than 2,000 years ago. God has already judged all your sins on the cross, because you believe in Jesus. It would now be totally unjust for God to demand further judgement. Jesus carried your sins on the cross so that you would never have to carry them again.

God has already judged all your sins on the cross, because you believe in Jesus. It would now be totally unjust for God to demand further judgement.

We receive God's *total* forgiveness by trusting in the finished work of Christ on the cross. When we trusted in Christ, God declared us righteous, not by our own works or efforts, but by his grace. This means our sins will never again be held against us by God. This truth is clearly expounded by Paul in *Romans chapter 4* as he quotes from one of the Psalms of King David.

Now to him who works, the wages are not counted as grace but as debt. But to him who does not work but believes on him who justifies the ungodly, his faith is accounted for righteousness, just as David also describes the blessedness of the man to whom God imputes righteousness apart from works: "Blessed are those whose lawless deeds are forgiven, and whose sins are covered. Blessed is the man to whom the LORD shall not impute sin."

Romans 4:4-8

This shows us clearly that forgiveness is *absolutely free* – it does not depend on our works. We are forgiven because we believe right, not because we live right. Forgiveness is also *total and complete*. God will not allow any sin (past, present or future) to count against us. God will never impute sin or hold us accountable for the sins we commit. Instead, he imputes to our account the infinite righteousness of Christ.

Holy living does not come about by living under the threat of judgment. It comes from knowing the genuine forgiveness of all our sins.

Some say that this is impossible because it means we can go on sinning and it will not matter. That is not true. Holy living does not come about by living under the threat of judgment. It comes from knowing the genuine forgiveness of *all* our sins. We live right because we *are* forgiven. Jesus said, "The one who has been forgiven much loves much." In other words, when we walk in the grace and forgiveness of the Father, we leave aside the old way of living – in fact, we die to the old way of sin when we escape from its guilt and condemnation. Look at the way Paul deals with this point.

Romans 6:1-2

What shall we say then? Shall we continue in sin that grace may abound? Certainly not! How shall we who died to sin live any longer in it?

We are set free from sin by walking in the forgiveness God has given us, and not by the constant thought that there are always more sins to be forgiven because we live imperfect lives.

We are made right with God through the once-for-all judicial forgiveness granted at the cross. But, walking in parental forgiveness means fellowshipping with the Father day by day, depending on his grace and the continual cleansing of the blood.

When Jesus tells us to ask the Father daily to forgive our sins, he is talking about *parental* forgiveness, not *judicial* forgiveness. We are made right with God through the once-for-all judicial forgiveness granted at the cross. But, walking in parental forgiveness means fellowshipping with the Father day by day, depending on his grace and the continual cleansing of the blood.

By calling God "our Father", we remind ourselves that all our sins have been dealt with at the cross. We come back to the principle of grace. Knowing the blood of Jesus *has* cleansed us and *keeps on* cleansing us from all sin, is the secret of walking in victory. John, the disciple who knew more about the love of Jesus than anyone else, teaches this principle in his letter to Christians:

1 John 2:1-2

My little children, these things I write to you, so that you may not sin. And if anyone sins, we have an Advocate with the Father, Jesus Christ the righteous. And he himself is the propitiation for our sins, and not for ours only but also for the whole world.

What does he say – we must confess our sins, otherwise we will be condemned? No! He reminds us that if we sin we have one *who speaks to the Father in our defence* – one who maintains our position of 'no condemnation' before God. Earlier in his letter, where John talks about the need to confess sins he is referring to how we came to Christ by confessing that we were sinners and needed God's salvation. John makes it clear that the 'blood of Jesus *keeps on cleansing* us from sin' *(1 John 1:7)*. Once we have confessed our sin and received God's gift of salvation we walk in the forgiveness of God.

1 John 1:8-10

If we say that we have no sin, we deceive ourselves, and the truth is not in us. If we confess our sins, he is faithful and just to forgive us our sins and to cleanse us from all unrighteousness. If we say that we have not sinned, we make him a liar, and his word is not in us.

Jesus came to set us free from the bondage of religious teaching that continues to hold us captive to sin – always more to do, always more sins to be forgiven, always more repentance needed.

Jesus came to set us free from the bondage of religious teaching that continues to hold us captive to sin – always more to do, always more sins to be forgiven, always more repentance needed. We have been saved from 'the uttermost to the uttermost' – from the state of uttermost sin and condemnation to the state of uttermost salvation. This uttermost salvation of total forgiveness is guaranteed by Jesus Christ our heavenly High Priest.

Hebrews 7:25

Therefore he is also able to save to the uttermost those who come to God through him, since he always lives to make intercession for them.

Once we are saved, our relationship with God is on a totally different footing. We now live under the blood of Jesus. Through the blood, God becomes our Father, and no longer deals with us according to the principle of the law. Through the blood, the condemnation of the law is removed forever from our lives. As a loving, heavenly Father, he draws us closer and closer to his heart, and leads us out of the works of darkness so that we can enjoy fellowship with him in the light. In other words, we *were cleansed* once for all at the cross and the blood of Jesus *keeps on cleansing* us as we walk in the light with him. When we sin, we bring it to the light, with full assurance that the blood is cleansing us and removing any hindrance to our fellowship with God. We own our sin in his holy presence only to disown it in the light of his grace and forgiveness. We never allow guilt or sin-consciousness to have a resting place in our hearts. We maintain a clear conscience before God by walking in the light of his love. This is true repentance – we reject our sin and embrace who we are in Christ.

We never allow guilt or sin-consciousness to have a resting place in our hearts.

Forgiving others

Jesus also broke the barriers of legalistic religion when he spoke about forgiving our enemies and all those who sin against us. The Law of Moses spoke about the rights of retaliation, 'an eye for an eye and a tooth for a tooth.' Jesus showed us a better way, the way of grace and forgiveness. He said,

Love your enemies, do good to them, and lend to them without expecting to get anything back. Then your reward will be great, and you will be sons of the Most High, because he is kind to the ungrateful and wicked. Be merciful, just as your Father is merciful. "Do not judge, and you will not be judged. Do not condemn, and you will not be condemned. Forgive, and you will be forgiven.

Luke 6:35-37

As we have seen, the Lord's Prayer teaches us the discipline of daily forgiving others. Jesus tells us to pray, "Forgive us our trespasses as we forgive those who trespass against us." Paul says that we are to, "Be kind and compassionate to one another, forgiving each other, just as in Christ God forgave you." This shows that one of the most important character traits in the family of God is our willingness to forgive others. It shows we are living in grace, and are true sons of our heavenly Father.

Forgiveness shows we are living in grace, and are true sons of our heavenly Father.

What does it mean then, 'to forgive one another, as God has forgiven us in Christ?' When God forgives us he makes a promise 'not to remember' our sins ever again. It is a promise to forget and it means that as far as God is concerned our sins never happened!

"This is the covenant that I will make with them after those days, says the LORD: I will put my laws into their hearts, and in their minds I will write them," then He adds, "Their sins and their lawless deeds I will remember no more."

Hebrews 10:16-17

When you forgive someone as God has forgiven you, it means you make a promise never to remember those sins again. In other words, forgiveness means you promise that you will never again bring up those sins or use them negatively against the person. You promise

LIVING FREE! ENJOYING FREEDOM AND VICTORY IN CHRIST

Jesus told us how to win a brother who has sinned against us. We approach them in an attitude of forgiveness and reconciliation.

never to remind the person concerned (or others, or even yourself) of their sins against you. That is how God has forgiven us.

The fruits of forgiveness

Forgiveness frees you up to love the offenders and help them with the underlying problem that gave rise to the offence in the first place. This is when we can lovingly help people according to Jesus teaching:

Matthew 7:3-5

And why do you look at the speck in your brother's eye, but do not consider the plank in your own eye? Or how can you say to your brother, 'Let me remove the speck from your eye'; and look, a plank is in your own eye? Hypocrite! First remove the plank from your own eye, and then you will see clearly to remove the speck out of your brother's eye.

Inner healing

Once we have dealt with our own faults and hardness of heart (including unforgiveness), we can begin to help restore others. The New Testament shows that we have a responsibility to do this, but we must first deal with our own offendedness before we can help the offenders.

Galatians 6:1-2

Brethren, if a man is overtaken in any trespass, you who are spiritual restore such a one in a spirit of gentleness, considering yourself lest you also be tempted. Bear one another's burdens, and so fulfill the law of Christ.

We can only work for restoration in relationships if we go about it with a Christ-like attitude of gentleness, with a complete lack of resentment and with a spirit of non-retaliation. Jesus told us how to win a brother who has sinned against us. We approach them in an attitude of forgiveness and reconciliation.

Matthew 18:15

Moreover if your brother sins against you, go and tell him his fault between you and him alone. If he hears you, you have gained your brother.

Walking in forgiveness frees you from all the negative effects of unforgiveness. It releases the power of God to work in that situation. Very often on our Encounter Weekends we see the powerful effects of forgiveness. We show people how forgiveness releases others from the offences they have committed against them.

As they do this, powerful things happen. People are healed and relationships are restored (often supernaturally) and families come back together. It seems as if forgiveness sets people free from the curse-like pronouncements that have kept people bound and imprisoned by negative experiences. The grace of God is released, often bringing dramatic change into the situation.

A father returns

The spiritual principles we have been discussing are real and practical. During a time of ministry at an Encounter Weekend one of the young women from the Youth Fellowship shared her feelings of hurt and disappointment with her father who had abandoned her and her mother some time ago. She had not heard from her father since he had left home.

The ministry time led the young woman through a process of inner healing for her hurt. She was helped to see that Jesus, who cared for her deeply, would never leave her or forsake her. She also found it within her heart to forgive her father and release him from the power of unforgiveness and resentment. She also prayed that God would speak to him.

The next day on the way home in the coach, she received a telephone call from her mother telling her that her father had repented and was coming home. That's the power of forgiveness.

Handling Your Hurt

We have begun to understand what a serious issue forgiveness is. Not only do we need the forgiveness of God in our lives, but we also need to give and receive forgiveness in our human relationships. *Luke 6:27-38* shows us some powerful pointers that take us in the direction of forgiveness and enable us to receive inner healing. Read that passage now as you prepare for to take the following steps.

When you have been sinned against or hurt by the offence of others, remember you are not responsible for what others have done to you. It is their offence against you. But you are responsible for your reaction to that offence. Your part is to refuse to live in anger, bitterness or resentment, and to forgive and release people from their offence – to demonstrate the same grace God has given you. The following shows how that process works in practice:

1. Acknowledge that you have been hurt
You cannot deal with your negative emotions by denying them. The first thing is to recognise that you are hurting, and this is not your fault. Your pain is real and must be acknowledged. This can be difficult at first, as you may not even be aware of it. You may have pushed the pain down for so long, and fear the further pain of facing it. But a realistic look at your life will surely show that you

When you have been sinned against or hurt by the offence of others, remember you are not responsible for what others have done to you. It is their offence against you.

But you are responsible for your reaction to that offence.

Ask God to reveal your inner hurts to you and help you face them his way.

cannot afford to carry on ignoring it. Remember, unresolved pain is very damaging to the personality. You may bury it, but when you bury unresolved pain, you bury it alive. It continues to live deep inside you and begins slowly but surely to disable you spiritually, emotionally and physically. Ask God to reveal your inner hurts to you and help you face them his way.

2. Give and receive forgiveness wherever necessary

Make sure you forgive all those who have sinned against you. If your pain is the result of your own sin, or if you have allowed your hurt to fester into bitterness, then let go of it and affirm God's forgiveness for yourself. This must be sincere and be accompanied by a willingness to take whatever steps necessary to put the matter right.

Let the Lord's healing power come and give you release from the pain of your inner hurt.

3. Ask Jesus to heal you of your inner pain

Jesus feels your every pain with you.

Hebrews 4:15

For we do not have a high priest who is unable to sympathise with our weaknesses

Your tears are recorded in heaven.

Psalm 56:8 (NIV)

Record my lament; list my tears on your scroll (or put my tears in your wineskin) – are they not in your record?

Let the Lord's healing power come and give you release from the pain of your inner hurt. You must be willing to let go of the pain and trust him. He will pour in the healing oil and dress your inner wounds.

Psalm 147:3

He heals the broken hearted and binds up their wounds.

4. Nurture God-honouring responses

See *Luke 6:27* & *Romans 12:17-21.*

Jesus said:
Love your enemies, do good to those who hate you, bless those who curse and pray for those who mistreat you.

5. Establish God-honouring relationships

As the following Bible verses show, we have been called to live at peace with our fellow human beings, forgiving those who wrong us and responding with compassion to those who hurt us.

2 Corinthians 13:11

Finally, brethren, farewell. Become complete. Be of good comfort, be of one mind, live in peace; and the God of love and peace will be with you.

TOPIC 6 INNER HEALING

If it is possible, as much as depends on you, live peaceably with all men. Beloved, do not avenge yourselves, but rather give place to wrath; for it is written, "Vengeance is mine, I will repay," says the Lord. Therefore "If your enemy is hungry, feed him; if he is thirsty, give him a drink; for in so doing you will heap coals of fire on his head." Do not be overcome by evil, but overcome evil with good.

Romans 12:18-21

Inner healing is an important part of living free in Jesus. It is important to keep reminding yourself that God's blessing and favour over your life is real and lasting. It does not depend on how you feel or on what is going on in your life. As you lay hold of God's grace at work in you, you will be more and more assured of his love and healing in your life.

As you lay hold of God's grace at work in you, you will be more and more assured of his love and healing in your life.

You can find a prayer of release from bitterness and resentment concerning someone who has sinned against you on page 258. Always remember to confess your righteousness in Christ as you walk in the forgiveness of God.

TOPIC 7

HANDLING YOUR EMOTIONS

Jesus came to undo the harm caused by sin and Satan and to bring his wholeness into every part of our lives, including our emotions.

In Topic 6, we looked at how we could find healing for our damaged emotions, especially those that come from being hurt or rejected by others. We found that God wants to heal us from all the emotional damage of the past. Now, we are going to see how we can grow in emotional wholeness by dealing with *all* our negative feelings and the things that cause them.

The Christian life is all about Christ. He is at the centre of everything. God sent his Son into the world to redeem us from all unrighteousness so that we might enjoy the abundant life found in him. Jesus came to undo the harm caused by sin and Satan and to bring his wholeness into every part of our lives, including our emotions.

The thief does not come except to steal, and to kill, and to destroy. I have come that they may have life, and that they may have it more abundantly.

John 10:10

Emotional wholeness is an important aspect of living life to the full in Christ. God wants us to have healthy emotions so that we can take pleasure in him and enjoy the life he gives us. The Holy Spirit teaches us to rise above the negative emotions that can so easily pull us down into misery. God does not want us to be a slave to our damaged emotions. In fact, as those who live under the favour and blessing of God, we should be the most positive, fulfilled and joyful of people on this planet.

God wants us to have healthy emotions so that we can take pleasure in him and enjoy the life he gives us.

Why do so many Christians seem to be in bondage to their emotions? One reason is denial. Many think that good Christians must deny their emotions, but that is wrong and can be quite harmful. God wants us first to acknowledge our emotions and then learn how to bring them under the control of his Spirit.

The path to emotional wholeness begins with identifying the negative emotions that are at work within us.

The path to emotional wholeness begins with identifying the negative emotions that are at work within us. Despite the fact that we live in a feeling-orientated world many people are not actually in touch with their emotions, especially the negative ones. Sometimes we are not aware of our emotions, how strong they are or why we are experiencing them in the first place.

Our Western education teaches us how to reason and to be aware of the intellectual realm of ideas. But there is very little education concerning our emotions. We are trained in the right way to think but we are not trained to be skilful in identifying the emotions at work deep in our lives or in the lives of others.

There are cultural issues to consider. We can speak of the British 'stiff upper lip' but other cultures also frown upon public displays of emotion. But imagine an emotion-free existence such as portrayed by Spock, the half-human, half-Vulcan character from the famous TV and film series *Star Trek*. What a boring and colourless experience that would be!

There is often a heavy price to pay for unexpressed feelings. Being unaware of our emotions can mean that we are unaware of how these emotions are affecting us and the people around us.

There is often a heavy price to pay for unexpressed feelings. Being unaware of our emotions can mean that we are unaware of how these emotions are affecting us and the people around us. But when we share our emotions and express our vulnerability we find it can help us connect with others, resolve conflicts and build genuine relationships.

Emotions – the signals of your heart

But there are even more important reasons why we must become skilled in recognising, identifying and owning our emotions. We all, from time to time, experience the effects of our damaged or negative emotions. And these emotions can be a clear indication of what is going on inside us. This self-understanding is vital if we are to deal with the deeper issues of our lives.

Our feelings are signals of what is taking place in our hearts. They point to our inner needs and tell us whether they are being met or not.

Our feelings are signals of what is taking place in our hearts. They point to our inner needs and tell us whether they are being met or not. If our needs are being met, we experience good emotions. We feel happy, pleased or satisfied. But if our needs are not being met, then we experience negative emotions, such as fear, anxiety, anger or sadness.

This does not mean that our feelings always tell us the truth. The world says, 'If it feels good, it is good.' But that is not always the case.

TOPIC 7 HANDLING YOUR EMOTIONS

Something may feel good for a time but may also be harmful. In the end, only the good things of God really satisfy. The answer lies in understanding that God is good and blesses us with good things. He has already given us his best gift – his one and only Son and he will not withhold any other good thing from us.

He who did not spare his own Son, but delivered him up for us all, how shall he not with him also freely [by grace] give us all things?

Romans 8:32

God knows what will bring us lasting satisfaction and fulfilment. If he forbids something, it is for a good reason. The only way we can avoid the disappointment that inevitably comes to us when we follow our own desires, is to discover that his way is best. It is the *only* path to blessing and fulfilment.

God knows what will bring us lasting satisfaction and fulfilment. If he forbids something, it is for a good reason.

Oh, taste and see that the LORD is good; blessed is the man who trusts in him!

Psalm 34:8

How can something that is harmful and ultimately dissatisfying feel so good and right to us at the time? The reason is, they conform to our wrong understanding of where happiness lies. If for example, we believe that the way to find love, acceptance or comfort is through sex, we will find it hard to pull away from immoral relationships, even when we know these are wrong and that they do not give us the deep satisfaction we are longing for. We will never really be free in this area until we realise that these things can never fully meet the true desires of our heart. We must dig down to our personal foundations and change our fundamental beliefs about what truly satisfies. The answer is to find our fulfilment in the abundant life Jesus gives.

We must dig down to our personal foundations and change our fundamental beliefs about what truly satisfies.

Take another example. If our reaction to being hurt by someone else is to retaliate, we may feel good for a time, but in the end, it will alienate us still further from that person. We soon find ourselves lonely and feeling more rejected than ever. What went wrong? We wrongly believed that we could feel better by getting even. The satisfaction of watching the other person feel bad for the wrong we perceive they did to us made us feel good for a little while. But the joy of self-vindication soon died and we were left with negative feelings of emptiness and isolation. This destructive cycle will repeat itself over and again until we change the false beliefs that feed it.

The answer is to find our fulfilment in the abundant life Jesus gives.

Can you see how utterly powerless we are to escape from these patterns of behaviour until we experience the deep love God has for us? Only the goodness of Christ can set us free. Trying harder to do the right thing only ends in frustration. Striving to live right and to obey God always fails. We cannot overcome the flesh by the flesh. We need a change of heart. Only the grace of God in Christ can do that. The Holy Spirit shows us the sheer breathtaking beauty of the Lord and all the riches we have in him, he directs our passions away from that which cannot satisfy and turns them towards the fulfilment found only in him.

Emotions reveal our beliefs

Our emotions help us see what is going on inside us. They reveal what we really believe will fulfil us in life. We feel good when we perceive our needs are being met and we feel bad when we perceive they are not being met. In other words, feelings point to what we perceive to be good or bad for us. Our emotions reveal what we believe will truly satisfy us.

Our emotions reveal what we believe will truly satisfy us.

Emotions are not self-generating. They are by-products and are always caused by something else. For example, if we value solitude and silence because we have a need for quiet reflection, we will feel irritated by constant interruptions. But if we are alone and our need is for companionship, we will feel good when someone calls us. We won't see it as an interruption at all. It will be a welcome opportunity for us to have our need for companionship met.

So our emotions are keys to understanding what is going on inside us. Once we understand that false beliefs lie at the root of our negative emotions we can begin to deal with these beliefs. People who feel depressed when others don't seem to appreciate them may find that this has to do with their belief that in order to feel good about themselves they must be liked by everyone around them. They are trying to find their self-worth through other people. This leads them to become over-anxious about what others think and they end up in bondage, trying to get everyone to like them.

The moment we grasp that fulfilment is found in Christ alone, we can abandon all destructive beliefs and deal with the negative emotions that plague us.

In order to be set free from these painful emotions they must change their belief about their self-worth. Once such a person understands their immeasurable worth in Christ they will be less dependent on other people's opinions. When they seem to be rejected by others they simply remind themselves of God's love and acceptance in Christ. The moment we grasp that fulfilment is found in Christ alone, we can abandon all destructive beliefs and deal with the negative emotions that plague us.

Unfulfilled goals are the root of negative emotions

Have you ever wondered why in certain situations unwanted emotions seem to rise to the surface? When our emotions are negative, we can feel guilty and uneasy about them even if we don't know exactly why we are experiencing these emotions in the first place. We feel bad about the anger that we feel inside us, we deplore our feelings of

TOPIC 7 HANDLING YOUR EMOTIONS

depression or anxiety – but often we do not know why we are feeling the way we do. We try to mask our emotions or justify them, but deep down we know things aren't right.

As we have seen, there is a helpful way of understanding what is generating our negative emotions. It has to do with what we believe will meet our needs and give us the feeling of wellbeing. Or, to put it another way, it has to do with our *goals*. Let me define what I mean by a 'goal' in this context:

A goal is something we value or desire because we believe it will meet a need in us.

For example, we will value friendship because we believe it will meet our need for companionship, and so we make it our goal to have and maintain friendships. Or, if we have a need for security, we will desire money or wealth because we believe these things will meet that need.

Only God can meet our deepest needs for security, significance and self-worth.

All this is well and good until these desires become idolatrous. That is, until they replace God and we find ourselves pursuing these things rather than him. After all, only God can meet our deepest needs for security, significance and self-worth. In Topic 4, we saw that human beings have three basic emotional needs:

Security – *to be safe in the presence of unconditional love and acceptance*

Significance – *to have impact and meaning, knowing we can make a difference and our being here matters*

Self-worth – *to know that we are people of infinite value and esteem.*

We also saw that the deep motivation of our lives lies in our belief concerning where these needs will be met. If we recognise that these needs can only be met by God then we will pursue him with all of our heart. But as fallen, sinful human beings we have developed the idolatrous belief that our needs can be met by things other than God and what he graciously provides for us. In other words, he is not enough.

As fallen, sinful human beings we have developed the idolatrous belief that our needs can be met by things other than God and what he graciously provides for us. In other words, he is not enough.

Jesus spoke about this in his parable of the sower. He describes the seed that fell on thorny ground and became fruitful. The thorns correspond to three things: the cares and anxieties of this world, the deceitfulness of wealth and the desires for other things.

Now these are the ones sown among thorns; they are the ones who hear the word, and the cares of this world, the deceitfulness of riches, and the desires for other things entering in choke the word, and it becomes unfruitful.

Mark 4:18-20

Can you see the basic teaching of Jesus here? He is saying that when we believe that our needs can be met outside of him, the word of God becomes unfruitful in us. We stifle it through the anxieties of life. We think that money brings us happiness and so we forget God and give ourselves to the pursuit of wealth. We set our heart on the pursuit of these 'other things' believing they will bring us fulfilment. Jesus exposes our idolatrous beliefs and shows their negative effects in our hearts.

Look at how this affects our emotional life. Because our idols will always fail us in the end, we are plagued by negative emotions of fear, anxiety, frustration, anger, sadness or depression. As long as we are looking to anything or anyone other than the Lord to meet our fundamental needs of security, significance or self-worth, we will always be unfulfilled. Only the Lord can meet these needs. Unfulfilled goals are always at the root of negative emotions.

Understanding different kinds of emotions

For the sake of clarity, it is helpful to group together the different kinds of emotions we experience. These categories show the full range of all possible emotions. They point to our goals – where we believe our needs will be met. They also reveal whether we feel our needs are being met or not.

According to this principle, there are four basic categories of emotions and these all indicate what is going on inside us:

Gladness – *a need or a goal is being met*

Fear or anxiety – *we are uncertain whether a need or a goal is going to be met*

Anger or bitterness – *our need or goal is blocked or prevented from being met*

Sadness – *we don't think our need or goal will ever be met.*

Because our 'emotional vocabulary' is so limited it is helpful to consult lists like the following in order to identify our emotions:

TOPIC 7   HANDLING YOUR EMOTIONS

Four categories of emotion with examples[5]

Category:	High:	Medium:
Feeling Glad	Ecstatic Elated High Delighted Strong Enchanted Powerful	Pleased Happy Cheerful Confident Contented Calm Affectionate
Feeling Afraid	Petrified Terrified Deeply shocked Horrified Panicky Frozen Muddled Confused Lost Apprehensive Threatened Vulnerable Scared	Anxious Insecure Nervous Shaky Cautious Unsure
Feeling Angry	Disgusted Furious Bitter Seething Provoked Sore Annoyed Fed-up	Angry Exasperated Frustrated Miffed
Feeling Sad	Depressed Defeated Devastated Empty Worthless Hopeless Crushed Battered Guilty Gloomy Fed-up	Discouraged Unhappy Low Bruised Disappointed Hurt Ashamed Upset

---

[5] Bayne, R., Horton I., Merry, T., Noyes, E and McMahon, G. (1999) *The Counsellor's Handbook*, Cheltenham, Stanley Thornes, pp 64-65

Taking responsibility for our feelings

One important reason for identifying our emotions is so that we can accept our responsibility for them. They are *our* emotions, nobody else's, and we are responsible for them.

What we feel is *never* the fault of others. Truly speaking, no one can make you feel anything. Your feelings are never caused by anything that anyone says or does to you. What others do to us, think about us or say to us, may be the *stimulus* of our feelings but they are never the *cause*. Our feelings result from how we choose to receive what others say and do, as well as our particular needs and expectations in that moment.

It is important to learn to accept responsibility for what we do to generate our own feelings. Whenever someone does or says something negative to us, we find it easy to respond negatively. We *blame ourselves* and accept that we deserve their negative action or evaluation. Or, under the pressure of what we perceive to be an attack from someone else, we *defend ourselves* by counter-attacking that person. Both these ways of responding are negative, fruitless and unproductive because they generate negative emotions and provoke further negative responses.

Dealing in the business of blame or judgmentalism, whether directed against yourself or others, is negative and damaging. Blaming yourself for your negative feelings – feeling bad about feeling bad – does not get to the root of the issue. Rather you need to practice self-compassion by asking 'What need am I trying to fill in this situation?' That way you can redirect your heart towards the Lord and his grace, finding fullness in him. Blaming others for the way you feel also misses the real point. The simple fact is that our emotions show us what is happening inside *us*. They point to our internal thoughts, perceptions and values. Blaming others for not meeting our needs is a negative judgement that will produce negative effects. It will stimulate the wrong kind of emotions in us – anger, resentment, self-pity, and so on, and provoke the wrong kind of reaction from them – hostility, rejection or cold indifference.

The needs at the root of our feelings

It is important to understand that our ultimate and most basic need as human beings is for God. Everything we long for in life is found in him and the things he lovingly provides for us. When we judge others, blame them, criticise them or vent our anger on them, we are really only crying out for our needs to be met. This is tragic miscommunication because they only hear our anger, and they immediately defend

TOPIC 7   HANDLING YOUR EMOTIONS

themselves or attack us back, in order to deal with the negative emotions we have just provoked in them!

Once we know that God will come through for us, we will stop looking to others to meet our deepest emotional needs. Satisfied in Jesus, we will experience far less by way of negative emotion. We will no longer be so quick to blame others for the way we feel. We will learn how to express ourselves and our emotions accurately. We will become less demanding of others and more secure in the love God has for us. We will cope better when people let us down, because we are not depending on them to meet our fundamental needs.

Once we know that God will come through for us, we will stop looking to others to meet our deepest emotional needs.

Satisfied in Jesus, we will experience far less by way of negative emotion.

This in turn will help us avoid the thoughts, words and actions that so easily alienate us from those around us. We will be more aware of and sympathetic to the needs of others as we learn to hear in their harsh and critical language their real heart cry for us to minister to their needs. We know that their needs as well as ours can only be fully met in the Lord, so we will change the way we communicate with others. Instead of using manipulative language calculated to get people to say and do the things that make us feel good, we will be more concerned to minister to their needs through our gracious and loving words to them.

We will be more aware of and sympathetic to the needs of others as we learn to hear in their harsh and critical language their real heart cry for us to minister to their needs.

Let no corrupt word proceed out of your mouth, but what is good for necessary edification, that it may impart grace to the hearers.

Ephesians 4:29

In this verse, the apostle Paul shows that corrupt unwholesome communication tears down the other person. We should rather be speaking positive words of encouragement directing people to the grace of God at work in their lives. Once we have learned to trust God fully to meet our needs, we are better prepared to minister to the needs of others.

Dealing with your idolatrous beliefs

We have seen that wrong beliefs concerning how our needs are met are at the root of many negative emotions. We press others to meet our needs according to our mistaken beliefs concerning what makes us happy. This leads to disharmony and breakdown in relationships because people can never fully meet these deep needs in us.

An idol is anything that replaces God, anything we depend on more than him.

We have also seen that these false beliefs are actually motivational goals. They drive us strongly in the direction of where we believe our needs will be met. Another word for this is idolatry. An idol is anything that replaces God, anything we depend on more than him. To understand this further, we need to look at some deep issues of the human heart. Jeremiah spoke of the tendency we have to be drawn away by things other than God. He said,

Jeremiah 17:9 — *The heart is deceitful above all things, and desperately wicked; who can know it?*

As Jeremiah makes clear, our problems lie in the deception resting deep in our hearts. We are influenced by false beliefs that lead us away from God. We have a strong desire to go in the direction determined by our beliefs concerning fulfilment – no matter how false these beliefs are. Our idolatrous goals set our direction in life. They usually arouse much passion in us and can even lead us into the realm of obsession. We must learn to re-direct this passion towards God, by identifying and renouncing the false beliefs that belong to our old way of thinking. That is what God means when he says,

> *Our idolatrous goals set our direction in life. They usually arouse much passion in us and can even lead us into the realm of obsession.*

Romans 12:2 — *Do not be conformed to this world, but be transformed by the renewing of your mind, that you may prove what is that good and acceptable and perfect will of God.*

Destroying your idols

Whenever we turn away from God we automatically follow idolatrous substitutes for him. Therefore, right belief concerning who God is and how he meets our needs is vital for a changed life. Wrong beliefs concerning where our true worth is to be found rob us of our passion for Christ. We need to regain this passion and reject all false ideas of happiness and fulfilment. Once we see how all-sufficient the Lord is for us, we will be willing to identify and abandon our idols and the negative beliefs that give them power over us.

> *Once we see how all-sufficient the Lord is for us, we will be willing to identify and abandon our idols and the negative beliefs that give them power over us.*

Usually, our idolatrous goals reveal our fundamental characteristics as people. These are the things that make us tick, the buttons others so easily press. Therefore, if we are to change from the inside out, we must challenge and deal with these idolatrous goals. Once we discover that our fullness is in Christ, the true path to life becomes clear and we begin to delight in that path. Then we can unmask our idols and go about destroying them. In other words, we will prove to ourselves that God's way works and that the highest good is to follow the Lord.

Jesus' conversation with the woman of Samaria is an example of this process.

The woman of Samaria

We find this remarkable story of Jesus and the woman of Samaria in John's Gospel chapter 4. In it, we see Jesus breaking through the religious, racial, cultural, social and personal barriers behind which this woman was hiding. And yet, she was a seeker. Her hide-and-seek approach is obvious throughout the story. She hides behind the fact that she is a woman and Jesus is a man, that she is a Samaritan and he is a Jew and that the Jews and the Samaritans had different religions and different beliefs about worship.

Then the woman of Samaria said to him, "How is it that you, being a Jew, ask a drink from me, a Samaritan woman?" For Jews have no dealings with Samaritans.

John 4:9

Jesus had asked her to draw water from the well and give him a drink, but his real intention was to reveal to her the living water that he alone could provide. He clearly saw through her religious cover-up and discerned the true needs of her heart.

She was the one who was really thirsty and was seeking for true satisfaction and fulfilment of life. Her religion did not provide it. She was worshiping what she did not know but a personal relationship with Jesus, the Messiah of all nations, was the true answer to her need. He cut through all her pretence and exposed the true need of her heart.

The woman of Samaria was really thirsty and was seeking for true satisfaction and fulfilment of life.

Her religion did not provide it.

"Go bring your husband," he said. She replied that she had no husband. Jesus agreed and said to her, "You are right in saying you have no husband. Because you've had five husbands and the man you have now is not your husband."

She was astounded. Jesus had spoken the truth, not only in that he had revealed facts about her, but also because he had exposed the secrets of her heart. He had uncovered her idolatrous goals. Later, she was to describe Jesus as a man who had told her everything she had ever done. In other words, the whole of her life could be summed up by her broken and unfortunate relationships with men. She was worshipping the wrong god.

The whole of her life could be summed up by her broken and unfortunate relationships with men. She was worshipping the wrong god.

It was a moment of life-changing revelation for her. Jesus saw into her heart and the need she was trying to fill. She had been looking for love and fulfilment but had never found it – either in any of her relationships with men or in her religion. She was the one who was really thirsty. No wonder Jesus said to her,

If you knew the gift of God, and who it is who says to you, 'Give me a drink,' you would have asked him, and he would have given you living water.

John 4:10

The woman did not seem to understand the spiritual significance of his words and was bound to the natural world. Like so many of us, she could only think in terms of the physical world and what it offers. But Jesus helped her focus on the real answer.

John 4:13-14

Jesus answered and said to her, "Whoever drinks of this water will thirst again, but whoever drinks of the water that I shall give him will never thirst. But the water that I shall give him will become in him a fountain of water springing up into everlasting life."

This woman, like all of us, had a problem finding where her needs could be truly met. We have turned away from God out of ignorance, deception and rebellion and, in doing so, we have abandoned the only way we can ever taste the cool, refreshing waters of satisfaction. Jeremiah prophesied about the people of Judah in his day, but these words apply to us all.

Jeremiah 2:13

My people have committed two evils: they have forsaken me, the fountain of living waters, and hewn themselves cisterns - broken cisterns that can hold no water.

Worshipping the true God, Abba Father, in spirit and truth, is like coming back to the true fountain and source of satisfaction. It means abandoning our idolatrous ways and rejecting the beliefs that lead us away from God. Real repentance means we renounce any beliefs we hold that lie to us about the source of true satisfaction and fulfilment. We come and drink at the only fountain of living water.

John 4:24

God is Spirit, and those who worship him must worship in spirit and truth.

What are your idolatrous beliefs? Where do you believe your needs will be truly met? How are you pursuing satisfaction and fulfilment in things other than God and his provision for your life?

Honest answers to these questions will reveal your heart and what drives you in life. Usually, this exposes the problem areas of your life, which will never be resolved until you recognise that you have been deceived. Lasting joy and fullness can only be found in Christ.

> *Worshipping the true God, Abba Father, in spirit and truth, is like coming back to the true fountain and source of satisfaction.*
>
> *It means abandoning our idolatrous ways and rejecting the beliefs that lead us away from God.*

Your negative emotions may be the best clues you have as to where you believe your needs will be met. These emotions reveal your secret beliefs as to where happiness can be found. As we have already seen, negative emotions point to needs in us that are *not* being filled. They are also linked to our beliefs, concerning where and how we can get these needs met. As we saw in Topic 4, these beliefs are often learned through repeated childhood experiences. It is time to reject these beliefs in the true spirit of repentance and grasp the revelation of God in Jesus Christ:

John 4:13-14

"Whoever drinks of this water will thirst again, but whoever drinks of the water that I shall give him will never thirst. But the water that I shall give him will become in him a fountain of water springing up into everlasting life."

TOPIC 7   HANDLING YOUR EMOTIONS

Dealing with negative emotions

Now we can see how God wants us to deal with our emotions. First, we need to be aware of what we are feeling. Ask yourself, 'What am I feeling right now?' Then, ask yourself why you are feeling that way. If you have good feelings ask yourself, is it a godly need being met in a godly way? Or, is it an example of the temporary satisfaction of idolatry? If so, repent of the belief that you could find satisfaction in something that diminishes God in your life.

If you are feeling angry or frustrated, ask yourself, "What need is being blocked?" Or, if you have fear or anxiety, ask "What need am I uncertain is going to be fulfilled?" Or, if you have feelings of hopelessness or depression, look for the need you have that seems utterly unattainable to you right now. The list on page 89 will help you identify your emotions. You will then be able to complete this sentence:

Recognising that your needs can only be met by the Lord, you can now redirect your passion to him and begin to seek him with all of your heart.

In order to find the satisfaction of_____, I believe I must _____ .

This reveals your idolatrous goal.

Now you can reject the idolatrous belief that is drawing you away from the Lord. Recognising that your needs can only be met by the Lord, you can now redirect your passion to him and begin to seek him with all of your heart, trusting him to meet this fundamental need in your life. The corresponding negative emotions will slowly lose their hold on you and positive emotions will soon follow.

Jesus gives you eternal security because he will never leave you nor forsake you.

Throughout this process, the most important thing is to taste the goodness of God by focussing on Christ, the only true source and fountain of lasting satisfaction. Find in him the answer to the deepest longings of your heart and soul. As you do this, you will discover that those old idolatrous beliefs lose their power over you. Remember, you are motivated to go in the direction you believe your needs will be met. Therefore, your beliefs determine your passion. You want something because you believe that it will meet your needs. Discover the real Jesus, the one who meets your deepest needs.

You are immeasurably significant in his eyes because you are greatly-blessed, highly-favoured and deeply-loved in him.

Jesus gives you *eternal security* because he will never leave you nor forsake you. You are *immeasurably significant* in his eyes because you are greatly-blessed, highly-favoured and deeply-loved in him. You are a person of *infinite worth* to the Father, because he gave his one and only Son who died on the cross to redeem you back to himself.

You are a person of infinite worth to the Father, because he gave his one and only Son who died on the cross to redeem you back to himself.

TOPIC 8

WALKING IN FREEDOM

In this chapter we learn how to experience the freedom Jesus Christ won for us. We discover that he gives us complete victory through his death on the cross and his resurrection from the dead. We learn how to walk in the grace of God and overcome every attempt of the enemy to bring us back into bondage.

Learn to walk in the grace of God and overcome every attempt of the enemy to bring you back into bondage.

The complete victory of Christ at the cross

Victory brings freedom, defeat leads to slavery. In ancient warfare the outcome of the battle determined whether you would remain free or be taken into slavery by enemy forces. The victorious nation would take captive the nation it defeated. So you were really fighting for your freedom. Before we accepted Christ we were living in defeat, in a permanent state of bondage. Read the following verses from Ephesians and ask yourself what you see there.

And you he made alive, who were dead in trespasses and sins, in which you once walked according to the course of this world, according to the prince of the power of the air, the spirit who now works in the sons of disobedience, among whom also we all once conducted ourselves in the lusts of our flesh, fulfilling the desires of the flesh and of the mind, and were by nature children of wrath, just as the others.

Ephesians 2:1-3

What do these verses describe? To my mind, only one thing – spiritual slavery and bondage. Before we came to Christ we were total enslaved to sin, death, hell and the grave. But that is not the end of the story! Let's read on.

Ephesians 2:4-7

But God, who is rich in mercy, because of his great love with which he loved us, even when we were dead in trespasses, made us alive together with Christ (by grace you have been saved), and raised us up together, and made us sit together in the heavenly places in Christ Jesus, that in the ages to come he might show the exceeding riches of his grace in his kindness toward us in Christ Jesus.

God has set us free through the grace and mercy shown us in Christ. Can you see just how gracious and kind God has been to us? Through Christ we have been lifted up out of the bondage of Satan and given the new life of Christ. We are actually seated with him, right now, in the heavenly places. This means we are seated on the throne of the universe – the place of victory, honour, authority and blessing. And what did we do to get there? Absolutely nothing! We just received God's gift of salvation by faith.

Through Christ we have been lifted up out of the bondage of Satan and given the new life of Christ.

We are actually seated with him, right now, in the heavenly places.

Also in ancient times it was customary for the conquering king to inscribe on the footstool of his throne the names of all the kings and kingdoms he had vanquished. He rejoiced that his enemies were under his feet. This helps us understand the image used of Jesus' victory in Ephesians chapter one.

Ephesians 1:22-23

And he [God, the Father] put all things under his feet [Jesus], and gave him to be head over all things to the church, which is his body, the fullness of him who fills all in all.

Now let's put these two thoughts together: Jesus is sitting on the throne of triumph with all things under his feet – and we are seated right there with him! That means his triumph has become our triumph, his victory has become our victory. We are free from all that once bound us and held us in slavery, through the once-for-all victory of Christ.

Through the blood of Jesus we have been redeemed from all the guilt and power of sin.

We have been set free from every bondage Satan held us under.

Our freedom in Christ comes from one source only – the victory Christ won for us on the cross. Through the blood of Jesus we have been redeemed from all the guilt and power of sin. We have been set free from every bondage Satan held us under.

Victory is a gift of God's grace

Victory and the freedom that flows from it are the gifts of God. We can do nothing to earn or deserve them. Our victory in Christ is totally by the grace of God.

1 Corinthians 15:56-57

The sting of death is sin, and the strength of sin is the law. But thanks be to God, who gives us the victory through our Lord Jesus Christ.

God has made us victorious by his grace – pure grace. And we receive it by simple faith. That's how we enjoy all the blessings of God – by simple faith. This means we can do nothing to try and achieve them through our own efforts. We simply enter into the victory of Christ. Many people find this hard to accept. They are held captive by religious legalism, which always focuses on what we have to do for God. Grace teaches us to focus on what God has done for us. Religious legalism is the arch weapon of the enemy. He convinces us that we have to earn or deserve God's blessings, and then accuses us when we fail. He tells us God is never really satisfied with us. We always have to do something more. And so we end up in bondage once again.

Keeping us under the bondage of the law is one of the main ways Satan tries to prevent us from seeing our true freedom in Christ. As long as he can convince us that we are still under the law, we will never rise out of our sense of guilt and condemnation. As long as he can persuade us to follow legalistic ideas he can keep us from seeing our deliverance and freedom in Christ.

Satan's tactic is always to accuse us and he uses the law to do it. As long as we believe that there is more for us to do in order to be free, more laws to obey, more changes we have to make before we live in victory, he will keep us forever in defeat. Legalism never allows us to escape from our sin. It keeps us under its power and brings us back under the curse-like influences of the law.

But the Holy Spirit gives us a revelation of the sufficiency of Christ and the total triumph of his cross. Jesus fought every battle we will ever face, he overcome every force of the enemy that could ever confront us. Jesus fought and won. His victory is complete and absolute. All we have to do is to receive Christ's victory as a gift and walk in it day by day by faith. You can never live free by attempting to qualify yourself for God's blessing. The truth is, as a Christian, you don't even have to try. It all comes by grace through faith. The Bible says that we have already been blessed with every spiritual blessing in heavenly places. We are already accepted and highly-favoured in the well-beloved *(Ephesians 1:3-6)*. We are more than conquerors through Christ who loved us *(Romans 8:37)*.

Being set free

As we have seen, believers in Christ are absolutely free. If you belong to Christ, you are seated with him in heavenly places. The devil cannot touch you. But you must learn to assert this position in your day-to-day confrontation with sin and evil – both within yourself and in the world around you. This means you have to 'take your stand' against the devil and all his works. The devil is a defeated enemy, but he is also a persistent and a resistant force. You must learn to resist him with all the power and spiritual strength God has given you.

Jesus' victory over the devil

Jesus was tempted by the devil in the wilderness. But in reality, it was the Spirit who led Jesus to go out into the wilderness in search of the devil to defeat him! Jesus returned to Galilee full of the power of the Spirit ready to take up his ministry of salvation, healing and deliverance. He did not yield to Satan on a single score. The same overcoming power of Jesus is living in you to give you victory over temptation and sin.

1 Corinthians 10:13

No temptation has overtaken you except such as is common to man; but God is faithful, who will not allow you to be tempted beyond what you are able, but with the temptation will also make the way of escape, that you may be able to bear it.

When Jesus died on the cross his victory over the devil was complete and when he rose from the dead that victory was manifested to all.

1 John 3:8

For this purpose the Son of God was manifested, that he might destroy the works of the devil.

Satan is defeated!

The following verses show Jesus complete victory of the enemy.

- Jesus has destroyed the devil nullifying his activity against us inoperable.

Hebrews 2:14

Inasmuch then as the children have partaken of flesh and blood, he himself likewise shared in the same, that through death he might destroy him who had the power of death, that is, the devil.

- Jesus has disarmed the devil taking away all his weapons and stripping him of his every pretension to power and authority.

Colossians 2:15

Having disarmed principalities and powers, he made a public spectacle of them, triumphing over them in it.

- Jesus has driven the devil out casting him out of his position in the heavens from which he blinded the nations.

John 12:31

Now is the judgement of this world; now the ruler of this world will be cast out.

And Jesus has given us this same victory over all the bondages and evil influences of the enemy!

Luke 10:19

Behold, I give you the authority to trample on serpents and scorpions, and over all the of the enemy, and nothing shall by any means hurt you.

Living in victory

The secret of living in victory is discovering and asserting who you are in Christ. You are already victorious, and you can live victoriously. You are already free in Christ and you can learn how to live in that freedom. This means you have to learn to stand your ground in the face of the enemy's attacks. Five times in *Ephesians chapter 6*, Paul tells us to stand firm in who we are in Christ. For example verse 13 says,

Therefore take up the whole armour of God, that you may be able to withstand in the evil day, and having done all, to stand.

Ephesians 6:13

The devil's best way of getting at us is to trick us into believing that we are not really free and that we have no protection against him. However the spiritual armour God gives us is totally effective against every attack of the enemy. We stand upon the victory Christ has won for us and live in the identity we have in him. That is how we wage war against the enemy.

We stand upon the victory Christ has won for us and live in the identity we have in him.

That is how we wage war against the enemy.

In all these things the true battle is in the mind. When you have the mind of Christ, you understand that the enemy has no power over you. But if you allow the devil to mess with your mind you can begin to doubt who you are in Christ. He loves to remind you of your sin and accuse you in your heart. He tells you that you are a guilty sinner and that God can never accept you. He shows you your failures and leads you back into the old patterns of condemnation. Successful spiritual warfare is all about bringing these thoughts captive and submitting them to the truth of who you are in Christ.

When you have the mind of Christ, you understand that the enemy has no power over you.

For the weapons of our warfare are not carnal but mighty in God for pulling down strongholds, casting down arguments and every high thing that exalts itself against the knowledge of God, bringing every thought into captivity to the obedience of Christ

2 Corinthians 10:4-5

Don't fall back into bondage

When we see how complete Christ's victory is over Satan, it's astonishing to think that he could ever bring us back into bondage. But that's exactly what *can* happen if we do not hold onto the freedom we have in Christ through his grace. Paul warns us against this in the book of Galatians. The believers he writes to have begun to put themselves back under the law and therefore find themselves once more in bondage.

Stand fast therefore in the liberty by which Christ has made us free, and do not be entangled again with a yoke of bondage.

Galatians 5:1

Notice that the yoke of bondage Paul speaks about is the law, which always brings bondage. When we put ourselves back under the law, we begin to lose our freedom. When we move away from the principle of grace in any aspect of our Christian life, we expose ourselves again to bondage.

The basic principle is this: when we focus on God's grace in our lives, we live in the blessings of faith. But when we take our eyes off Jesus, we begin to rely once more on our works. We think that God will only bless us if we deserve it. When we re-introduce the principle of the law into our lives we open the door to the constant accusations of Satan who reminds us of our failure and unworthiness. We give him a golden opportunity to mess with our lives again. Once we succumb to the temptation to leave the principles of grace, we find we cannot enjoy the promises of God. We feel more and more unworthy and find it increasingly difficult to believe that God can bless us. Consequently, we find it harder and harder to defend against the devil's attacks on us.

Blessing and freedom come through the righteousness of faith and not the works of the law.

We are blessed because we have become the righteousness of God through faith in Christ – not because we deserve to be blessed.

Blessing and freedom come through the righteousness of faith and not the works of the law. We are blessed because we have become the righteousness of God through faith in Christ – not because we deserve to be blessed. As long as we hold onto that, the devil cannot touch us. But if we yield again to the demands of the law we surrender once more to the control of the flesh. Remember, the law will always enslave you to sin and bind you to the flesh.

As long as we hold onto that, the devil cannot touch us.

The most important deliverance we can ever experience is deliverance from the law. The law keeps sin alive in us. It opens the way for the devil to torment us with guilt and condemnation. Every single bondage in our lives operates through the principle of the law. When we understand that we have been set free from the law, we can truly walk in the freedom of Christ.

Once you grasp the principle of grace-through-faith you realise that God has completely set you free from all the demands and consequences of the law. Walking by faith means depending on God's grace and not your own merits. Freedom comes by the Spirit of God, not through fleshly self-effort. When you let go of all your efforts to keep the law and yield yourself to the Holy Spirit's work in you, you walk in freedom and the devil cannot touch you. Freedom from sin means being set free from the law. Look at the mistake the Galatian believers were making:

Galatians 3:3-4

Are you so foolish? Having begun in the Spirit, are you now being made perfect by the flesh?

TOPIC 8   WALKING IN FREEDOM

Don't give the devil access!

The devil tries to keep you bound by convincing you to live the life God requires through the efforts of your flesh. As long as you are trying to perfect yourself through the law, you will remain in bondage to the flesh. The efforts of the flesh can only produce what is according to its nature.

Now the works of the flesh are evident, which are: adultery, fornication, uncleanness, lewdness, idolatry, sorcery [witchcraft], hatred, contentions, jealousies, outbursts of wrath, selfish ambitions, dissensions, heresies, envy, murders, drunkenness, revelries, and the like...   Galatians 5:19-21

Frankly, those who are still trying to live under the law are the most likely people to succumb to the bondages of the enemy. But if we live by the principle of grace we will overcome sin, enjoy real freedom and be victorious over every attempt of the devil to bring bondage back into our lives.

Having understood that we are victorious and free in Christ, we now look at how we can defeat every attempt of the enemy to bring us back under bondage. We are going to cover the following areas:

- Freedom from demonic powers
- Freedom from soul ties
- Freedom from curses
- Freedom from hereditary bondages.

At the end of each section, there is a freedom declaration. Learn to speak these out frequently, believing that every word applies to you. That way, you will gradually re-train your thinking, overcome Satan's accusations and develop a freedom mentality.

> *As long as you are trying to perfect yourself through the law, you will remain in bondage to the flesh.*
>
> *The efforts of the flesh can only produce what is according to its nature.*

FREEDOM FROM DEMONIC POWERS

One of the ways Satan tries to steal your freedom is through demonic attack. To combat these attacks we must be sure of our absolute victory and freedom in Christ. We must know we have been totally delivered from all the powers of darkness and have been transferred us into the kingdom of God.

He has delivered us from the power of darkness and conveyed us into the kingdom of the Son of his love   Colossians 1:13

This means that no demon of hell can ever possess you or take over your life, ever again. But, if the devil can convince you that sin still has some hold over you, he can gain access into your heart. You lose sight of your authority over his works and you lack confidence in resisting him and the forces that wish to invade your life. The devil tries to make you focus on the negative influences that are in your life – your sin, your problems and your weaknesses. Once he makes you sin-conscious he finds it easy to convince you that you are subject to his attacks and his demonic influences. Sin takes many forms and the enemy will try to use every single one of them to accuse you and to open up the door to the demonic in your life:

- Generational sin – the sins of the fathers visited on their children

Deuteronomy 5:9-10

For I, the LORD your God, am a jealous God, visiting the iniquity of the fathers upon the children to the third and fourth generations of those who hate me, but showing mercy to thousands, to those who love me and keep my commandments.

Notice that generational sin applies only to those who reject the Lord. Once you come to Christ, its power is broken. God established a new bloodline of mercy and grace extending to thousands of generations. This is what the apostle Peter speaks about:

1 Peter 1:18-19 (NIV)

For you know that it was not with perishable things such as silver or gold that you were redeemed from the empty way of life handed down to you from your forefathers, but with the precious blood of Christ, a lamb without blemish or defect.

The blood of Jesus sets you free from every unrighteous thing you may have inherited from your ancestors. Once you assert this freedom over your life and your family, the enemy can never hold you in bondage to generational sin. This access point for the devil's activity in your life and family is closed forever.

- *Occult powers* – clearly any link with the occult in our lives exposes us to demonic bondage. But the moment we realise that the blood of Jesus cleanses us from this sin, we can reject every demon that tries to gain entrance through occult involvement.

- *Habitual sin* – sin habitually performed can provide cover for the invading forces of the enemy. Often habitual sins becomes life dominating like sexual bondage and drug or alcohol addiction. But, once we realise that Christ has set us free from the power of sin, we find deliverance from these bondages and the devil has no hold over our lives.

- *Idolatry* – the worship of idols always attracts demonic activity. The devil craves the worship that is due to God alone. But, cleansed from your sin, you become a true worshipper of the Father, and the power of idolatry is broken in your life.

TOPIC 8 WALKING IN FREEDOM

- *False religion and belief* – the devil is behind the teaching of all false philosophies and false religions, but when we understand that grace and truth came by Jesus Christ, these false beliefs lose their hold over us and the enemy's work in us is destroyed.

- *Curses* – the enemy works through demonic pronouncements made over us to try and bring harm to us. But once we realise that we are blessed and not cursed, we can combat every curse over our life.

- *Mental affliction* – this is often the oppression of the enemy. Not all mental illness is caused by a demon but most of it seems to be exploited by the devil. The answer to this is that "we have the mind of Christ" *(1 Corinthians 2:16)*. The sound mind of Christ will protect us from every mental affliction.

- *Unforgiveness* – this is one of the biggest causes for demonic attack. The moment we refuse to forgive others, we invoke our 'rights' under the law. We put ourselves back under the principle of the law and this can open the door for the devil. But when we walk in grace, we exchange the spirit of retribution for the spirit of forgiveness and the devil loses his hold.

> *When we walk in grace, we exchange the spirit of retribution for the spirit of forgiveness and the devil loses his hold.*

The path to freedom from demonic powers

The simple truth is that, as we walk with the Lord, we walk free from demonic bondage. The following points are not a step-by-step formula for deliverance. Rather they are important reminders of your freedom in Christ and how you can assert that freedom over every power of the devil.

1. Confess your righteousness in Christ

For he made him who knew no sin to be sin for us, that we might become the righteousness of God in him.

2 Corinthians 5:21

Learn to confess that you are the righteousness of God in Christ. All your sin is nailed to the cross. The blood of Jesus has dealt with it completely. Because you are in Christ, you are free and the devil has no hold over you. The devil has no more hold over you than he has over Christ. Look at what Jesus said of himself, just before he went to the cross.

I will no longer talk much with you, for the ruler of this world is coming, and he has nothing in me.

John 14:30-31

He then went straight to the cross, was crucified and was raised again from the dead so that the devil could never again have a reason to accuse us.

1 John 4:17

Love has been perfected among us in this: that we may have boldness in the day of judgment; because as he is, so are we in this world.

The proper focus of our lives is Christ and all that he has achieved through the cross.

2. Focus on Christ, not your sin

The whole of the Bible is about how God deals with our sin by the power of his grace. The Holy Scriptures were given to show us how to be saved from sin through faith in Christ *(2 Timothy 3:15)*. The proper focus of our lives is Christ and all that he has achieved through the cross. Living a *sin-conscious* existence plays into the hands of the devil. We must learn to live *righteous-conscious*. When we see everything that Jesus has accomplished for us and who we are in him, sin loses its grip on us.

This righteous-conscious attitude is what real repentance is all about.

This righteous-conscious attitude is what real repentance is all about. As we turn to Christ, we turn our back on the past with all its sin and failure. It is as good as saying 'Get behind me Satan! You have no hold on me!' this is what it means to overcome Satan with the blood of the Lamb and the word of your testimony.

Revelation 12:11

And they overcame him by the blood of the Lamb and by the word of their testimony

Your testimony is not what you have done for God, but what he has done for you through the blood of the Lamb. You don't need to plead the blood, the blood pleads for you. Hebrews says that we have come,

Hebrews 12:24

...to Jesus the Mediator of the new covenant, and to the blood of sprinkling that speaks better things than that of Abel.

The blood of Abel pleaded vengeance, but the blood of Jesus pleads mercy! God has made every provision for our sins – past, present and future. Stop looking at your sin and your failure. Look to Jesus, your heavenly advocate and the devil will turn his head away in shame!

1 John 2:1-2

My little children, these things I write to you, so that you may not sin. And if anyone sins, we have an Advocate with the Father, Jesus Christ the righteous. And he himself is the propitiation[the one who turns away God's wrath] for our sins, and not for ours only but also for the whole world.

3. Show grace to all those who have sinned against you

In Topic 6 we saw that if we deal with others according to the law of vengeance we expose ourselves to that same principle. The Bible shows us that God has totally forgiven us our sins and we will never meet him as Judge to receive his condemnation. He now deals with us as a loving Father deals with his children. If you walk in unforgiveness you will lose your confidence in the Father's love and blessing. He will not judge you, but he will discipline you. We have already looked at these words found at the end of the Lord's Prayer.

For if you forgive men their trespasses, your heavenly Father will also forgive you. But if you do not forgive men their trespasses, neither will your Father forgive your trespasses. — Matthew 6:14-15

We see this same principle in the parable of the unmerciful servant who was unwilling to forgive a small debt owed to him even though his master had forgiven him his enormous debt.

And his master was angry, and delivered him to the torturers until he should pay all that was due to him. So my heavenly Father also will do to you if each of you, from his heart, does not forgive his brother his trespasses. — Matthew 18:34-35

The only way to enjoy the blessing and intimacy with the Father that flows from his forgiveness is to extend that same forgiveness to others. The moment we use the law against others, making them 'pay' for their misdeeds against us, we weaken our own confidence in the grace of God. We begin to doubt his love to us and we expose ourselves to the enemy's torments of guilt and unworthiness. Forgiven people forgive others.

4. Resist and expel every evil presence in your life

One of the most important truths God's people need to know is that they have power to resist the devil. We no longer need to submit to him. In fact, he has to submit to us. But there is one condition. Humility. We must submit in humility to God, as James makes clear,

Therefore submit to God. Resist the devil and he will flee from you. — James 4:7

The kind of humility James is speaking of here is surrender to God's grace. This is just about the most humbling thing of all. Grace brings down the arrogance of the flesh. Once we realise that we can do nothing to merit God's favour, we are ready to give up trying, and we can yield ourselves to God's grace and mercy.

But he gives more grace. Therefore he says: "God resists the proud, but gives grace to the humble." — James 4:6

Humble yourselves in the sight of the Lord, and he will lift you up. — James 4:10

As you humble yourself under God's gracious hand, he lifts you up out of every bondage and gives you strength to overcome every evil attack.

When you humble yourself, James says, you receive more grace! God gives you everything you need to turn away from evil and to overcome it in Jesus name. As you humble yourself under God's gracious hand, he lifts you up out of every bondage and gives you strength to overcome every evil attack and to reject every demonic presence in your life.

5. Praise and magnify the Lord

When you see your glorious position in Christ, your heart will be filled with gratitude and your mouth will be filled with praise. This is one of the most powerful antidotes to all demonic activity.

Psalm 8:2

Out of the mouth of babes and nursing infants you have ordained strength [praise], because of your enemies, that you may silence the enemy and the avenger.

God silences the enemy through your praise. The avenger cannot bear to hear God praised.

God silences the enemy through your praise. The avenger cannot bear to hear God praised. He cannot stand in the presence of those who know who they are in Christ and praise him for it. When we praise the name of Jesus, the devil has to bow the knee.

6. Seek a fresh infilling of the Holy Spirit

No demon can resist the Holy Spirit. When you are full of the Holy Spirit, the devil has to run away. The Holy Spirit will make you Christ-conscious – conscious of his presence and power. Some people are so preoccupied with demons that they could almost be described as demon conscious! No wonder the enemy plagues them with demonic attack. But if you keep filled with the Spirit you will always be more conscious of Christ than of the devil. You will know the joy of loving him and serving him.

Ephesians 5:18-19

...be filled with the Spirit, speaking to one another in psalms and hymns and spiritual songs, singing and making melody in your heart to the Lord

Freedom from Demonic Power
Deliverance Declaration

I confess and declare that I know and enjoy the absolute freedom of God. Jesus Christ has set me free from the guilt and power of sin! And I am free indeed! I have been crucified with Christ, and have been raised into his resurrection life of perfect liberty. I know that the Son of God was manifested with the purpose of destroying all the evil works of the enemy. And I know that he has done this in me. I walk in the freedom of the Spirit, and have been liberated by the law of love. I have been delivered from the curse of the Law, and I am no longer bound by sin, or by the flesh, or by the devil. I announce

that I am now free to do right, to obey God's will, and to serve my Lord and Saviour with every part of my being. I know that I'm not my own, for I was bought by a great price, the precious blood of Jesus. I now belong to Jesus, and am eager to do his bidding. I renounce sin, Satan, and all his evil works. I stand firm in my freedom, and live in the victory of Christ forever.

Freedom from Soul Ties

There are different kinds of bondages which can affect us in different ways. For example bondages can be:

- Physical – *drugs and alcohol addiction*
- Emotional – *soul ties*
- Spiritual – *demonic.*

Soul ties are mental or emotional links to a situation, person, or place that keep you attached to the old life.

We need to understand all three dimensions to deal with life-dominating problems. Often the one that escapes our notice is the 'soul tie' – the psychological and emotional bondage that come from our involvement with sin. This mental and emotional bondage or 'soul tie' is often the strongest part of the bondage.

In drug addiction, for example, the physical dependence on the drug (say heroin) can be 'cured' in a matter of days of medical treatment and detoxification. But the psychological dependence on the drug will take a lot longer to deal with as will the underlying mental, emotional and motivational reasons for the person taking the drugs in the first place.

What are soul ties?

Soul ties are powerful bonds operating at the level of the human soul. They tie us to the people, places and objects, which link us to our former way of life. The human soul has three main faculties – mind, emotions and will. Soul ties are mental or emotional links to a situation, person, or place that keep you attached to the old life. Soul ties draw your eyes away from Jesus and keep your mind focussed on our past. Our emotions become distorted and our hearts distracted from who we are in Christ. Consequently, we find it difficult to break from old habits – former patterns of thinking and behaving. Soul ties keep us linked with our past by providing a lifeline that keeps our old bondages alive. Soul ties are part of the binding and seductive power of sin and they must be broken in order for us to enjoy the full freedom we have in Christ.

Soul ties are part of the binding and seductive power of sin and they must be broken in order for us to enjoy the full freedom we have in Christ.

Soul ties go deeper than mere sentimental attachment and often can be charged with spiritual power. This spiritual or demonic element is similar to that of addictive or compulsive behaviour. Deliverance can happen in a moment, 'in the name of Jesus!' But often the underlying issues in a person's life can take a little longer. One of these issues can be soul ties that must be broken through repentance and faith.

Soul ties go deeper than mere sentimental attachment and often can be charged with spiritual power.

How soul ties operate

Soul ties can develop whenever there is a sinful connection with a person, place or object relating to your previous sinful behaviour patterns. An emotional, psychological and (sometimes) spiritual dependency develops tying you to the sins of the past. It acts like a bridge to the past life.

Paul warns us about the dangers of turning back to the ways of our past life. He says it is like going back on your freedom in Christ.

Romans 6:16

Do you not know that to whom you present yourselves slaves to obey, you are that one's slaves whom you obey, whether of sin leading to death, or of obedience leading to righteousness?

If we go back to the sins from which we have been delivered we can bring ourselves back under bondage. We rebuild the bridges to sin that Christ has destroyed.

If we go back to the sins from which we have been delivered we can bring ourselves back under bondage.

We rebuild the bridges to sin that Christ has destroyed.

- Soul ties can come through sexual sin, or emotional ties that are bordering on sexual sin.

What you do with your mind can be almost as damaging as what you do with your body. Mental immorality and adultery is as serious as physically doing it – it is sin.

Matthew 5:28

I say to you that whoever looks at a woman [or man] to lust for her [or him] has already committed adultery with her [or him] in his heart.

- Soul ties bind you to former patterns of thinking and behaving.

Sometimes people find it difficult to give up former sexual partners (or people who bear a similarity to them in appearance and character). They find it difficult to put things into the past and truly move on with God. The soul tie must be broken.

- Soul ties are sometimes the real issues of the heart that lead the person into the sin in the first place.

The needs we are seeking to be filled draw us away into sinful paths. As we saw in Topic 4, we are transformed by the renewing of the mind. We must break the power of our idols and deal with the strongholds of the mind in order to break free from the sin holding us in bondage.

- Soul ties are often rooted in unforgiveness

If you harbour unforgiveness you will be tied to the situation, people or circumstances linked to your unforgiveness. You must forgive if you want to be released from this bondage.

Judge not, and you shall not be judged. Condemn not, and you shall not be condemned. Forgive, and you will be forgiven. Give, and it will be given to you: good measure, pressed down, shaken together, and running over will be put into your bosom. For with the same measure that you use, it will be measured back to you.

Luke 6:37-38

Breaking free from soul ties can be impossible until you see that in Christ you have died to sin and its every connection and association in your life.

The measure you use on others will be used on you. It will be measured back to you. This means that if you hold onto unforgiveness, you will never be completely free from the thing that you are refusing to forgive. Untold damage comes to you emotionally and spiritually when you withhold forgiveness. It gives the devil access into your life.

How to be free from soul ties

Breaking free from soul ties can be impossible until you see that in Christ you have died to sin and its every connection and association in your life. Freedom in Christ means that not only have you been set free from sin, but also that the bridges that lead to it were destroyed. Jesus defeated every aspect of sin in your life, including all the ties to your past. You have died with Christ and therefore sin has no more hold over you than if you were physically dead!

God wants us to break off all contact with our past sinful life, by presenting ourselves to him as servants of righteousness.

Knowing this, that our old man was crucified with him, that the body of sin might be done away with, that we should no longer be slaves of sin. For he who has died has been freed from sin.

Romans 6:6-8

The only way we can go back into the bondage of sin is by actively inviting sin to reign over us again. Paul is very clear on this point.

Do not present your members as instruments of unrighteousness to sin, but present yourselves to God as being alive from the dead, and your members as instruments of righteousness to God.

Romans 6:13

God wants us to break off all contact with our past sinful life, by presenting ourselves to him as servants of righteousness. In other words we forsake all the sins of the past and, conscious of our righteousness in Christ we live in the light of who we are – we present ourselves to God as servants of righteousness.

Soul ties belong to the old way of living which we have renounced in Christ – they have nothing to do with our life in Christ.

Galatians 5:23-24

And those who are Christ's have crucified the flesh with its passions and desires.

The following list is not a formula, but a review of the principles of freedom. As you follow these principles you will re-discover who you are in Christ and you will destroy all the bridges to sin you have re-built in your life.

1. Bring the soul tie before the Lord – the physical or emotional contact you have maintained with the person, the place or the physical object relating to your past life.

2. Renounce the contact – name the person or situation.

3. Forsake it utterly from your heart.

As you follow these seven principles you will re-discover who you are in Christ and you will destroy all the bridges to sin you have re-built in your life.

4. Forgive all who have offended you, used you and abused you.

5. Break all unhelpful contact with the person – physically, including tokens, keepsakes, gifts, photos, and so on.

6. Affirm your freedom in Christ – confess you are the righteousness of God in Christ.

7. Turn your heart to the Lord for all your needs.

One of the most dangerous aspects of soul ties is that they take your eyes off Jesus. Do not let that happen. The most important thing to do is to re-focus your heart on all that you are and have in Christ. The following verses from Colossians will help you.

Colossians 3:1-4

If then you were raised with Christ, seek those things which are above, where Christ is, sitting at the right hand of God. Set your mind on things above, not on things on the earth. For you died, and your life is hidden with Christ in God. When Christ who is our life appears, then you also will appear with him in glory.

Soul Ties
Declaration of Release

Father God, I thank you that you will sanctify me through and through and present me faultless at the coming of Christ. You will save my whole spirit, soul and body. I thank you that Jesus and his sacrifice are all-sufficient for me. I confess that I do not need anything to do with my old life of sin to satisfy me. Jesus alone satisfies all the needs of my heart. I now reject, renounce and totally repudiate every contact, every connection, and every association with this soul tie. I forsake all sin and wrong-doing linked with it. I declare that I am released, cut off and totally set free from this soul tie. I am no longer bound by any previous attitude, thought, emotional feeling, act or habit associated with this soul tie. I am now free to move on in my life. I turn my heart back to you Lord Jesus. You are Lord, over my spirit, my soul and my body! Amen.

Deliverance from every different kind of curse is part of the victory of the cross for your life.

Freedom from Curses

God has set us free from the curse of sin, the curse of the law, and any other form of curse the enemy tries to put on us.

The Bible teaches us how to be free from all curses and how to live in the blessing of God. Deliverance from every different kind of curse is part of the victory of the cross for our lives. God has set us free from the curse of sin, the curse of the law, and any other form of curse the enemy tries to put on us. Even the curses that have been passed down to us from generation to generation have been dealt with by the blood of Jesus!

The Old Testament shows that the effects of generational sin operate both in the immediate family and in the wider, extended family.

The Lord is long-suffering and abundant in mercy, forgiving iniquity and transgression; but he by no means clears the guilty, visiting the iniquity of the fathers on the children to the third and fourth generation.

Numbers 14:18

For I, the Lord your God, am a jealous God, visiting the iniquity of the fathers upon the children to the third and fourth generations of those who hate me, but showing mercy to thousands, to those who love me and keep my commandments.

Deuteronomy 5:9-10

Notice that even the Old Testament shows God's grace is stronger than the power of curses. The sins of the fathers are visited upon their children to the third and fourth generations; whereas God's blessing lasts a thousand generations of the righteous!

But even more than that, the New Testament reveals that Jesus has set us free from all generational curses. This includes the worst curse of all – the original curse of death that came through Adam's sin and passed onto all who came after him.

Romans 5:17

For if by the one man's offense death reigned through the one, much more those who receive abundance of grace and of the gift of righteousness will reign in life through the One, Jesus Christ.

The curse on sin was death. It came upon us all through Adam's transgression. But God, in the abundance of his grace sent the Second Adam, Jesus Christ who bestows upon us the gift of righteousness. Delivered from death we now reign in life through Christ. This means that no curse can touch us. We reign over every curse the enemy can throw at us.

Proverbs 26:2

Like a flitting sparrow, like a flying swallow, so a curse without cause shall not alight.

Jesus has dealt with the curse of sin and therefore no curse can have any effect on us. We are the righteous sons and daughters of the Most High God. Jesus qualifies us for blessing in place of cursing.

The blessings of God

Ephesians 1:3 states that we have been blessed with every spiritual blessing in Christ. The word 'blessing' means 'speaking well of' someone. God speaks well of us because we are in Christ. Because we inherit the blessings of the Son, the Father can say over us the same thing he spoke over the life of Jesus: "This is my beloved Son in whom I am well pleased." After all, we are "highly favoured in the well-beloved" *(Ephesians 1:6)*.

God continually blesses us through the word of his mouth spoken by the breath of his Spirit.

God continually blesses us through the word of his mouth spoken by the breath of his Spirit. He pronounces blessing on us – blessing upon blessing, through Christ. We are not blessed according to our merits and cursed according to our wrong-doing. We are only blessed – by God's grace.

John 1:16 NIV

From the fullness of his grace we have all received one blessing after another.

This means that we are blessed because God has spoken or breathed his blessing into our lives. The book of Deuteronomy lists many of the Old Covenant blessings *(Deuteronomy 8:13-15 and 28:1-14)*. These include:

God pronounces blessing on us – blessing upon blessing, through Christ.

- Fertility
- Health
- Victory
- Prosperity
- Good reputation
- Family harmony
- Success.

TOPIC 8   WALKING IN FREEDOM

As we have seen in the New Testament, the Old Covenant blessings are extended to include "every spiritual blessing in Christ" *(Ephesians 1:3)*.

The Old Testament physical blessings have never been revoked. Instead, they now come to you alongside all the spiritual blessings that the Holy Spirit pours into your life. You can read about these blessings in *Ephesians 1:4-14*. They include:

- Election
- Freedom
- Forgiveness
- Holiness
- God's presence
- Adoption.

> *The Old Testament physical blessings have never been revoked. Instead, they now come to you alongside all the spiritual blessings that the Holy Spirit pours into your life.*

The Old Covenant blessing came to Israel when they obeyed the Law of Moses. But under the New Covenant all God's blessings are ours by grace through faith in Christ.

What is a curse?

When we bless someone, we announce God's well-being over his or her life. But God always pronounces a curse on sin. God's first curses were pronounced in the Garden of Eden. His curse on sin brought the whole human race under condemnation. Even creation itself was subjected to futility. As a result, we live in a fallen world of suffering and heartache. But when God announced the original curse, he also revealed his mercy and grace. He told the serpent:

> *When God announced the original curse, he also revealed his mercy and grace.*

I will put enmity between you and the woman, and between your seed and her Seed; he shall bruise your head, and you shall bruise his heel.   Genesis 3:15

This was humanity's first promise of freedom from the curse on sin. God said that 'the Seed' of the woman would crush the serpent's head. God was pointing to Jesus' victory on the cross – where he removed our sin, defeated Satan, and paid the price for the curse of sin to be lifted! As believers on earth, we begin to experience the freedom of the cross. And, when we reach heaven, we'll find that the curse on sin will have been totally eradicated from our lives.

God will wipe away every tear from their eyes; there shall be no more death, nor sorrow, nor crying. There shall be no more pain, for the former things have passed away.   Revelation 21:4

This shows us how Satan operates. He works through sin and the curse. This is his only territory! But he is a defeated enemy under the judgment of God. Once sin has been dealt with, Satan's power is completely broken. He can influence only those who are under the curse. Where there is no curse, the devil has no power. Jesus defeated Satan on the cross by dealing with the curse on sin.

The curse of the Law

When Jesus died on the cross, he was made a curse according to the Law of Moses. He took the curse of the Law onto himself and opened the way for the blessing of God to come upon us by faith.

God gave the Law to the people of Israel. It kept them apart from other nations and taught them the holiness of God. Their obedience to the Law released God's blessing, and their disobedience attracted God's judgment – or curses. You can read about this in *Deuteronomy chapters 28 & 29*.

Jesus has dealt, not only with the curse of sin, but also the curse of the Law. When he died on the cross, he was made a curse according to the Law of Moses. He took the curse of the Law onto himself and opened the way for the blessing of God to come upon us by faith.

Galatians 3:13-14

Christ has redeemed us from the curse of the Law, having become a curse for us (for it is written, 'Cursed is everyone who hangs on a tree') that the blessing of Abraham might come upon the Gentiles in Christ Jesus, that we might receive the promise of the Spirit through faith.

This means that the curse of the Law has been lifted from all those who believe in Jesus. Life in the Spirit is a curse-free existence! Because of this freedom in Christ, we are now free from the curse of sin and the curse of the Law. And if these curses cannot affect us, how can any other curse pronounced by people or the devil affect us?

Life in the Spirit is a curse-free existence!

Some people live in fear and superstition concerning curses. They are terrified if they hear that a person is cursed. They tremble if they are told that a certain place or object carries the power to bring a curse. Is not Christ greater than all this? Has he not triumphed over all things? A believer has nothing to fear from any curse.

'Then what's the problem?' you might ask. There is no problem! We only need to rest in the security and protection of Christ and his blood. We have been set free by the blood of Jesus from every negative influence – including all curses made against us, but we have to be prepared to resist the enemy and stand fast in our freedom.

Do curses operate today?

I am not saying that curses do not exist. They do and are real. A curse can carry a supernatural element in addition to the natural harmful power of the tongue. We know that gossip, slander and negative

TOPIC 8 WALKING IN FREEDOM

speaking do great harm. Words can hurt more, and do much more damage, than a physical attack.

When someone speaks with the intention of hurting a person, family or situation, his or her words possess a certain natural power. They probably don't realise, however, that their hurtful words can also be a 'prayer' which the evil one may choose to enforce. By saying, 'I wish you were dead', they may mean only to hurt the person emotionally. But the destroyer can take their request literally – and start to act upon it physically. The devil delights to defame and destroy people, and curses can arouse his negative influences. The Bible teaches that those who utter a curse are ready to arouse demonic influence.

Every negative word or curse-like pronouncement provides Satan with an opportunity to defame and destroy someone.

May those curse it who curse the day, those who are ready to arouse Leviathan.   Job 3:8

Leviathan was a sea monster, and this description can be interpreted as a picture of Satan. This verse shows that the devil can be roused into action when one person curses another. Every negative word or curse-like pronouncement provides Satan with an opportunity to defame and destroy someone.

What causes a curse?

Any word that you speak against yourself, or against others, exposes you and them to the destructive power of the enemy. But the Bible shows us that curses are ultimately rooted in sin. Curses come upon people because they are exposed to something that makes a curse stick.

The following is a list of the things that bring a curse. We must renounce these things if we want to live in the freedom of Christ.

When you learn to live in the freedom of the cross you can rise above every curse, no matter its origin.

- Anti-Semitism – *Genesis 12:1-3*
- Worship of false gods – *Deuteronomy 27:15*
- Disobedience to God – *Deuteronomy 27:26*
- Misusing God's name – *Jeremiah 29:23*
- Dishonouring parents – *Exodus 21:17*
- Sexual sin – *Leviticus 20:10-16*
- Occult activity – *Leviticus 20:27*

Freedom from curses

The good news is that *all* curses were destroyed at the cross. They lost their power over you when you came to Christ in repentance and faith. We have been released in Jesus' powerful name! When you learn to live in the freedom of the cross you can rise above every curse, no matter its origin. If people curse you, you can bless them, knowing that their words cannot affect you. When the devil curses, you can laugh, because the devil cannot curse those whom God has blessed *(Numbers 23:8)*. In fact, those who curse us, bring a curse on themselves *(Numbers 24:9)*.

Stand firm in Christ and focus on his goodness and blessings.

Part of living curse free is to focus on the blessings of Christ and not become preoccupied with any evil influences you think may be coming from your family, your neighbours, your colleagues at work, or even from your enemies. Stand firm in Christ and focus on his goodness and blessings. All your concerns about the enemy's desire to curse you will be lost in the light of his glory and his grace.

Freedom from Curses
Deliverance Declaration

Father God, in the all-powerful name of Jesus Christ, I take authority over every negative word which has ever been spoken against me. I cancel and nullify them now. By the blood of Jesus, I am released from every evil influence, and from every curse, which has been made against me. I return blessing for cursing, and declare that I am blessed with every blessing in Christ. Amen.

Walking in the freedom and blessing of God means dealing with every spiritual blockage in your life and removing every argument the enemy uses against you.

Freedom from Hereditary Bondage

Walking in the freedom and blessing of God means dealing with every spiritual blockage in your life and removing every argument the enemy uses against you. Sometimes the enemy accuses you of being unworthy of God's blessing because of the sins committed by your ancestors or your relatives. Consider this New Testament passage.

1 Peter 1:18-19

You were not redeemed with corruptible things, like silver or gold, from your aimless conduct received by tradition from your fathers, but with the precious blood of Christ, as of a lamb without blemish and without spot.

Look carefully at the phrase, 'your aimless conduct received by tradition from your fathers'. It refers to something which is handed down to us from past generations – things which affect how we live and what we experience today. The New International Version translates this as, 'you were redeemed from the empty way of life handed down to you from your forefathers'.

TOPIC 8   WALKING IN FREEDOM

Problems from past generations

We all carry some sort of baggage from the former generations of our families which pulls us in the direction of 'an empty way of life' – a life outside God's blessing. We need to be redeemed – to be set free, from these things. This is exactly what Jesus has done for us through the blood of his cross. He has redeemed us from every inherited pattern of emptiness, futility and fruitlessness. The blood has taken care of it!

Why, then, do so many Christians still live empty lives without much evidence of God's rich blessing? The answer is that it's one thing to quote a good verse, but quite another thing to live in the good of that verse! As with every divine promise, it may be necessary to take God's Word and to grasp it aggressively. You have to stand up for your rights in Christ, and enforce them against the wishes of the enemy.

As with every divine promise, it may be necessary to take God's Word and to grasp it aggressively.

You have to stand up for your rights in Christ, and enforce them against the wishes of the enemy.

The people of Israel had to dispossess the Promised Land of its enemies before they could possess it for themselves. They could only take possession of their inheritance, when God had given them rest. God invites us to enter into his rest. In other words, the battles are over, the enemy has been driven out and all we have to do is to step into God's rest.

There remains therefore a rest for the people of God. For he who has entered his rest has himself also ceased from his works as God did from his.

Hebrews 4:8-10

God's rest is the fruit of his accomplishments for us in Christ. You know you are resting in the finished work of Christ when you cease from your own striving and efforts for victory. Once you learn to rest in the promises of freedom and victory, they begin to operate in your life. Let your altitude determine your attitude! Let your position in Christ govern all your thinking.

We tend to be attached to the things we inherit – attitudes as well as antiques!

Natural attachments

Learn to overcome the natural inclinations of your mind. First, there's your own attitude to these generational problems. It stands to reason that generational issues run very deep. We tend to be attached to the things we inherit – attitudes as well as antiques! Family traditions die hard. Attitudes and beliefs which we picked up from our parents (which they learnt from their parents and their parents before them) can be firmly embedded in us. We may not even be aware of them.

Supernatural dimension

There is also a powerful spiritual dimension to generational problems. If God loves to bless the family bloodline, you can be sure that the devil wants to curse it. Curses and other forms of spiritual bondage often run in families. Remember, we're not islands in the sea of life. Our actions and attitudes affect others – especially our children. The sins of the parents really are visited upon the children. The devil loves to get behind this 'family dynamic' and assert a family or generational bondage through it.

Jesus' blood is so powerful that it reaches even to the generations which have gone before.

It sets us free from any inherited effects of the sins of our parents.

We have seen that it is impossible for these negative elements to control us once we have been born again and cleansed by the blood of Jesus. We are redeemed. We have been set free by the blood of Jesus from all these things. This is a spiritual reality and an accomplished fact! But we must learn to enjoy our freedom and live in the good of Christ's work personally. You are in a fight. A battle is raging in your mind, your will and your emotions.

You must stand firm and live according to your position. You must actively lay hold of your blessings and possessions in Christ. Sometimes this is a simple matter of claiming the promise of the Word and you experience God's freedom immediately! At other times, though, you must stand firm and keep resisting until you experience personally the victory that is yours by right. Once more the answer is to turn your eyes away from yourself and back onto Christ – where your blessing and favour come from.

Freedom from the past

The glorious good news of the gospel proclaims that you were set free from your past when you trusted Jesus as your personal Lord and Saviour. Every single thing that you've thought, or said, or done, which is contrary to God's will, has been totally removed by his blood!

But what about the sins of your ancestors? Are you free from their effects? If God visits the parents' sins upon their children to the third and fourth generation, what happens to these 'generational sins' when we trust in Jesus? The good news is that he provides a full and complete salvation. Nothing is left out. This means that all our sins are removed – including the ones we have inherited.

Jesus' blood is so powerful that it reaches even to the generations which have gone before. It sets us free from any inherited effects of the sins of our parents – even to the third and fourth generations. This is included in what Peter means when he says,

TOPIC 8   WALKING IN FREEDOM

You were redeemed from the empty way of life handed down to you from your forefathers… with the precious blood of Christ   1 Peter 1:18-19 (NIV)

A great deliverance

There's only one force which can release us from our forefathers' negative influence. It's not the latest self-help book, nor is it a psychological technique, but it's the precious blood of Jesus. The blood has done its powerful work. Think for a moment about the sheer magnitude of your deliverance. If the iniquities of the parents are visited upon the children to the fourth generation, we can be affected by the sins of up to eight people in our family tree. And this number is doubled when we marry!

Without the blood of Jesus, what hope would there be for our freedom? Sin pollutes and destroys, it spreads its evil influence and it carries a curse that brings devastating consequences. All these negative effects pass down the generations – until Christ's blood wipes them out. These negative influences come in many forms. They can be both physical and spiritual.

- Hereditary sickness

Sickness can be passed down the generations. Even the medical profession now accepts that many diseases are hereditary. Some illnesses may affect several generations simply because the parents' sins are being visited upon their children – without a recognised medical cause.

- Inherited sin

All kinds of sinful bondages appear to be passed down the family bloodline. Alcoholism, sexual immorality, divorce, criminal activity – they all influence the generations to come.

- Demonic influence

Demonic activity can also be passed down the generations. It seems that even the devil tries to afflict us with demons through the family bloodline.

Perfect freedom

The good news is that you've been set free from all these things by the perfect blood of Jesus. When, by faith, you lay hold of everything that his blood has achieved for you, the result is perfect freedom. This doesn't mean, of course, that there's nothing for you to battle against in these areas. In fact, you may have to take a very strong stand against hereditary influences from your past.

Sin pollutes and destroys, it spreads its evil influence and it carries a curse that brings devastating consequences.

All these negative effects pass down the generations – until Christ's blood wipes them out.

You may have to 'fight the good fight of faith' to experience your freedom from the enemy's efforts to enslave you in some form of fear or bondage.

You may have to 'fight the good fight of faith' to experience your freedom from the enemy's efforts to enslave you in some form of fear or bondage. Remember your position. Know what Jesus has achieved for you on the cross. Recognise that you really have been set free from the empty way of life handed down to you from your forefathers.

- You don't have to endure the same diseases as your parents.
- You don't have to be afflicted by the bad temper that you inherited from your father.
- You don't have to give in to the temptations which have ruined others in your family.
- Your marriage doesn't have to end in divorce like your parents, or their parents before them.
- You don't have to be affected by the demonic fears which have plagued your family for generations.

Remember your position.

Know what Jesus has achieved for you on the cross.

You've been set free. So take your stand today against the wiles of the devil. Resist his every tactic and strategy. Jesus is Lord over your spirit, so no other spirit can ever lord it over you!

Freedom from Hereditary Bondage Deliverance Declaration

Father, I thank you that the blood of Jesus has set me free from the empty way of life which was handed down to me from my forefathers. I now stand firm in my freedom and liberty in Christ. I declare that I'm released from every curse and bondage of my bloodline. I'm cleansed from the iniquity of my forefathers. I'm set free from all forms of negative hereditary influence. I command my whole person to live in the good of this promise. And I declare that I'm sound in body, mind and spirit. My emotions and my will are fully subject to God's Holy Spirit. Jesus is Lord over my entire being. Praise his Holy Name! Amen.

TOPIC 9

THE SPIRIT-FILLED LIFE

2,000 years ago, the Church of Jesus Christ was baptised in power and clothed with a supernatural enabling to fulfil her role in the world, just as Jesus had promised.

2,000 years ago, the Church of Jesus Christ was baptised in power and clothed with a supernatural enabling to fulfil her role in the world, just as Jesus had promised.

Behold, I send the Promise of my Father upon you; but tarry in the city of Jerusalem until you are endued with power from on high. — *Luke 24:49*

God never intended that we should go naked into the battle but that we should be fully equipped with God's power on our lives. This is the divine enablement we need to live for God and to witness to Jesus Christ.

But you shall receive power when the Holy Spirit has come upon you; and you shall be witnesses to me in Jerusalem, and in all Judea and Samaria, and to the end of the earth — *Acts 1:8*

Baptised in the Spirit

We must carefully examine this statement of Jesus, as it is pivotal to our understanding of the role of the Holy Spirit in empowering believers for witness.

The book of Acts is the second volume in a two part series about the work of Jesus. Luke, the author, explains that in the first part of his work he described the things that Jesus "began to do and to teach" *(Acts 1:1)*.

By this he indicates that the second volume is going to be about the things Jesus 'continued' to do and teach. After a few verses Luke shows how Jesus was taken up into heaven. And from there he sends the Spirit to equip the infant church to continue his works on the earth.

We can see exactly what Jesus intended for the Spirit to do from the opening verses of Acts. First, we see Jesus after his resurrection showing himself to his disciples, proving that he was alive and teaching them about the kingdom of God.

Acts 1:3

...to whom he also presented himself alive after his suffering by many infallible proofs, being seen by them during forty days and speaking of the things pertaining to the kingdom of God.

The Holy Spirit comes to enable us to produce the proof that Jesus is alive.

During this 40-day period, Jesus was his own witness, producing the proof that he was alive. He didn't argue. He simply appeared to them physically, showing himself to be alive. But then he explained that he wasn't going to do this anymore. Instead, he was returning to the Father and from there he would send the Spirit. That's why the disciples had to wait in Jerusalem until they had been clothed with the Spirit's power.

Jesus describes this as being baptised in (or with) the Spirit.

Acts 1:5

...for John truly baptised with water, but you shall be baptised with the Holy Spirit not many days from now.

John the Baptist pointed to Jesus as the Lamb of God that takes away the sins of the world. He also said Jesus would baptise believers in the Holy Spirit. Now Jesus reveals the purpose of this baptism in the Spirit. He says, "You shall receive power" *(Acts 1:8)*. The Greek word for 'power' is *dunamis* and this means 'enablement'. It is receiving the ability to do what you could not normally do. So, the Holy Spirit comes to enable us, to give us the power to do what we could never do on our own. But what specifically does the Holy Spirit enable us to do?

Proof producers

The Holy Spirit enables us to produce the proof that Jesus is alive. When someone acts as a witness in a court of law they are called to give evidence. A witness is a proof producer. First, Jesus was his own witness producing the proof that he was alive. But then he went back to heaven, received the promised Holy Spirit and poured him out onto the waiting church below.

TOPIC 9   THE SPIRIT-FILLED LIFE

As his witnesses, they began to produce the proof that he was alive. In other words, they began to do what they could not do before. On the Day of Pentecost, Peter preached to the multitudes and thousands came to Christ. Later he and John pronounced healing for the lame man at the gate of the Temple. The Apostles did great signs and wonders – the dead were raised, the crippled walked, deaf were healed and the blind were given sight.

The Holy Spirit brought the power the Church needs to make Christ known through the preaching of the gospel followed by signs, wonders and gifts of the Holy Spirit, as Hebrews makes clear.

The Holy Spirit brought the power the Church needs to make Christ known through the preaching of the gospel followed by signs, wonders and gifts of the Holy Spirit, as Hebrews makes clear.

... so great a salvation, which at the first began to be spoken by the Lord, and was confirmed to us by those who heard Him, God also bearing witness both with signs and wonders, with various miracles, and gifts of the Holy Spirit, according to his own will...   Hebrews 2:3-4

This isolates the principal purpose of the coming of the Spirit to the Church. Jesus explained that the Holy Spirit was going to be given to us, for them. That is, the Spirit is given to us believers, for the purpose of reaching those who do not yet know Christ. Jesus made it clear that it is impossible for unbelievers to receive the Holy Spirit,

...the Spirit of truth, whom the world cannot receive, because it neither sees him nor knows him; but you know him, for he dwells with you and will be in you.   John 14:17

Before we come to Christ we are dependent upon the work of the Holy Spirit to convict us of sin, and to bring us to Christ, just as Jesus said,

And when he [the Holy Spirit] has come, he will convict the world of sin, and of righteousness, and of judgment.   John 16:8

However, there is a further work of the Spirit in our lives. It's not enough to have the Spirit's influence bringing you to Christ, or have the rebirth experience in which the Spirit of God comes into your life and gives you a new nature – a spiritual nature like his. You need to experience a further work of God in your life. You need to be born again, but you also need to be baptised in the Spirit. You need to know the Spirit's work in regeneration by which you become a Christian by being born of the Spirit into the kingdom of God. But you also need to be baptised in the Spirit so that you can receive power to witness to Christ.

You need to be born again, but you also need to be baptised in the Spirit.

You need to know the Spirit's work in regeneration by which you become a Christian by being born of the Spirit into the kingdom of God.

But you also need to be baptised in the Spirit so that you can receive power to witness to Christ.

One common mistake that some Bible teachers make today is to assume that every believer has the Holy Spirit's power in fullness once they have become a Christian. But the New Testament's teaching is very clear. The Spirit of God is given to believers. First, you believe in Christ, and then you receive the Spirit. This means that there is something more for you to experience once you have come to Christ. You need to be filled with the Spirit.

Subsequence and evidence

The experience of the Holy Spirit is something that follows faith. It is subsequent to believing.

We have seen that the purpose of the Spirit coming into our lives is to give us power for witness. But there are two other key points to understand about being baptised in the Spirit, and these are, 'subsequence' and 'evidence'. These tell us when we receive the Spirit and what happens when the Spirit comes.

Now, as I have been emphasising, the Spirit comes upon those who believe. He is given to believers. The experience of the Holy Spirit is something that follows faith. It is subsequent to believing. This means that being baptised in the Spirit is not automatic. Just because you have become a Christian it doesn't mean that you have automatically been baptised in the Spirit. The Spirit is promised to all who believe, but usually, you have to ask Jesus, the Baptiser, to baptise you in the Holy Spirit. Sometimes he gives the Spirit without someone having to seek this experience but this is not usual in the book of Acts. Jesus gives the Holy Spirit to those who ask him *(Luke 11:13)*.

Receiving follows believing

The book of Acts is the only book in the New Testament which records the actual experience of people receiving the Holy Spirit. And we see repeatedly how the receiving follows believing.

Just because you have become a Christian it doesn't mean that you have automatically been baptised in the Spirit.

In *Acts chapter 2* the disciples receive the Spirit as they wait for him to come, just as Jesus told them. In *Acts chapter 8*, we read of the Samaritan believers who received the Spirit some days after they had believed and after the Apostles had come down from Jerusalem to pray for them to receive the Spirit. *Acts chapter 9* shows Saul (the apostle Paul) receiving the Spirit after he had believed in Jesus and when Ananias, the disciple, laid hands on him. The Ephesians of *Acts chapter 19* also received the Holy Spirit after they had believed in Jesus and when Paul laid his hands on them and prayed.

But there is one example of people receiving the Holy Spirit in Acts which seems to contradict this teaching on subsequence. In *Acts chapter 10* we read of Cornelius and his household being baptised in the Spirit while the gospel was being preached to them. It seems as if they received the Holy Spirit, when they believed – that is, at the same moment they came to faith in Christ.

TOPIC 9   THE SPIRIT-FILLED LIFE

While Peter was still speaking these words, the Holy Spirit fell upon all those who heard the word.

Acts 10:44

But when we look closely at this incident it is clear that here also the Holy Spirit was given to those who had first believed. Peter later used this fact to show that Cornelius and his family were true believers. The Spirit had come upon them and this was proof that God had first purified their hearts by faith. In other words, they first believed and then, immediately afterwards, they received the Holy Spirit.

And when there had been much dispute, Peter rose up and said to them: "Men and brethren, you know that a good while ago God chose among us, that by my mouth the Gentiles should hear the word of the gospel and believe. So God, who knows the heart, acknowledged them by giving them the Holy Spirit, just as he did to us, and made no distinction between us and them, purifying their hearts by faith."

Acts 15:7-9

This is exactly what Paul teaches in the book of Ephesians when he says that the Holy Spirit is God's authentic seal of approval upon those who have believed in Christ.

In Him you also trusted, after you heard the word of truth, the gospel of your salvation; in whom also, having believed, you were sealed with the Holy Spirit of promise

Ephesians 1:13

What happens when the Spirit comes?

Way back in 1901, a man called Charles Parham called his Bible College students in Topeka, Kansas back from their Christmas holiday to report on their homework assignment. A few days earlier he had told them all to study the New Testament and find out what happens when the Spirit comes into someone's life. When they returned, they reported their findings: when the Spirit comes, many things happen, but one sure thing is that people speak in tongues. In response to this one student, by the name of Agnes Ozman, asked for prayer and began to speak in tongues, just as in the New Testament.

Soon many thousands of people had experienced the baptism of the Spirit according to the book of Acts. This was the beginnings of the Pentecostal movement that has touched millions of people worldwide. There are around 600 million people, in every Christian denomination all over the world, that claim to have experienced the Holy Spirit as Agnes did all those years ago.

In every place where the book of Acts records people receiving the Holy Spirit there are clear visible or vocal evidences of the Spirit's presence.

In every place where the book of Acts records people receiving the Holy Spirit there are clear visible or vocal evidences of the Spirit's presence. There were manifestations of a rushing mighty wind and flames of fire *(Acts 2)* and the shaking of the building where the believers were praying *(Acts 4)*, which were clearly special manifestations for those people and which may (or may not) be repeated for us today. But as

The book of Acts makes clear that the gift of tongues was the accepted sign that people had been baptised in the Holy Spirit.

well as these things there is a recurring pattern. Every time the Spirit comes, people speak with tongues and prophesy. Jesus said, "Out of the overflow of the heart, the mouth speaks" *(Matthew 12:34)*. When your heart is full of something, it overflows out of your mouth. When you are full of love, you speak words of love. When you are full of anger, angry words come out of your mouth. And when you are full of the Holy Spirit, spiritual words – words belonging to the Spirit, overflow from your mouth.

Tongues as a sign

The book of Acts makes clear that the gift of tongues was the accepted sign that people had been baptised in the Holy Spirit. On the Day of Pentecost, they spoke with tongues.

Acts 2:4

And they were all filled with the Holy Spirit and began to speak with other tongues, as the Spirit gave them utterance.

The Samaritan believers received a definite sign of the Spirit's presence and Simon, the magician, wanted to pay money to be able to give the Spirit to people in the same manner he had just seen it demonstrated. Many Bible scholars (including non Pentecostals) believe it was the gift of tongues Simon witnessed. We know the apostle Paul, who received the Spirit in *Acts chapter 9*, spoke with tongues (although it is not recorded in Acts chapter 9 that he did so).

1 Corinthians 14:18

I thank my God I speak with tongues more than you all…

Cornelius and his household also spoke with tongues when the Spirit came upon them. And this was definite proof that they had received the Spirit.

Acts 10:45-46

And those of the circumcision who believed were astonished, as many as came with Peter, because the gift of the Holy Spirit had been poured out on the Gentiles also. For they heard them speak with tongues and magnify God.

The believers of Ephesus spoke with tongues and prophesied when the Holy Spirit came upon them.

Acts 19:6

And when Paul had laid hands on them, the Holy Spirit came upon them, and they spoke with tongues and prophesied.

All this shows that the gift of tongues is a sign that God gives people as an evidence that they are baptised in the Spirit.

TOPIC 9   THE SPIRIT-FILLED LIFE

The Spirit-filled life

Being filled with the Spirit is not a once-for-all experience. It is true that we should be able to point to an initial experience with God when we were baptised into the Holy Spirit. But as we saw in Topic 2, this baptism is meant to be an ongoing experience. We must remain in the flow of the Holy Spirit.

Just as a sponge soaks up the water when it is immersed, so we must learn how to soak in God's presence and power. We are called to live in the presence of God being continually filled with the Spirit.

Just as a sponge soaks up the water when it is immersed, so we must learn how to soak in God's presence and power.

And do not be drunk with wine, in which is dissipation; but be filled with the Spirit   Ephesians 5:18

This verse compares the effects of being drunk with being filled with the Spirit. Excessive use of alcohol can lead to an addiction that negatively affects and totally controls the person's life. However, the effects of being filled or controlled by the Spirit are entirely positive.

God tells us to be continually filled with the Spirit. Just as it takes habitual abuse of alcohol in order to become an alcoholic so also you must be continually surrendered to the Holy Spirit in order to become truly 'addicted' or filled with the Holy Spirit.

We are called to live in the presence of God being continually filled with the Spirit.

The command, "Be filled" in *Ephesians 5:18*, is in the present imperative, and it means literally that we are to be 'continually filled' with the Holy Spirit.

This means that we are to constantly yield our lives to more of him and his influences in our lives. The Holy Spirit wants to take over and direct the whole of our lives. He wants to lead us closer and closer to Jesus, to reveal more and more of Christ's word to us and to make us more like him every day.

The gifts of the Spirit

Throughout this process he is continually equipping us with his ability through his supernatural working in our lives. The gifts of the Spirit in *1 Corinthians chapter 12* show us the tool kit for workers in the kingdom. These supernatural endowments are available to all who are walking with the Spirit.

But the manifestation of the Spirit is given to each one for the profit of all: for to one is given the word of wisdom through the Spirit, to another the word of knowledge through the same Spirit, to another faith by the same Spirit, to another gifts of healings by the same Spirit, to another the working of miracles, to another prophecy, to another discerning of spirits, to another different kinds of tongues, to another the interpretation of tongues.   1 Corinthians 12:7-11

But one and the same Spirit works all these things, distributing to each one individually as he wills.

So it's the Holy Spirit who leads you to live the supernatural lifestyle of the kingdom of God. And this is a growing experience. Never be content to remain at the same level in the things of the Spirit. God always has more for you. There are levels of the Holy Spirit's power and enabling and there are depths of divine encounter with Christ that you have yet not begun to even dream about. Be open to everything that the Holy Spirit has for you in your Christian life.

There are levels of the Holy Spirit's power and enabling and there are depths of divine encounter with Christ that you have yet not begun to even dream about.

TOPIC 10

SERVING GOD

Everything that we have seen and discovered in this book has been building up to this point: *we have been called to serve God by taking up the ministry of Jesus Christ.* Jesus has set us free so that we might fulfil the ministry he has given to each of us.

The focal point of discipleship in the New Testament is the call to follow Christ's example and to do what he did while he was on this earth. This is more than a good behaviour agreement, and much, much more than merely enjoying our freedom and the blessings he has given us. It means that we join with him in the great mission and purpose of his heart. We become his ambassadors in this world.

It is a high and holy calling to be Christ's agents and his representatives in this world. And without the Holy Spirit it would be impossible. Jesus himself said, "Without me you can do nothing" *(John 15:5)*. But this implies that joined to him we can do all things.

The focal point of discipleship in the New Testament is the call to follow Christ's example and to do what he did while he was on this earth.

Using your freedom

Much of this book has been about finding healing and learning how to enjoy your freedom in Christ. But there has also been a deeper purpose: using your freedom to serve Christ because you have been healed to serve. This is illustrated by the simple story of the healing of Simon Peter's mother in law. She was lying in bed sick with a fever, and we read how that Jesus,

It is a high and holy calling to be Christ's agents and his representatives in this world.

Mark 1:31

...came and took her by the hand and lifted her up, and immediately the fever left her. And she served them.

Jesus healed her and she immediately set about serving him. In the same way, Jesus is calling you to live your life in service to him. He has left us a task so great that it will take nothing short of total dedication and building all the priorities of our life around the fulfilment of his plan for our lives.

Matthew 28:19-20

"Go therefore and make disciples of all the nations, baptizing them in the name of the Father and of the Son and of the Holy Spirit, teaching them to observe all things that I have commanded you; and lo, I am with you always, even to the end of the age." Amen.

Both Jesus' command and the accompanying promise are absolutely clear. He has left us in no doubt about his promise to be with us always to help us fulfil his will.

The Great Commission

If you want to be a real follower of Christ, you cannot ignore the Great Commission or place it at the sidelines of your life. It has to become your purpose on this earth, taking precedence over everything else. That means you no longer selfishly pursue your own plans and ambitions. Rather, you follow Christ's plan for you.

If you want to be a real follower of Christ, you cannot ingnore the Great Commission or place it at the sidelines of your life.

Many Christians fail to understand the seriousness of this command of Christ, but we must remember who is speaking here. It is the risen Christ, who is Lord of all. He is the one who says, "All authority has been given to me in heaven and on earth" *(Matthew 28:18)*.

It has to become your purpose on this earth, taking precedence over everything else.

Tragically, most churches do not make Jesus' last command their first concern. Church life is often about anything but the effective fulfilment of the Great Commission. It has become the 'great omission' in the lives of God's people both individually and corporately. We have to change all that and to so structure our personal and our church life that we actually obey the command of our Lord and the Head of the church.

Many believers think that if they do put God's priorities first in their lives they will miss out. Nothing could be further from the truth! This is pure deception from the evil one. Take this fact deep into your heart: you never miss out by going God's way. You cannot lose. Look at what Jesus said in the Sermon on the Mount.

You never miss out by going God's way. You cannot lose.

Matthew 6:33

Seek first the kingdom of God and his righteousness, and all these things shall be added to you.

He promises you that if you put him first and pursue his will above all else, that 'all these things' will you given to you as well. What are the things he is referring to? The very things that people seek for and run after to attain in life. So the way to the total provision of God's abundance and blessing in every part of your life is to take up and fulfil God's plan for you.

Many people allow their ambition and desires in life to push out God's purposes. Christian living becomes mere church attendance and trying to keep up the appearance of a Christian lifestyle. But that is not enough. We will appear before the judgement seat of Christ on that Day to answer one question, "What have you done with what I told you to do?"

Therefore we make it our aim, whether present or absent, to be well pleasing to him. For we must all appear before the judgment seat of Christ, that each one may receive the things done in the body, according to what he has done, whether good or bad.

2 Corinthians 5:9-10

Instead of merely pursuing our career or the direction we have set for ourselves in life, God wants us to ask 'how we can serve him?' We have been sent into the world with the same call and commission that Jesus had, as we can see from the prayer of Jesus to his Father in *John chapter 17*.

As you sent me into the world, I also have sent them into the world.

John 17:18

This means we are called to influence the world as much as we possibly can by being a disciple of Jesus wherever he places us in the world. Your career in life is the platform for you to fulfil the Great Commission of Jesus. Your place of work, your college, your school, your home, your family, and your whole community are your mission field.

Once you grasp this fact your life will never be the same. Even your recreational life and your hobbies take on a new dimension. These things are like bridges into the lives of people who don't yet know about Jesus and are waiting to see him in your life.

Christ must first be formed in us before he can be reproduced in others we are discipling.

Let's look at God's plan for you in more detail. Matthew chapter 28 speaks of Jesus' command to 'make disciples of all nations'. This means we must first become a disciple ourselves and be an example of Christ's life to others. There can be no effective disciple-making without this. Christ must first be formed in us before he can be reproduced in others we are discipling. Remember the call is not just to lead people to become believers but followers of Christ.

Therefore the command to make disciples actually involves 3 things: making, maturing and mobilising disciples.

This is a process that we can divide into 4 stages:

- Win – *leading people to faith in Christ*
- Consolidate – *helping them become established in Christ*
- Disciple – *forming Christ in them and equipping them to lead others*
- Send – *releasing people into the work of Christ.*

The Great Commission:
- *Win*
- *Consolidate*
- *Disciple*
- *Send*

All these things are implied in the Great Commission. The call begins where we are but it can take us to the very ends of the earth as Jesus leads us.

Dealing with hindrances

When people hear about their calling, almost always their first reaction is, 'I can't do this. It's too hard!' They look at their weaknesses or failures and think of all the demands of life and turn away from the plan of God. My friend, please understand that is not a viable option. There is no alternative. We must obey the Lord and not allow our lives to become unfruitful like the seed sown among thorns in Jesus' Parable of the Sower.

Mark 4:18-19

Now these are the ones sown among thorns; they are the ones who hear the word, and the cares of this world, the deceitfulness of riches, and the desires for other things entering in choke the word, and it becomes unfruitful.

In a sense this book is all about dealing with the thorns in the soil of your life. We have seen how to be free from our idolatrous goals which bring nothing but fruitless dissatisfaction. Why go on pursuing these things? Why not take up the call of God and go for him one hundred per cent! It's the path that leads to fruitfulness and blessing.

Mark 4:20

But these are the ones sown on good ground, those who hear the word, accept it, and bear fruit: some thirtyfold, some sixty, and some a hundred.

We must obey the Lord and not allow our lives to become unfruitful like the seed sown among thorns in Jesus' Parable of the Sower.

Also, remember, you are not on your own. Help is on the way! Jesus spent much valuable time during his last hours with the disciples teaching them this very thing – how to withstand the pressures of the world and become fruitful.

Bearing fruit

God's will for you is fruitfulness. And the way to fruitfulness is by abiding in Christ.

TOPIC 10   SERVING GOD

Abide in me, and I in you. As the branch cannot bear fruit of itself, unless it abides in the vine, neither can you, unless you abide in me.

John 15:4

This is a command that we have to do something in order to obey. Fruitfulness is not automatic. It doesn't come to you just because you are a Christian. You must consciously abide in him. You must dwell in him and make him your habitation. You must draw from him his life, strength and power. Only then will his life begin to touch your life and see the fruit of a Christ-filled life come to pass.

I am the vine, you are the branches. He who abides in me, and I in him, bears much fruit; for without me you can do nothing.

John 15:5

The nature of the fruit

If we are abiding in him and he is abiding in us, the kind of fruit we are going to bear is fruit that resembles him! This is Christ being produced in us so that he may be reproduced through us in others. This is the principle of multiplication and is essential to discipleship.

If we are abiding in him and he is abiding in us, the kind of fruit we are going to bear is fruit that resembles him!

Fruitfulness also carries with it a promise – the fulfilment of our deepest desires.

You did not choose me, but I chose you and appointed you that you should go and bear fruit, and that your fruit should remain, that whatever you ask the Father in my name he may give you.

John 15:16

Abiding in the Vine and bearing fruit for Christ means you have an intimate relationship with him and he will fulfil the desires of your heart and life.

If you abide in me, and my words abide in you, you will ask what you desire, and it shall be done for you.

John 15:7

Jesus shows us in *John's Gospel chapter 15* many other blessings of obedience and fruitfulness.

Bearing fruit:

- Glorifies the Father

Verse 8: "By this is my Father glorified…that you bear much fruit…."

- Proves your discipleship

Verse 8: "so, thus, in this way… you will be my disciples"

- Makes you a friend of God

Verse 14: "You are my friends if you do whatever I command you."

Fruit that remains

Jesus promised us fruit that remains *(John 15:16)*. In other words, our lives are not wasted when we follow him and make disciples according to his command. All others works will be burned up and we will suffer loss *(1 Corinthians 3:14-15)*. But the work we do for Christ as we pursue the call of making disciples will last and endure forever. Through spiritual reproduction we leave a lasting legacy. We will build generations of disciples as we disciple them and teach them to do the same.

The work we do for Christ as we pursue the call of making disciples will last and endure forever.

Many believers who understand this call do not have the support of a church that is organised entirely around the command of Christ to make disciples. This is tragic because we can only achieve the will of God as we work together towards the goal of making, maturing and mobilising disciples.

Let's see how a church can be organised if it is going to obey the Great Commission.

Cells

First there must be a context for believers to gather together in groups committed to discipleship. These are the cell groups where disciples are made and the work of God takes place. The cell groups are places of nurture, care, encouragement and preparation for the service of the Master.

The cell groups are where disciples are made and the work of God takes place.

These cell groups are ideal places for evangelism as people reach out to their friends or those on their 'Evangelism of 3' (see Topic 3).

There are also leadership cells, where leaders receive on-going training and discipleship in the same way Jesus trained and led his 12 disciples. Jesus is still blessing this principle of discipling in groups of 12 today.

Leadership School

But there is also a need for practical training so that new believers can take up their call to leadership. Every Christian is called to be a leader. We are all called to lead other people to Jesus and to lead them deeper into their Christian faith. The leadership school is where you can be trained and developed for your ministry.

Remember, God's people are called to do God's work, and the body of Christ is the only agent of Christ in this world. That means all believers, including you, are called to serve Christ. You should take the next step today and enter into your training for leadership. This will prepare you to win people to Christ and take up the call to the ministry God has given you. You can grow and mature in your Christian life and take up the leadership role God has for you. Not every believer is called to be an apostle, a prophet, an evangelist or, a pastor or a teacher. But we can all learn how to form Christ in others. We can all learn how to lead a cell and fulfil our calling that way.

Make this commitment to Christ today. Yield to his will for you and determine to live the rest of your life as a disciple of Jesus Christ and a disciple-maker of others. Think of the blessing that awaits you on that Day when having followed Christ all the days of your life, you hear these words,

"Well done, good and faithful servant; you were faithful over a few things, I will make you ruler over many things. Enter into the joy of your lord."

Matthew 25:21

The amazing effects of grace

In another sense, this book has been all about God's amazing grace that has set us free from the penalty and power of sin. By grace we have been saved through faith. By grace we walk the walk of faith. By grace we are set free from every bondage and impediment of the devil. And by grace we serve God through faith, as we depend on his power working so energetically within.

I don't believe grace produces lazy Christians. People will labour hard giving their lives for many different things – for money, for success, for promotion and for fulfilment in life. But the greatest motivation of all is love. I have seen people labour tirelessly for the Lord over the years. I know that no amount of money in the entire world could produce such a labour of love.

Once you have seen the pure, boundless and perfect love of God shown to you in Christ, you can't help yourself – you just fall in love with him. Nothing that he asks you to do is too small or too big. Grace teaches you to be a selfless worker for Christ – not out of duty or fear, but out of love. The apostle Paul said that he owed everything he was to the grace of God. He also said that it was grace that had led him to live a life of totally dedicated service to God. This was the amazing effect grace had on him.

But by the grace of God I am what I am, and his grace toward me was not in vain; but I laboured more abundantly than they all, yet not I, but the grace of God which was with me.

1 Corinthians 15:10

God's passion becomes your passion, his vision for the nations of the world, becomes the vision for your life.

You too can say, "By the grace I am what I am." Think about all you are and possess in Christ. This is the miracle of amazing grace. But the miracle does not end there! You are who you are, by the grace of God and, like Paul, this grace will continue to produce its effects in your life. God's grace in never in vain. The more you dwell on his grace, the more you meditate on God's goodness to you, the more you will find yourself serving him. His passion becomes your passion, his vision for the nations of the world, becomes the vision for your life. You move out in the power of his grace, burning with the message of his love – the love that you know and have experienced personally. This love is contagious. People are fed up with religion – they want the reality of Christ's love. And you have it!

You move out in the power of his grace, burning with the message of his love – the love that you know and have experienced personally.

Take up this high call on your life today. Surrender to the Holy Spirit within you, sit back and watch him work. You will soon find yourself going where you would not ordinarily go, doing and saying what you would not ordinarily do and say. But it will not be *you* – it will be the *Holy Spirit* activating and energising you through the grace of God at work in you.

EPILOGUE

A WORD OF ENCOURAGEMENT

> *You have caught a glimpse of the mountain top – your true place in the heavenly realms, seated with Christ on the throne of the universe.*

The Lake District in Northern England is one of the most beautiful parts of the British Isles. I know a certain place in one particularly striking corner of this countryside, surrounded by hills and mountains, valleys, lakes and streams. Set back on the edge of a hill is a bench strategically placed to give the best view across the dale of the imposing peaks that command the head of the valley. Engraved on the bench are the opening words of Psalm 121:

I will lift up my eyes to the hills - from whence comes my help? My help comes from the LORD, Who made heaven and earth.   *Psalm 121:1-2*

Sitting on this bench you can easily imagine those mountain peaks representing your high and holy calling in Christ – so tantalisingly close and yet completely out of reach. To attain those heights you have to leave the comfort of the bench, set out across the valley and begin to slowly make your way to the top. It takes effort, but it's worth it! Each step takes you upward and onward. From time to time, you discover convenient resting places where you can pause for reflection and take in the view. You can look back to the valley behind you and see the ground you have covered so far and you can look up towards the mountain peak ahead renewing your determination to make it to the top.

> *You have begun your journey of adventure – becoming in your daily life who you are in Christ.*

The *Living Free!* course presented in this book is a kind of journey. Over the weeks you have caught a glimpse of the mountain top – your true place in the heavenly realms, seated with Christ on the throne of the universe. You have also begun your journey of adventure – becoming in your daily life who you are in Christ. You have learned how to work through a major issue in your life and slowly bring about the changes God wants yielding your mind, emotions and will to his Spirit at work in you. It has not been easy, and no doubt at times you wondered whether it was all ever going to work. But you persevered by his grace and here you are!

No matter how fierce the battle appears or how impossible the journey seems, the Lord is with you to help you and to strengthen you.

Let me offer some words of encouragement for you – no matter how fierce the battle appears or how impossible the journey seems, the Lord is with you to help you and to strengthen you. He will never leave you nor forsake you. If you persevere you will succeed, you will attain to your high and heavenly calling. Remember, "I can do all things through Christ who gives me strength" *(Philippians 4:6)*. Your help truly comes from the Lord, the Maker of heaven and earth.

Your ever-watchful keeper

The verses following those engraved on the bench on the valley's edge I spoke of earlier remind you that you are not alone – he who has saved you, is the one who also keeps you, ever watchful over your every step, not to condemn you or criticise you but to lift you up and help you take the next step.

Psalm 121:3-4

He will not allow your foot to be moved; he who keeps you will not slumber. Behold, he who keeps Israel shall neither slumber nor sleep.

This is confirmed by those encouraging words found in Jude's open letter to believers.

Jude 1:24

Now to him who is able to keep you from stumbling, and to present you faultless before the presence of his glory with exceeding joy...

Facing your trials

The saying goes, 'When the going gets tough, the tough get going.' That's a great motivational statement, but not a helpful one for those living by grace! Grace teaches us to rest in Jesus' finished work on the cross and to depend on his power to bring us to our destination – the Father's kingdom. Quite simply, we can't, but God *can*. This means we rely on Christ's faithfulness to us and place no confidence in our own ability or self determination. He will keep us faithful and close to him, but even when we fail, he remains ever faithful and will never abandon us.

Even when we fail, he remains ever faithful and will never abandon us.

2 Timothy 2:11-13

This is a faithful saying: For if we died with him, we shall also live with him. If we endure, we shall also reign with him. If we deny him, he also will deny us. If we are faithless, he remains faithful; he cannot deny himself.

A WORD OF ENCOURAGEMENT

Perseverance, inspired by the Holy Spirit's work in your heart, no matter what the difficulties, the setbacks and the obstacles in your way will always bring the reward. James encourages us to stay the course in the midst of tiresome trials and temptations.

Blessed is the man who endures temptation; for when he has been approved, he will receive the crown of life which the Lord has promised to those who love him. — James 1:12-13

Throughout this book I have set out in a practical way the life of freedom that Jesus has for those who come before him in simple faith. We have seen that this freedom is available through his victorious death and triumphant resurrection. We too have died with Christ and have been raised to new life in him.

The secret of discipleship is to become passionate about abundant life in Christ that we are willing to surrender totally to his will. That way we can find both strength for the journey and joy in travelling it. This high and holy calling will cost you everything you have but it is worth it. The Holy Spirit urges us daily to press on to perfection and maturity and fulfil the command of Jesus: 'be perfect as your heavenly father is perfect'. Spiritual attainment is nothing more than living out your call to be free, working it out day by day, until you reach the end of the journey.

> *The secret of discipleship is to so desire the abundant life of freedom in Christ that we are willing to surrender totally to his will.*

The pace of grace

As you finish this course you will be aware that the journey has just begun. There are other battles to fight, other mountains to climb. I want to encourage you to go forward step by step, fearing nothing but relying totally on the grace at work in you in Christ.

Learn the secret of walking with Jesus – I call it the 'pace of grace'. We must learn 'the unforced rhythms of grace – learn how to keep pace with the Spirit's work in your heart. You cannot go further than the revelation you have received – you cannot lead the Spirit, only follow him. Through constant and increasing revelation of who you are in Christ, God's grace opens up the way for every step you take in your journey towards spiritual attainment and freedom in Christ. Your part is to keep up with him and by responding to his promptings within. This is how we discover his enabling power to keep on going. It is by being yoked to Christ that we discover spiritual rest and conquer the strivings of the flesh.

> *Through constant and increasing revelation of who you are in Christ, God's grace opens up the way for every step you take in your journey towards spiritual attainment and freedom in Christ.*

Come to me, all you who labour and are heavy laden, and I will give you rest. Take my yoke upon you and learn from me, for I am gentle and lowly in heart, and you will find rest for your souls. For my yoke is easy and my burden is light. — Matthew 11:28-30

May God richly bless you as you continue on your journey, both personally and in fellowship with your brothers and sisters in Christ. May he ever be with you helping you through every struggle against the weaknesses of the flesh. And may you always remember that you have a faithful and compassionate High Priest who is always available to help you and pour fresh grace upon you until you reach the summit.

Hebrews 4:14-16

Seeing then that we have a great High Priest who has passed through the heavens, Jesus the Son of God, let us hold fast our confession. For we do not have a High Priest who cannot sympathise with our weaknesses, but was in all points tempted as we are, yet without sin. Let us therefore come boldly to the throne of grace, that we may obtain mercy and find grace to help in time of need.

> *Real change comes when you get out of the way, cease from your striving and preoccupations with your imperfections and simply gaze on the wonder and marvel of you and Jesus seated together on the heavenly throne of God.*

Always remember you will never be transformed into the image of Christ by looking at yourself. Don't allow anything or anyone to distract your eyes from gazing at Jesus. Don't let the spirit of legalism take over. You are already the righteousness and the holiness of Christ in him. You cannot change by your own efforts. Real change comes when you get out of the way, cease from your striving and preoccupations with your imperfections and simply gaze on the wonder and marvel of you and Jesus seated together on the heavenly throne of God. When you get out of the way, you release the Holy Spirit to make the righteousness and holiness of Jesus effective in your life. It the Holy Spirit who brings you freedom, the Holy Spirit who changes your heart and the Holy Spirit who transforms you into the image of Christ.

2 Corinthians 3:18

But we all, with unveiled face, beholding as in a mirror the glory of the Lord, are being transformed into the same image from glory to glory, just as by the Spirit of the Lord.

LIVING FREE! Transformation Track

TRANSFORMATION TRACK

Be transformed by the renewing of the mind   *Romans 12:2*

Each week you will work through the following material section by section in small groups. A facilitator will be assigned to your group to help you introduce the process of transformation God wants to bring in your life.

The 'transformation track' will lead you through three areas of change through a 10-week programme. This will then equip you to continue the process of change as you go on in your life of discipleship in Christ.

LIVING FREE! TRANSFORMATION TRACK

WEEK 1

WHY CHANGE?

Most people find the thought of change off-putting and even threatening. We usually find our security in the things that are familiar even if they are not ideal. But when the Holy Spirit reveals to you the glory of Christ he inspires within you a deep desire to become like him. By keeping your eyes on Jesus, you will be able to overcome the resistance of the flesh and to surrender to the Holy Spirit's transforming power – you will be changed from glory to glory!

Change is essential if we want to grow. We cannot expect to enjoy the benefits and blessings of spiritual growth unless we know the dynamics of change and how to apply them to our life. And, most important of all, we must be willing to change and to move out of our comfort zone.

The rewards of change

There is nothing more foolish than to want something different while continuing to do the same things. If you want something you've never had, you have to do something you've never done.

Before you commit to any process of change you need to have 4 things clear in your mind. You need to know:

- What it is you want to change
- What that change will look like
- How that change will take place
- Why you want to change.

Beginning with that last point first, can you see how important it is to know why you want to change? Unless you know that, change will not come about, or at least not permanently.

Think for a moment and ask yourself.

- What changes do you want to come into your life?
- Why do you want those changes?
- What will be the benefits of those changes?
- What will be the consequences of not changing?
- Some people say that the only thing worse than change is the consequence of not changing. Do you agree?

Remember, in all this talk about transformation, the Holy Spirit is the real agent of change in our lives. Without him we cannot do it.

2 Corinthians 3:18 — *But we all, with unveiled face, beholding as in a mirror the glory of the Lord, are being transformed into the same image from glory to glory, just as by the Spirit of the Lord.*

Some of the reasons for bringing the changes God wants in your life are:

- Peace
- Blessing
- Joy
- Fruitfulness
- Better relationships
- Healthier life
- More fulfilment
- Prosperity
- Purpose
- Knowing God
- Bringing God glory.

Group Exercise

What changes do you want to come into your life?

WEEK 1   WHY CHANGE?

Why do you want those changes?

What will be the benefits of those changes?

What will be the consequences of not changing?

Homework

Read through the *LIVING FREE! Daily Devotional* and keep the journal every day for the next 7 days. Be ready to share this in your group next week.

LIVING FREE! TRANSFORMATION TRACK

WEEK 2

THE DYNAMICS OF CHANGE

Change is not a complicated process. It is happening to us all the time. Every day we are establishing habits – either by making new ones or by confirming existing ones. A habit is something that we have learned to do and practiced enough times to be able to do it without thinking about it.

A number of years ago, when the car seatbelt regulations came into force, we all had to think hard to remember to fasten our seatbelts. Now we do it without thinking. It has become a habit. When you get a new job, it all seems very strange to you. You have to think about everything you do – beginning with the new bus route you have to take to work each day, you have to remember that things are different now. But gradually you get used to it and your new job becomes second nature to you.

This shows us the dynamics of change. First, the new things are strange and we feel awkward, even unnatural as we do them. But gradually we get used to the new thing, and finally we cannot remember what it was like to be without it. For example, some people who accidentally leave their mobile phones at home wonder how they will get through the day without one! They have become used to being able to make and receive telephone calls anywhere at any time.

The basic principles of change

From all this we can grasp certain principles of change. Change implies stopping doing something that we are familiar with and replacing it with something else that is unfamiliar. But, when we keep doing this on a daily basis it becomes a new habit. We have replaced one habit by developing a new one in its place. Look at the following summary:

1. Change implies stopping doing something
2. Starting to do something different
3. Continuing in the new thing until it the new habit replaces the old habit.

The 'three week' rule

Psychologists tell us that it takes three weeks of doing something every day in order for it to become a habit, or a new pattern of behaviour. And it takes a further three weeks to confirm that habit so that it can become part of your lifestyle. Of course you must persist in the new way – otherwise you will break your new habit and revert to your old ways again.

This shows us that the first three weeks are crucial in the introduction of change in your life. This Transformation Track takes that fact into account. That's why we have chosen to introduce change in three major areas of your life:

First – *we seek to help you develop an enjoyable daily devotional life, which will help you keep your eyes on Jesus.*

Next – *we help you discover the attitudes and beliefs that are at the root of the behaviour you want to change in your life. Changing these attitudes is the key to long-term change.*

Finally – *we help you experience real, lasting change in one area of your life and give you an example of how you can continue to grow and keep up the process of change as a disciple of Jesus Christ.*

The cell group ministry

Remember, you are not alone; you are called to be part of the family of God. Learn to develop trusting relationships with your brothers and sisters in Christ. Your Group Facilitator is there to help you. He or she is not in the role of a police officer to check up on you, but a fellow soldier to help fight your battles with you.

That is why we have cell groups in the church. The cell is where you can find help and encouragement and where you can begin to be a lessing to other people.

WEEK 2　　THE DYNAMICS OF CHANGE

Group Exercise

Feed back on the daily devotions from last week.
Have you begun to enjoy your daily time with the Lord?

What did God say to you in your devotions last week?

Discuss your progress in your daily devotions.
What difficulties did you encounter?

What obstacles do you find that make it difficult for you to develop a daily discipline in your devotional life?

How can you deal with these obstacles?

Being part of a cell.
Are you part of a cell? Do you regularly attend and participate fully in the ministry of the cell? If not ask your Group Facilitator to advise you.

HOMEWORK

Do your devotions this week every day, applying the insights gained from the group discussion. Keep the journal, and be ready to share something God is doing in your life in the next group session.

LIVING FREE! TRANSFORMATION TRACK

WEEK 3

SHARING YOUR TESTIMONY

The teaching session this week deals with the fact that you are called to witness to Jesus Christ. The facilitator will help you draw up your list of 10 and help you choose people for your Evangelism of 3 list. You will also begin to write down your testimony and learn to share it with someone this week.

GROUP EXERCISE

The list of 10
Make a list of 10 people who don't yet know the Lord Jesus. These must be people who you know and can see fairly easily and regularly so that you can deepen your friendship with them and introduce them to Christ.

1	6
2	7
3	8
4	9
5	10

Your Evangelism of 3

Now, you are ready to choose people to be on your Evangelism of 3 list. Pray and ask the Holy Spirit to show you 3 names from your list of 10 who you see regularly and to whom you can witness about Christ and invite to your cell or to some other Christian activity where there will be testimony made for Jesus.

1	
2	
3	

Writing out your testimony

You learnt about how to prepare your testimony in this week's teaching session. Work from the section *How to give your testimony* beginning on page 40 and begin to write down your testimony:

Before I came to Christ my life was...

Since I came to Christ I...

When I look forward to the future I know...

WEEK 3   SHARING YOUR TESTIMONY

Sharing your testimony
Be prepared to share your testimony when you have finished writing it. You can do this in the week with your Christian friends, and also with a friend who doesn't know Christ yet. Be prepared to share it with your group in next week's group discussion.

Your devotional life
This is now the second full week of developing your devotional life. How have you done this past week? What have you learned? What help do you still need? What do you want to share with the group?

Homework

Throughout this week, continue to work on your list of 10 and your Evangelism of 3 list. Start praying every day for these people. Share this list with your fellow cell members.

Continue to develop your testimony and practice sharing it with people during the week and be ready to share in your group next week what happened when you told someone your testimony.

LIVING FREE! TRANSFORMATION TRACK

WEEK 4

RENEWING YOUR MIND

This week's teaching shows that real change comes through the renewing of the mind. The verse that keeps coming up is,

And do not be conformed to this world, but be transformed by the renewing of your mind, that you may prove what is that good and acceptable and perfect will of God.   Romans 12:2

Renewing your mind means changing old, negative thoughts, attitudes and beliefs that are the root of the sinful patterns of living, and exchanging this 'stinking thinking' for new attitudes and beliefs. That way you can go on and bring the changes God wants in your life, from the inside out. Remember all this flows from who you are in Christ. The more you understand how much he loves you the more you will live according to the grace of God revealed to you in Christ. You will stop striving to be different and let the Holy Spirit change you from within.

Discovering your 'stinking thinking'

How do you identify the negative thought patterns at the root of the behaviour you now want to change in your life? First of all, you can do this by looking at the things you are dissatisfied with in your life. What is it that you want to change? In what ways do you want to be different?

Seeing yourself as God sees you

Change is about becoming in your practical life who you are in Christ. You begin by practicing to see yourself in Christ. Always think of yourself as the righteousness of God in Christ. See yourself as who you are and not who you were before you came to Christ.

Then begin to replicate the person you are in Christ in your daily life. We are going to focus on one major area of change that needs to take place in you so that this area of life will more fully reflect who you are in him.

Some people find it helpful at this point to write a letter to Jesus beginning with 'Dear Jesus, thank you for what you have done for me...' Then you write a description of who you are in Christ.

Finally list some areas of your life in which you want to become more like Christ.

If you do this honestly, you will begin to highlight problem areas of your life. But remember, you can only deal with these through the revelation of who you are in Christ and by the power of his Spirit working in you.

WEEK 4   RENEWING YOUR MIND

Dear Jesus, thank you for what you have done for me...

Please help me to change...

The next step is to look for any patterns that emerge from the list of things you want to change. These patterns will lead you to the underlying beliefs that are governing your life. These will be the false beliefs you have held concerning where to get your needs met.

Write down what you have discovered.

Review No 1

Congratulations! You are now one third of your way through this course. It is time for a review.

1. You have been learning how to develop a delightful devotional life. You have been establishing a daily habit of seeking God in prayer, Bible reading and listening to God.

2. You have begun to see who you are in Christ and learnt to think of yourself in the light of the new person God has made you.

3. You have also been learning how change comes about in your life. By the Spirit's power, you change old ways of thinking and behaving and exchange them for new ways of thinking and behaving.

4. You have learned that to change a habit you must cease to do the old thing (put off the old) and practice doing the new thing every day (put on the new). When you do this every day for three weeks, you begin to form a new habit or pattern of behaviour.

5. You have also learned that the real change begins when you deal with the thoughts, attitudes and intentions that are at the root of the problem.

Write down how you think you have progressed in these areas and share this with your Group Facilitator.

WEEK 5

GOD MEETS ALL YOUR NEEDS

The teaching on page 52 highlights the three major personal needs we have as human beings: security, significance and self-worth.

What do you believe will meet your needs?

Ask yourself honestly where do you most naturally look to have these needs met. This will show you the idolatrous thought patterns and beliefs that you need to change in order to pursue God with all of your heart.

The following questionnaire will help you examine your heart honestly. Do this questionnaire and begin to discuss the results in your group session.

SECURITY

In your practical experience, where do you derive your basic sense of security in life?

- Job
- Family
- Friends
- Other relationships
- What else?

How do you react when any of these things are under threat?

SIGNIFICANCE

Significance has to do with impact. We need to feel that our being on planet earth matters, that we make a difference and that we have purpose.
Where do you find yourself most often deriving your sense of impact?

- Job
- Family
- Friends
- Other relationships
- What else?

How do you react when any of these things are under threat?

WEEK 5   GOD MEETS ALL YOUR NEEDS

SELF-WORTH

We need to feel that we are people of worth and value, that we are held in esteem in somebody's eyes.

What is the state of your self-esteem?

- High
- Medium
- Low

What do you attribute this to?

Who or what do you look to in order to feel good about yourself?

- Job
- Family
- Friends
- Other relationships
- What else?

How do you react when any of these things are under threat?

Now, spend some time thanking God that you are the righteousness of God in Christ. That is who you really are. See yourself as being totally complete in Christ. That way your actions will begin to conform more and more with your true identity in Christ.

LIVING FREE! TRANSFORMATION TRACK

WEEK 6

DISCOVERING YOUR IDOLATROUS BELIEFS

The teaching on pages 52–54 showed that often we learn idolatrous beliefs concerning how to get our needs met from our early childhood experiences.

Repeated childhood experiences, both positive and negative, can lead to learned beliefs concerning what to do or to avoid doing in order to engender feelings of security, significance or self-worth.

For example, if you were always praised when you did well at school and were shamed by your parents when the school gave you bad reports you could easily learn to believe that 'in order to feel good about myself I must not fail, but always match the standards and expectations of others'.

This has the makings of an idolatrous belief that states, 'In order to be a person of value and worth I must be a person of achievement.' This means your self-esteem is linked to other people's opinions and expectations of you and indeed to your own expectations of yourself.

This is idolatrous bondage. It is idolatrous because you are trusting in something or someone else other than God for your fundamental sense of worth or well-being. It is bondage because as long as your acceptance or sense of worth depends upon you fulfilling certain conditions laid down either by yourself or by others, you are locked into having to fulfil those conditions. If you don't you will not have your need for acceptance or self-worth met.

But the situation is actually worse than that. Because only God can meet your fundamental needs for self-worth, security and significance, pursuing your idolatrous goals will never bring satisfaction. And until you change your beliefs about where or how you can get your needs met the pattern of your life will always be:

pursuit... attainment... *dissatisfaction*... pursuit... attainment... *dissatisfaction*... pursuit... attainment... *dissatisfaction*...

Do you recognise this pattern in your life? What areas of your life do you find dissatisfying? Can you discern the underlying false beliefs that you are holding onto concerning where your needs can be met? How will you correct the tendency to look away from Christ to other things to meet your needs? When you begin to focus daily on Christ you will discover a new pattern emerging:

pursuit... attainment... *satisfaction*... pursuit... attainment... *satisfaction*... pursuit... attainment... *satisfaction*...

Group Exercise

Discerning childhood patterns of belief

The exercise below can sometimes show you what you think will bring you fullness or satisfaction. This can sometimes help explain to you why you do what you do and how you try to avoid negative emotions or experience positive ones.

Think of an experience or something that happened to you as a child that 'made you feel good.' Summarise it below noting especially the circumstances and the emotions you had.

CIRCUMSTANCES:

EMOTIONS:

WEEK 6 DISCOVERING YOUR IDOLATROUS BELIEFS

Now think of an experience or something that happened to you as a child that 'made you feel bad'. Summarise it below noting especially the circumstances and the emotions you had.

CIRCUMSTANCES:

EMOTIONS:

Can you see from these experiences how you may have learned what to pursue, and what to avoid in order to get your needs met?

WRITE OUT THAT FALSE BELIEF:

My false belief is that in order to meet my need for...

I must...

GROUP MINISTRY:

1. Ask the Holy Spirit to show you experiences that have led you to go in the wrong direction to have your needs met and ask him to heal you from these negative experiences.
2. Ask him to help you abandon these false patterns of thinking and behaving.
3. Spend time with the Holy Spirit and ask him to help you discover new depths of intimacy and relationship with Christ.

LIVING FREE! TRANSFORMATION TRACK

WEEK 7

WALKING IN FREEDOM

By now you have begun to discover the deeply-rooted beliefs that you need to change in order to walk in freedom. You have discovered that the key to change is to take a step of faith and begin to act on your new belief that God (and he alone) can meet your needs.

Now it is time to begin to apply this to a specific area of life that you want to change. It is best to choose one major issue in your life that has most to do with the fundamental area of idolatrous belief you have discovered and begun to deal with in the earlier sessions. Your Group Facilitator will help you identify this.

Group Exercise

Look at the Life Issues section and begin to think about which issue you will select to work on for the rest of this course (see pages 187-188). It is important to choose an issue in which you clearly see the need to change and that you really want to deal with. Motivation is paramount at this point. Then write down your selection below.

My life issue I want to change is:

Describe what specifically you want to change:

I want to change from

WEEK 7   **WALKING IN FREEDOM**

I want to change to

173

Review No 2

Congratulations! You are now two thirds of your way through this course. It is time for another review.

1. You have been continuing to delight yourself in the Lord during your daily devotions. You have been learning how to build this discipline permanently into your life.
2. You have been learning to see how complete you are in Jesus and that you are defined by who you are in Christ, not by your weaknesses and imperfections.
3. You have also been learning how change comes about in your life. This is by changing old ways of thinking and behaving and exchanging them with the new ways of thinking and behaving in Christ.
4. You have learned that to change a habit you must cease to do the old thing (put off the old) and practice doing the new thing every day (put on the new). When you do this every day for three weeks you begin to form a new habit or pattern of behaviour.
5. You have also learned that the real change begins when you deal with the thoughts, attitudes and intentions that are at the root of the problem.
6. You have also been reminded that living for Christ involves living out your identity in Christ in your daily life.

Write down how you think you have progressed in these areas and share this with your Group Facilitator.

WEEK 8

CHOOSING TO CHANGE

Now you have selected the area of change you are going to work on over the next few weeks. The final three sessions will focus on this area of change.

GROUP EXERCISE

Write down again the life issue you are going to be dealing with.

My life issue I want to change is

Describe specifically how you are going to change.

I want to change from...

to...

In any process of change it is important to identify the steps you need to take in order to bring that change about. This means knowing both what you must do and the things that you must avoid doing in order to facilitate the change.

Begin to list the things that will help and the things that will hinder the change:

Things that will help me change:

WEEK 8   CHOOSING TO CHANGE

Things that hinder me from changing:

LIVING FREE! TRANSFORMATION TRACK

WEEK 9

PUTTING-OFF AND PUTTING-ON

Continue working through your chosen area of change according the directions found in the appropriate *Life Issues* section. Remember, real change comes from delighting yourself in the Lord and his glory. This is the right focus as it releases the dynamic of change in your heart.

Group Exercise

This week you are going to:

Make a list of all the things you have to PUT OFF (stop doing) in order to bring God's change into your life.

And then you are going to:

Make a list of all the things you have to PUT ON (start doing) in order to bring God's change into your life.

Things I have to PUT OFF in order to bring God's change into my life:

WEEK 9　　PUTTING-OFF AND PUTTING-ON

Things I have to PUT ON in order to bring God's change into my life:

LIVING FREE! Transformation Track

WEEK 10

MAKING CHANGE STICK

Continue working through your chosen area of change according the directions found in the appropriate *Life Issues* section.

What are the most important things you must concentrate on over the next few weeks in order to make sure God's changes stick in your life?

Group Exercise

Now that you have successfully completed this Life Transformation Course, it is vital that you make the right decision as to where you go from here.

By now you should understand the importance of taking up further leadership training in order for you to fulfil your ministry and your calling as a disciple of Jesus. This is an important next step for your life.

Sign up today for the next Leadership School course beginning soon!

Your Facilitator will help explain more of this to you and answer your questions.

God bless you abundantly in all your service for the Master!

Review No 3

Congratulations! You have now completed your 10-week course! It is time for your final review.

1. Over the past 10 weeks you have been bringing about change in three major areas of your life.
2. You have developed a healthy habit of seeking God in your daily devotional life.
3. You have learned how to listen to God and to obey what he says to you from his Word and through the leading of the Holy Spirit.
4. You have confronted your former negative beliefs that drew you away from God, and have replaced these with godly beliefs that encourage you to go God's way with joy.
5. You have begun to deal with a major issue in your life and have learnt how the process of change works so that you can grow daily to be more like Christ.
6. Now you can continue to walk in the path of freedom and go on to other areas of change as the Holy Spirit shows you.
7. Remember to be an active part of your cell and share these things with your cell leader who will be taking over from your Group Facilitator as your helper in your spiritual life.
8. Sign up to the Leadership School so you can continue to find and fulfil your destiny as a disciple of Jesus Christ.
9. Always remember to keep your eyes on Jesus. You will grow spiritually to the degree to which you see yourself in Christ.
10. With the help of your cell leader, you can now work on other areas of change covered in this book.

Describe the things that you will continue to work on and share this with your cell leader.

WEEK 10 MAKING CHANGE STICK

Write down your testimony of how this course has helped you change and grow as a Christian disciple.

LIFE ISSUES

Be transformed by the renewing of the mind   *Romans 12:2*

You will work from the material found in this section after week 7 in the course. You will be asked to choose one of these areas from the pages that follow. Each week your Group Facilitator will help you apply the teaching and practical assignments relevant to your chosen area of change.

Remember to do these exercises prayerfully relying on the help of the Holy Spirit who alone can bring about the change that God requires in your life.

Through the teaching in this book, you have learned that the root of our negative and harmful behaviour patterns is our sinful, idolatrous beliefs. You will have learned to identify at least one major belief you once held about how to get your needs met and how to replace that negative belief with a godly belief which points you towards the Lord, who alone can meet your needs.

Summarise here one or two of these basic beliefs you have discovered you held in your heart and how you have come to change those beliefs.

I used to believe that in order to find security or significance or self-worth I must...

But I now believe that I can only have these needs met by...

Choosing a Life Issue

For the rest of this course you will be dealing with one particular life issue. You will learn how to 'put off' the old attitudes, intentions and actions that lie at the root of the problem you want to deal with. And you will learn how to replace these with the new ways of Christ and 'put on' new attitudes, intentions and actions. That way you will know what it is to be transformed in this area of life by the renewing of your mind.

How to choose the life issue to work on

Your Group Facilitator will help guide you through the process of selecting a life issue to focus on as the next step in your spiritual growth. Here are some guidelines to help you choose:

- Choose one Life Issue covered in the following pages
- Take an area of your life where you recognise there is a pressing need to change
- Choose an issue where you can see the connection between change and the renewing of your mind
- Choose an issue where you can see the link between the behaviour you want to change and the idolatrous goals of your heart
- Choose an area where you can see yourself beginning to introduce meaningful change over the next three weeks
- Choose a key area of your life that will bring you a sense of victory and achievement and become a model for more change to come in your life.

My area of change

Write down your chosen area of change:

Begin to picture what that change will look like in reality. See yourself becoming and being that new person you desire to be. It will match who you really are, the new you in Christ. Keep that picture in your mind and in your heart. Meditate on it every day until it is firmly embedded in your spirit.

Now describe what that change will look like:

FROM WHAT? (what you have to put off)

TO WHAT? (what you have to put on)

For the rest of this course you will be focussing on how to deal with this particular problem. Now go to the relevant material that deals with your problem.

LIFE ISSUES 1
....
EMOTIONAL PROBLEMS

Emotional problems are often the result of our deep needs not being met[6] particularly in the areas of security, significance and self-worth.

- Problems of *fear and anxiety* are caused by you being *uncertain* whether your fundamental needs will be met.
- *Bitterness and anger* are the result of you being *blocked* from having your goals met.
- *Depression or feelings of hopelessness* come from you judging that your needs are *unlikely* ever to be met.

Much of the time, when negative experiences trigger negative emotional responses in us, we are able to deal with them quickly and move on.

But sometimes we are aware that we have negative emotions almost all the time and we cannot always identify why. Our emotions seem to be so easily provoked and our reactions appear (either to ourselves or to others) to be out of all proportion to the stimulus we are responding to. Remember the stimulus is never the *cause* of our emotions but simply an event that *triggers* a response in us.

---
[6] But there are some problems that may need medical help. Please see Appendix 2 on pages 293-294, where serious emotional problems that require medical care as well as biblical counselling are described.

Accepting responsibility

It is important for you to accept the responsibility for your own emotions. The cause of your emotions is always in you and not in any situation outside yourself. Accepting responsibility for your emotions is not so that you become overloaded with a burden of guilt and blame. It actually brings dignity, release and hope, because it shows you that you are not a helpless victim of your emotions and shows you how you can handle these negative emotions.

Describe the negative emotions that are a problem to you.

Describe the negative effect they are having on you and other people.

Do you accept ownership and responsibility for these emotions?
Yes / No

If yes, state why:

LIFE ISSUES | EMOTIONAL PROBLEMS

If no, state why:

Now you will be ready to focus on the particular group of emotions you are dealing with.

Choose one of the following emotional groupings that best describes your problem. To help you decide, look at the emotions listed on page 89 and see which grouping they come under.

Choose one of the following:

1. Fear and anxiety
2. Bitterness and anger
3. Depression and loss of hope

Now go to the relevant material below that deals with this problem.

Fear and anxiety

These emotional problems can be crippling and can affect your wellbeing. They both have the same root: an uncertain goal.

The roots of fear and anxiety

At the root of all negative emotion is unmet need. But the matter is complicated by our seeking to get our needs met through idolatrous means, that is, we are seeking to find fulfilment in things other than God.

When we are not sure whether our need is going to be met the emotional response that is triggered is fear or anxiety. We are fearful and worry what tomorrow will bring. Will our needs be met?

That's why Jesus said,

Therefore do not worry about tomorrow, for tomorrow will worry about its own things. Sufficient for the day is its own trouble. — Matthew 6:34

That is why the antidote to fear and anxiety is trust – trusting God to meet our needs as we deal with life's issues one day at a time. But this also implies that we are going his way and putting him first in our lives. To trust God means to obey him because we know that going God's way not only honours him but also shows we trust him to meet all our needs.

Whether these needs are emotional, physical, spiritual or financial, we know that as we go God's way we can have confidence that he will provide the fulfilment of every need we have.

Philippians 4:19 *And my God shall supply all your need according to his riches in glory by Christ Jesus.*

But notice the conditions found in *Philippians chapter 4* that we must fulfil in order for this promise to be fulfilled in our life:

1. Stand fast in the Lord – do not let your attention or focus wander from the Lord, but rather pursue him with all your heart *(v1)*
2. Walk in unity and peace with your brothers and sisters *(v2)*
3. Rejoice in the Lord always – knowing that he alone can meet your needs *(v4)*
4. Walk in gentleness – this means dealing with negativity and judgementalism and dealing gently and mercifully with others *(v5)*
5. Don't worry about anything – worry is a sin, as is fear, therefore, put off every attitude that reflects these things *(v6)*
6. Learn to pray about everything – this brings you into the reality of divine, supernatural capacity of God *(v6)*
7. Cultivate a mentality and lifestyle of thanksgiving *(v6)*
8. Let God's peace be the 'umpire' or ruler of your heart keeping out the negative, fearful and anxious thoughts *(v7)*
9. Meditate on the positive, life-enriching things God has for you in your life *(v8)*
10. Learn how to live a godly, peace-filled lifestyle from your leaders and from mature Christians *(v9)*
11. Learn to be content with your circumstances and don't let the world's ambition or greed take hold of you *(vs10-12)*
12. Be confident of God's power in you *(v13)*
13. Develop a lifestyle of loving generosity especially towards God's work and to those in need *(vs14-18)*
14. Trust God to meet your every need *(v19)*
15. Learn to focus on God's glory rather than on yourself or your problems *(v20)*.

What do you have to stop doing in order to fulfil these principles in your life?

What do you have continue to do or start doing?

Develop a practical plan of action to bring these changes about and follow your plan every day for the next three weeks.

After 3 weeks, review your progress and describe the changes that you have experienced.

Bitterness and anger

These emotional problems can be crippling and can affect your wellbeing. They both have the same root: a blocked goal.

The roots of bitterness and anger

At the root of all negative emotion is unmet need. But the matter is complicated by our seeking to get our needs met through idolatrous means. That is, we are seeking to find fulfilment in things other than God.

When we are prevented from obtaining something that we believe will meet our needs anger is the emotional response that is triggered.

See *Mark 3:5, Psalm 7:11, Ephesians 4:26-32, Proverbs 26:21-28*.

Two forms of anger

The emotion of anger, characteristically, works in two ways. First, there is the *explosive* expression of anger in which the emotion is directed outwards, usually against the person or situation judged to be causing the anger. And second, anger can be *implosive* and turned inwards, taking hold in the heart in the form of bitterness, resentment or malice.

Usually these two forms of anger are found together in the same person although some may tend towards the one method or the other in order to deal with this emotion in their lives. Angry people tend to hold malice in their heart and it deeply affects their attitudes, speech and behaviour towards the person, situation, organisation or institution that is judged to have caused the hurt or offence.

Even those who never raise their voice, lose their temper or express their anger physically can reveal their anger through the language of criticism, judgementalism, coldness or withdrawal.

Signs of implosive anger

Imagine a seething pot of stew on the gas burner. It may look calm and cool on the outside, but if you take the lid off you discover a boiling mass inside. Signs of anger turned inward are:

- Clamming up
- Refusing to communicate

LIFE ISSUES | EMOTIONAL PROBLEMS

- Shutting someone out or cutting them off
- Pretending nothing is wrong
- Hiding behind spiritual language
- Sugary sweet responses
- Ignoring someone
- Harbouring hurt feelings
- Vengeance, getting even
- Playing the victim, offended party or the martyr
- Brooding over the offence
- Self-pity
- Self-righteousness
- Keeping a record of sins
- Self-vindication
- Blame shifting
- Projecting your thoughts, actions or faults onto someone else
- Bearing a grudge
- Spreading gossip and slander
- Blocking a person's blessing
- Working against someone
- Bearing malice
- Entertaining hateful thoughts and hard attitudes against the person
- Unforgiving and judgmental spirit
- Faultfinding
- Sarcasm
- Despising looks
- Rolling the eyes
- Put-downs
- Hostility.

Signs of explosive anger

Imagine an exploding bomb! Anger is just like that. It can explode, tearing things apart and bringing destruction:

- Blowing up
- Shouting
- Rage
- Mocking
- Angry facial expressions
- Angry physical gestures
- Losing your temper
- Angry, destructive words
- Swearing and cursing
- Abusive words
- Accusations

- Exaggerations
- Blaming
- Sarcasm
- Put-downs
- Arguing
- Hateful talk
- Hurtful talk
- Fighting
- Physical violence
- Verbal violence
- Throwing things
- Retaliation
- Acts of revenge.

The Bible says,

Ephesians 4:26-32

"Be angry, and do not sin": do not let the sun go down on your wrath, nor give place to the devil. Let him who stole steal no longer, but rather let him labour, working with his hands what is good, that he may have something to give him who has need. Let no corrupt word proceed out of your mouth, but what is good for necessary edification, that it may impart grace to the hearers. And do not grieve the Holy Spirit of God, by whom you were sealed for the day of redemption. Let all bitterness, wrath, anger, clamour, and evil speaking be put away from you, with all malice. And be kind to one another, tenderhearted, forgiving one another, just as God in Christ forgave you.

These verses show you how to deal with anger both of the explosive and the implosive kind:

1. Accept responsibility for your anger. Anger is never the fault of others, but has to do with how you perceive others
2. Deal with your anger in the right way. Don't let it take the negative path that brings hurt and destruction
3. Deal with your anger immediately and don't let it fester
4. Recognise the necessity for forgiveness and the resolving of disagreements
5. Control your anger and direct it towards the proper goal
6. Focus compassionately on the needs of others, understanding why they do what they do
7. Ask yourself what need the other person is trying to meet and be committed to helping that person meet their need in Christ
8. Ask yourself what need of yours is behind your emotion of anger
9. Seek God to meet this need
10. Forgive unreservedly and unconditionally
11. Seek reconciliation
12. Reject all malice in your heart
13. Seek the well-being of the other person
14. Pray for the other person.

LIFE ISSUES | EMOTIONAL PROBLEMS

What do you have to stop doing in order to fulfil these principles in your life?

What do you have continue to do or start doing?

Develop a practical plan of action to bring these changes about and follow your plan every day for the next three weeks.

Then, review your progress and describe the changes that you have experienced.

Depression and loss of hope

These emotional problems can be crippling and can affect your wellbeing.

They both have the same root: an unrealisable goal.

The roots of depression and loss of hope

At the root of all negative emotion is unmet need. But the matter is complicated by our seeking to get our needs met through idolatrous means, that is, we are seeking to find fulfilment in things other than God.

When we begin to believe that our need is never going to be met the emotional response that is triggered is depression or feelings of hopelessness. The future looks terribly bleak and we can spiral down into a deep depression. But when we learn to trust God to meet our fundamental needs we can take life's disappointments knowing that our hope is in him.

God is always speaking hope into his people no matter how dire the circumstances. Meditate on the following Bible verses and write down how they relate to you and your personal circumstances:

Jeremiah 29:11

For I know the thoughts that I think toward you, says the LORD, thoughts of peace and not of evil, to give you a future and a hope.

Psalm 31:24

Be of good courage, and he shall strengthen your heart, all you who hope in the LORD.

Psalm 42:5

Why are you cast down, O my soul? And why are you disquieted within me? Hope in God, for I shall yet praise him for the help of his countenance.

LIFE ISSUES | **EMOTIONAL PROBLEMS**

For you are my hope, O Lord GOD; you are my trust from my youth. By you I have been upheld from birth; you are he who took me out of my mother's womb. My praise shall be continually of you. I have become as a wonder to many, but you are my strong refuge. Let my mouth be filled with your praise and with your glory all the day.

Psalm 71:5-8

But I will hope continually and will praise you yet more and more.

Psalm 71:14

Therefore, having been justified by faith, we have peace with God through our Lord Jesus Christ, through whom also we have access by faith into this grace in which we stand, and rejoice in hope of the glory of God. And not only that, but we also glory in tribulations, knowing that tribulation produces perseverance; and perseverance, character; and character, hope. Now hope does not disappoint, because the love of God has been poured out in our hearts by the Holy Spirit who was given to us.

Romans 5:1-5

For we were saved in this hope, but hope that is seen is not hope; for why does one still hope for what he sees? But if we hope for what we do not see, we eagerly wait for it with perseverance.

Romans 8:24-25

Now may the God of hope fill you with all joy and peace in believing, that you may abound in hope by the power of the Holy Spirit.

Romans 15:13

LIVING FREE! LIFE ISSUES

Titus 2:11-14

For the grace of God that brings salvation has appeared to all men, teaching us that, denying ungodliness and worldly lusts, we should live soberly, righteously, and godly in the present age, looking for the blessed hope and glorious appearing of our great God and Saviour Jesus Christ.

How to deal with sadness, depression and loss of hope

1. Identify and replace the messages of hopelessness and negativity you are repeating to yourself:

   - Hopelessness – *"What's the use of trying – it never works"*
   - Alienation – *"I am all alone – no-one really cares"*
   - Rejection – *"I'm not wanted"*
   - Powerlessness – *"There's nothing I can do"*
   - Worthlessness – *"I'm useless."*

These are the kind of messages you must learn to change. Start working on this now by listing some of the specific messages you have playing to yourself over and over again and alongside them the new messages you are going to repeat to yourself which reflect the truth about you in Christ:

I must replace the following negative false messages:

With these messages of truth and hope:

2. Identify the need at the root of your feelings of despair

What need of yours is being unmet to the point that you are beginning to wonder if it will ever be met?

You can find the answer to this question by looking at the things that have brought you disappointment in life and then tracing these back to the needs you were hoping these things might meet in you.

So for example, if you are feeling depressed because you haven't found your life partner, understand that your feelings of sadness or depression are not caused by these circumstances. Rather they come from the mistaken belief that you need to be married and to have a family in order to be happy.

The mistaken belief here is, 'In order to be a person of worth and to be fulfilled I must be married and have children.' But the truth is that marriage or family life cannot meet these needs. Only God can fulfil your deepest needs for companionship and relationship.

He gives you meaning and purpose in life and your fundamental need for these things cannot be met in marriage, children, career, material possessions or wealth.

List your disappointments:

I am disappointed in life because…

Now identify the real need at the root of these disappointments revealing the false belief that is at the root of your struggle with the negative emotions related to loss of hope in these areas:

I recognise that I have been looking for my need of…

...to be met by the following people, conditions and circumstances of life...

3. Recognise that these needs can only be met by God and begin to redirect the passions of your heart towards the Lord and pursue him to fulfil these needs in you directly.

Record the practical changes this will mean for your life:

Instead of looking for my need of...

...to be met by...

...I will now pursue the Lord for the satisfaction and fulfilment he alone can bring by seeking him in the following ways:

Practically, this means...
(List the practical changes this will mean for you by showing what you would have done when faced with certain situations and how you will now handle those same circumstances).

When faced with _____

Before I would:					But now I will:

i.

ii.

iii.

iv.

v.

4. Commit your life into his hands on a daily basis trusting him to direct your life into his will and fulfilment in all these areas.

My son, do not forget my law, but let your heart keep my commands; for length of days and long life and peace they will add to you. Let not mercy and truth forsake you; bind them around your neck, write them on the tablet of your heart, and so find favour and high esteem in the sight of God and man. Trust in the LORD with all your heart, and lean not on your own understanding; in all your ways acknowledge him, and he shall direct your paths.   Proverbs 3:1-6

After 3 weeks of practicing these principles, what differences can you see in your life?

LIVING FREE! LIFE ISSUES

LIFE ISSUES 2

SEXUAL PROBLEMS

Learning to Handle your Sexuality

Sexuality is an important part of our humanity as male and female. It is God's precious gift for intimacy between married couples and for the procreation of children. Unfortunately, sexual wholeness is often marred by society's turning away from the principles of God's word. Sex is cheapened when it is removed from the context of the loving relationship between a man and a woman in marriage.

The following outline gives a biblical framework for understanding sex and its place in our lives.

God created sex as a good gift for humankind

Genesis 1:27-28

- God created humanity – male and female
- He designed the human body including male and female sexual organs
- Your sexuality is God's gift
- It is blessed by God.

Sex is given solely for within marriage

Genesis 2:24-25

- Male and female (one husband or wife – not bigamy or polygamy)
- In marriage relationship
- Premarital sex is outside God's will (fornication)
- Extramarital sex is outside God's will (adultery)
- Same gender sex is outside God's will (homosexuality).

The purpose of sex

Genesis 1:28
Song of Solomon 2:4-7
1 Corinthians 7:3-4

- Procreation – for offspring
- Intimacy and unity in marriage
- Sexual joy and happiness in marriage
- Fruitfulness and multiplication
- Sex is given for the loving relationship between husband and wife
- In sex, as in everything, the emphasis of love is on giving
- This means your sexuality does not belong to you, but to your marriage partner.

Sexual sin

1 Corinthians 6:16-20

- Acknowledge it, if it is present
- Forsake it, do not justify it
- Purity is God's plan
- Sex is a blood covenant seal on the marriage relationship
- Immorality binds the person to the one they have had sex with – physically, emotionally and spiritually
- Casual, non-covenantal sex brings harm, hurt and misery
- Danger of sexually transmitted diseases, demons, bondages and curses.

How to overcome sexual sin

Matthew 5:27-30
1 Thessalonians 4:3

- Determine to live a life of sexual integrity
- Control your thoughts
- Avoid the things that lead you into temptation
- Be accountable to your leader and fellow cell members
- Pray and depend on the Holy Spirit
- Focus your energy on positive things.

Surveys have shown that 10% of men have no problem with sexual sin in any form. 10% are in bondage or addicted to sexual sin. And 80% are somewhere in between. That means the majority of men (even Christian men) have a problem in this area.

For the majority of women sexual temptation tends not to happen through visual stimulation but through the need for intimacy and security. Women are tempted to give sex to gain love, while men are tempted to give love to gain sex.

The following are often at the root of sexual temptation:

- Sexual images
- Sensuality
- Pornography
- Seduction
- Loneliness
- Search for intimacy
- Need for acceptance
- Security
- Comfort
- Need for family.

What is sexual purity?

Sexual purity means enjoying God's gift of sex with the boundaries of his plan and purpose.

This is a good definition because it focuses on the positive aspects. Sex is a gift of God to be shared between loving partners in the covenant of marriage. Sexual sin destroys marriages and hurts people, including those who engage in it.

To overcome sexual sin you must learn to guard your:

- Eyes
- Thoughts
- Actions
- Heart

Ask yourself what need are you trying to fill when you fall into sexual sin. The surface need is the physical need, but lack of control in the physical area is due to a deeper need.

The need I am trying to fill when I fall into sexual sin is...

How to be free from sexual sin

- *Make a decision*

You want to be free because you see what you have become. You realise the things that you are doing are harmful and damaging. Sexual sin is bondage. It wastes your time and saps your spiritual vitality. You are plagued with a sense of guilt and failure. You know you are grieving the Lord. There is only one solution and that is to turn from sexual sin and determine to live a pure life.

- *Receive deliverance*

Often demons attach themselves to sexual sin and bring a supernatural dimension to the bondage.

- *Deal with the need at the root of the sexual sin*

When you see what need you are trying to fill when you pursue sexual sin you realise that you will never get your need met this way. So how will you now handle that need?

Instead of pursuing sexual sin I will now learn to meet my need by...

- *Discipline yourself – learn new habits*

Begin by turning your eyes away from any sexual image (Job 31:1). Then bring your thoughts under control and make every thought captive. Take your sexual thoughts prisoner.

For women the discipline in the area of thoughts and emotions is particularly important. Learn to replace old habits of negative and destructive thoughts, which damage your self-image. Avoid TV soaps, sloppy romantic novels and magazines, which promote sexual fantasy.

Sexual desire can begin to take you over when you feed yourself a diet of sexual images, thoughts, words or sexually stimulating actions. This ultimately becomes unmanageable and can bring a sense of an uncontrollable urge for sexual release. But when you abstain from these sexually stimulating thoughts and actions your sexual urge can become manageable. Six weeks of controlling what you see with your eyes and taking your thoughts captive will bring new habits of sexual purity.

- *Discipleship*

Make yourself accountable to your primary leader, your cell leader and your cell members – groups of three are good. This form of accountability is more than simply checking up on each other, it is also for prayer, encouragement and for helping one another fight the battle for purity.

- *Dignity*

Being a man and being a woman is not defined by sexual activity. Bringing your desires under control is the true measure of masculinity and femininity. Learn to respect your dignity and that of members of the other sex. Learn to treasure your present or future husband or wife and keep yourself pure for them.

- *Develop intimacy with God*

Sex is often a search for intimacy. As you grow in your intimacy with God, you will develop a capacity to be intimate with your wife or husband and sex will be a generous not a selfish act. You will be giving intimacy and sharing love with another person and not just looking to have your own needs met.

Remember, you will never find freedom by focussing on yourself. It sounds like a strange thing to say, but the more you try to be free, the worse it gets. Of course, discipline is necessary. We must actively turn away from sin and immorality, but the answer is never to focus on your sin. If you do that, you are facing the wrong way – towards what you *were*. God wants you to focus on what you *are* – the righteousness of God in Christ. As you turn your focus on Christ, you leave all these things behind. Don't just try to stop committing sin,

LIVING FREE! LIFE ISSUES

pursue righteousness, direct your life towards Christ and his pure love for you. Paul's advice to Timothy shows us the key to sexual freedom:

2 Timothy 2:21-22

Flee also youthful lusts; but pursue righteousness, faith, love, peace with those who call on the Lord out of a pure heart.

Freedom from Homosexual Sin

What God Says About Same Sex Relationships

This is a controversial topic! Christian teaching on this subject goes against the trend visible in many societies. Many people around the world are actively working to make same sex relationships acceptable in the eyes of their society. They see the Bible as an obstacle to their goals. Activists for homosexual rights blame the negative approach of Christians to homosexuality for the prejudice, bigotry and discrimination shown towards homosexual people. And, in some instances, they are right.

We must remind ourselves that our gospel is about the good news of God's love. We cannot minister the gospel to the world while we carry hypocritical, negative and judgemental attitudes towards those in the world, or any particular group of people in the world. Homosexuality is not the unforgivable sin. There is grace and forgiveness available in Christ for everyone. The blood of Jesus has the power to cleanse from *all* sin. Jesus came to lift us all out of our sin and moral failure, so that we might find forgiveness and new life in him.

The problem occurs when we rise up in moral indignation against what we perceive to be the worst kinds of sin. This self-protective measure serves to puff ourselves up in our sense of self-righteousness. We condemn certain sins and condone others. We reject some things and tolerate others. We treat people according to the nature of their sin – reserving the harshest words and attitudes for the things we personally detest the most. This goes against the character of God - who is just not like that. It also goes against the fundamental principles of the love and grace we preach in the gospel.

Let us attempt to put all prejudices aside and see what God says in his word. The Bible presents many positive pictures of same sex relationships as the following examples show.

David and Jonathan
1 Samuel 18:1-4
1 Samuel 20:41-42
2 Samuel 1:26

Naomi and Ruth
Ruth 1:16

These same sex relationships were:

- Close
- Loving
- Family-like (Mother-daughter or brother-brother)
- Covenantal
- In the purpose of God – not selfish or inward-looking.

The Bible also shows that marriage is uniquely between a man and a woman. The covenant of marriage is first described in Genesis 2:24. This verse is repeated four times in the Bible and at no time is there any indication that it was extended to include same sex relationships.

Marriage

- Is a covenant of companionship
- Meets a man and a woman's need for complete companionship
- Includes sexual intimacy
- Is given for fruitfulness (multiplication)
- Is not identical to any other kind of relationship – mother and daughter, father and son, brother and sister, or special friends of the same sex.

The boundaries of same sex relationships

There is no evidence that sex was a part of any close, same sex friendships described the Bible. John, the disciple whom Jesus loved, reclined on Jesus' chest at the last supper. That was physical closeness, friendship, even an expression of intimacy, but it was not sexual. The centurion had a servant who was sick, and it is recorded that there was a relationship of love between them. But there is never mention of sex being a part of that relationship.

The problem is that today sex is so over-emphasised that people cannot accept that it is possible to be close physically and emotionally without it becoming sexual. On the other hand, some justify homosexual activity as a legitimate expression of love. However, sex outside the covenant of marriage is not within the plan of God. This includes sexual acts between members of the same sex.

Some argue that the Bible condemns only unnatural homosexual acts, which excludes people whose natural inclination is towards members of the same sex. Verses such as *Leviticus 20, Romans 1, 1 Corinthians 6* and *1 Timothy* are explained as referring to sexual perversion found in pagan religious practices or other forms of sinful exploitation of unnatural sex. But this does not explain why there is no positive affirmation of homosexual union anywhere in the Bible. There is no provision for it. We can only lovingly conclude that these things are outside the plan and purpose for God.

We must remember, God has set boundaries for our own good. He created us and knows us intimately, and he knows what will bring us joy and fulfilment. If he excludes something, he does so because it is not good. It does not bring the happiness and satisfaction it promises.

Accepting responsibility for your sexuality

It is important to acknowledge your attraction to members of the same sex and accept responsibility for your actions. Nothing can be served by living in denial or by blaming others for the way you live.

There may be many factors that contribute to making you the person you are today. Among these are the choices you have made and your responses to the circumstances or conditions you experience in life. Many things may have contributed to your attraction to members of the same sex including:

- Environmental factors
- Psychological factors
- Your upbringing and childhood experiences
- Some possible genetic or bio-chemical element.

But none of these things mean that you are free to express your homosexual inclination any way you wish. God has set clear boundaries and we must honour these.

Much publicity has recently been given to the existence of the so-called 'gay gene'. But homosexuality is a complex human experience that does not fit into any set or predetermined pattern. God has given us the dignity of freewill and created us to be morally responsible human beings. That means, no matter what the influences upon us – whether cultural, environmental, biological or genetic – these do not remove our responsibility to choose lifestyles that honour God.

Holiness is possible for the homosexual

How then can people who have homosexual inclinations honour God and deal with this issue in their lives?

1. You are not defined by your sexual orientation

Many speak of basic sexual orientation still being present in some form after many years and many attempts to change it through prayer, fasting, Bible study, counselling and deliverance. Christians are foolish to deny the existence of desires of the flesh in them, but we should never allow ourselves to be defined by our sinful desires or allow these desires to shape our identity.

2. You can resist and do not have to give into temptation

Every Christian is faced with this situation. We all have to deny ungodliness and worldly lusts.

3. You need to deal with the issues at root level

Many approaches to holiness are superficial. Sin is seen to be acts that the individual has deliberately chosen – consciously, intentionally, knowing them to be wrong.

But sin is much deeper and far more complex than that.

- Sin is not just what you do as an individual – there's a corporate dimension to it.
- Sin is not confined to conscious acts – we can sin unconsciously.
- Sin is not merely rejection of known standards – the Old Testament speaks of sins of ignorance.
- Sin does not consist only in acts of deliberate choice. Some say that if you have no power to stop yourself then you cannot be held responsible for your actions. But sin is a compelling power. It is a habitual, compulsive and driving force acting from within us. Often it feels as if we cannot help doing what we do, but we are still responsible for our actions.
- Sin is not limited to outward, observable acts. It is, ultimately, a state of heart.

This shows that we are all in the same position – all have sinned and fall short of the glory of God *(Romans 3:23)*.

All sin has its roots in how we perceive our needs and what we believe will make life work for us – which normally means we think it will give us what we want and what we believe will satisfy us.

Romans chapter 1 shows us the all-encompassing downward spiral of sin and judgment that applies to the whole of humanity, and not just one section of it, such as homosexual men and women. The whole downward spiral begins with refusing to hold onto the knowledge of God and substituting him with false ideas and concepts of God. It is about idolatry – seeking satisfaction through means and things other than God.

At the root of sin are the deep, idolatrous desires of the human heart. They are deep because they lie at the motivational centre of our lives and they are idolatrous because we seek to meet these needs in people and things other than God and his provision for our lives.

The chief motivational needs of our lives are:

- Security
- Significance
- Self-worth.

Looking to have these needs met in same sex affirmation can lead to a sexualising of your desires for same sex friendship. This is particularly so if your physical attraction to members of your own sex comes from a misplaced desire for legitimate intimacy. Sometimes homosexuality develops out of the pursuit for the love that you needed, but you never had, from your mother or your father in your early years. Homosexual feelings can then be re-enforced by childhood or adolescent relationships in which same sex affirmation was experienced. These in turn can set up patterns of sexual behaviour lasting into adulthood.

If you have homosexual desires, ask yourself what is happening beneath the surface of this attraction. Write down your thoughts:

My attraction to members of my sex has to do with my search for... (complete the sentence)

But I desire above all things to pursue God and his ways in my life, so I will now begin to trust God to meet this need by... (fill in the things that you will do differently)

One helpful psychological theory addresses the issue of a person's psychosexual development. It states that the opposite sex parent is particularly important in the early years of a child's development, helping that child build a healthy view of the opposite sex, this is necessary for the formation of healthy heterosexual relationships later on in life. In adolescence, it is said that the same sex parent is important for the discovery of your own sexual identity as a male or a female. If you never had the affirmation of your same sex parent in adolescence, then the chances are that you began to look for it elsewhere. And for some people, this forms the foundation for their same sex attraction.

If this rings true in your experience it may be necessary to deal with the issue of forgiveness first. You must forgive your parents for not giving to you what you needed to help you be affirmed in your masculinity or your femininity.

I recognise I need to forgive my mother/father for not... (complete the sentence)

Forgive that parent now (For more on forgiveness, see page 251)

4. Build godly same sex relationships
Finally, it is also good to develop same sex relationships, but this time, make sure they are built on godly principles and not just sexual attraction.

1. Same sex relationships are part of healthy living and have their place in childhood, adolescence and adulthood.
2. Be blessed by these friendships.
3. It is an important part of mental and emotional maturity to be able to develop and sustain same sex friendships.
4. Build a godly relationship of honour, respect and friendship with same sex parent or 'parent-figure'.
5. Be sure that these are serving God's purposes and that they are not selfish or self-serving.

6. Don't try to make same sex relationships fulfil the God-given role of marriage. Single people can seek God for the gift of singleness, which is a gift of God to be so taken up with him and so full of Christ's ministry to your heart that you are able to live a fulfilled single life – either permanently or until God calls you into the state of marriage.

Forgive others for their hate, rejection and prejudice

Many people who admit to having homosexual feelings experience hostility and rejection rooted in the fear, ignorance or prejudice of others. Sadly, even some Christians lack compassion and grace, despite the fact that God has dealt with *them* so mercifully in Christ. They judge others harshly instead of pointing them to the love and forgiveness in Christ. They inconsistently expect immediate change in other people's behaviour while they tolerate in their own lives many things that are equally displeasing to God.

If you have been hurt by such people, don't retaliate. Forgive them. We are all broken people on the way to wholeness. Remember, Jesus knows everything about you. He loves you and accepts you totally and unconditionally by his grace. That grace is what changes your heart. We love him because he first loved us. If you fail, he helps you start afresh. When you feel weak and helpless, he is with you to strengthen you. When desires rage within you, he can calm the storm. He will never give up on you, never reject you and never abandon you. Jesus accepts you as you are and although others may reject you, you are always accepted by God in his well-beloved Son. He is your friend that sticks closer than a brother *(Proverbs 18:24)*. Your nearest and dearest may look down on you or even abandon you, but God is will never treat you like that.

Psalm 27:10 — *When my father and my mother forsake me, then the LORD will take care of me.*

Set your heart on Christ and the provisions of his grace

Reject all harmful advice pressuring you to bury your feelings and to conform outwardly to other people's expectations. Resist the temptation to rush into marriage as the 'answer' to your problems, which is the superficial advice and intense pressure some people will put on you. Avoid the teaching that suggests simplistic answers. Often these are legalistic in nature – pray more, fast more, get more deliverance, suppress your thoughts, put on a heterosexual front. If your church tells you to do these things, it is probably a religious, legalistic church. Find another one! Look for a grace church which teaches people to accept others on the basis of who they are in Christ – a church that teaches heart-transformation, not behaviour-modification.

Above all, look to Jesus to meet your needs. Keep focussed on him and let the Holy Spirit direct the desires of your heart. Don't try to change yourself. Focus your attention on Jesus. He is the only source of deep satisfaction and fulfilment. Ultimately, this is the love we are all seeking. As you see yourself in Christ, who seated at the right hand of the Father, full of grace and truth, the desires and attractions of this world will gradually lose their hold over you because you are being transformed in your inner being *(2 Corinthians 3:18)*. The glory and beauty of Christ will become the over-riding passion of your heart.

LIVING FREE! LIFE ISSUES

LIFE ISSUES 3

MARRIAGE AND FAMILY PROBLEMS

The Key to Success in Marriage and the Family

God's love and grace extends to all our relationships. We are blessed and highly favoured in Christ and this favour of God is the key to success in every area of life. Most, if not all, problems in marriage and the family would be solved if we learned to walk in the grace and love of God. Grace makes us more tolerant, more giving and more forgiving. Before you read any further, ask God to fill you once more with the palpable sense of his grace and forgiveness. Humble yourself before your heavenly Father and ask for more grace for you, your marriage and your family.

But he gives more grace. Therefore he says: "God resists the proud, but gives grace to the humble." — James 4:6

Now let's look at some Bible basics on marriage.

Marriage is a covenant of companionship

Marriage is a covenant in which a man and woman pledge to be one another's exclusive companion for life. God's purpose for marriage is that we should develop deep unity within the bonds of marriage because the two are one flesh.

Read *Genesis 2:18-25*.

Marriage is instituted by God

It is not a mere social convention or human arrangement for convenience. God ordained marriage in order to meet the fundamental need of companionship that men and women have.

Read *Proverbs 2:17 and Malachi 2:14*.

Marriage is public not private

Marriage is not some informal, private relationship. It is to be honoured openly and is the bedrock of society. It is for the honourable procreation, nurture and upbringing of children and is the only institution capable of doing so. There is no substitute.

Marriage is exclusive

It is between one man and one woman. Marriage is monogamous and no other relationship, not even the parent-child relationship should take precedence over it.

Marriage is permanent not temporary

Marriage is the pledge that a man and woman make to each other to be together, 'till death us do part.' Jesus said, "That which God has joined together let no one separate."

Marriage is divine sign for humanity

Marriage points beyond itself to our relationship with God. The union between a man and a woman in marriage is a sign of the relationship between Christ and his Church.

Read *Ephesians 5:30-33*.

Having seen all this it is little wonder that Satan wants to dilute, disrupt and destroy God's institution of marriage. It is vitally important that believers know how to build a strong and healthy family life. This means strong marriages and God-honouring relationships in the home.

Dealing with Marriage Problems

The scope of this course is limited but we will touch on three simple issues that can, nevertheless, make a profound impact on our families: the role of the husband, the role of the wife and issues relating to children.

God has given men and women different, yet complimentary roles in marriage. Marriage is a partnership between equals who have different roles. Men and women are equal, but different. The husband is called to be the loving leader and the wife is called to the submissive helper. He is the initiator, and she is the responder. See *Genesis 2:18* and *1 Corinthians 11:11-12*.

Most marriage problems can be solved by breaking the sinful patterns that undermine the relationship and the stability of marriage. These patterns developed as a result of humanity's sin in the Garden of Eden *(Genesis 3:16)*.

The wife usually wants to take the control from the husband and to usurp his authority and position. Often this cannot be through sheer force or physical strength, so she tries through psychological means, such as *manipulation*.

The husband wants to avoid his position of responsibility and so he shirks it by *capitulation* ('I do what you say') or wrongly asserts it by *domination* ('You do what I say').

But the answer is for both the husband and wife to accept God's order and submit to it. Both must accept their God-given roles.

To deal with your marriage problem, begin to fulfil your role as a husband or as a wife.

Read *Ephesians 5:22-33*.

Husbands love your wives

We begin with the husbands: "Husbands, love your wives" When Paul speaks of the role of the wife, he says: "Submit to your husbands." But when he comes to the men, he does not say, 'Husbands take authority over your wives'. The husband's authority is clearly implied. However, the outworking of that authority does not imply authoritarianism, but leading through love. The husband's leadership is all about accepting responsibility, not as a dictatorial overlord but as a loving servant.

Husbands are to love their wives as Christ loved the Church, and he showed his love for the Church by sacrificing himself for it. Christ's bride came first and he sacrificed everything for her. The whole relationship between Christ and the Church is based on the self-sacrificial love of Christ.

Love makes special

Christ's love made us special by setting us apart for a special relationship with him. The one loved is made beautiful and acceptable by the love they receive. This is how husbands are called to love their wives. Husbands are also responsible to provide spiritual care and protection for their wives and to uphold their spiritual welfare. This means taking their place as spiritual leaders in the relationship and at home.

Love brings to fullness

Jesus' love for the Church does not stifle it. Rather, he brings her to fullness. He is growing the Church to maturity, and preparing us as his bride.

So it is to be with husbands. They are called through love to build up their wives to see them come to the fullest expression of who they are in Christ in the home, in their abilities and in their spiritual gifting in the Church.

Love puts others first

Husbands are called to love their wives as their own bodies. Treat your wife as if she were part of you – an extension of your own body, and a part of your very self. This means you must provide for her, care for her, consider her, respect and nurture her.

Just as Christ's love is the key to our being members of his body, so the husband's love is key to developing the deep unity of the one flesh relationship in marriage.

LIFE ISSUES 3   MARRIAGE AND FAMILY PROBLEMS

FOR HUSBANDS – How I can love my wife

Study the previous section and write down the ways in which you are failing to love your wife as Christ loved the church.

Now write down the things you are going to do to show your wife that love.

Wives submit to husbands

Wives are called to submit to their husbands in all things as unto the Lord, because 'the husband is the head of the wife' *(Ephesians 5:23)*. There is a purpose in the divine order. Headship belongs to the husband for a two-fold purpose: responsibility and care.

The work of the wife as a 'submissive helper'

The term 'helper' is not a word implying inferiority. The Holy Spirit is also called a helper. In marriage, the husband is the leader and initiator, and the wife is helper and responder. In this partnership between equals, the husband has final responsibility. He provides the care, nurture, protection and covering for his wife. She functions best and blossoms under this kind of loving protection and leadership.

Summary

As the leader, the husband is called to love his wife sacrificially and serve her so that she becomes all that God wants her to be. The wife is called as the helper to support and encourage her husband so that he becomes all that God intends him to be. Together, they can display Christ's love to the world. That is how they shall together 'have dominion' as God commanded in the beginning.

Genesis 1:26-28

Then God said, "Let Us make man in Our image, according to Our likeness; let them have dominion over the fish of the sea, over the birds of the air, and over the cattle, over all the earth and over every creeping thing that creeps on the earth." So God created man in his own image; in the image of God he created him; male and female he created them. Then God blessed them, and God said to them, "Be fruitful and multiply; fill the earth and subdue it; have dominion over the fish of the sea, over the birds of the air, and over every living thing that moves on the earth."

FOR WIVES – Becoming the helper your husband needs you to be

Write down the things you do that are a hindrance to your husband

Now write down the things that you are now going to start doing that are going to make you the helper he needs you to be

Children and the Family

God has a special love for children and a special responsibility for parents that corresponds to it. The fruit of the womb is blessed by God – that's his special favour for all families, but especially for Christians. Children of Christian parents are the special focus of God's care and protection. They are described as 'holy' or special to the Lord – even if only one parent is a believer:

1 Corinthians 7:14

For the unbelieving husband is sanctified by the wife, and the unbelieving wife is sanctified by the husband; otherwise your children would be unclean, but now they are holy.

Let's look at what the Bible says about the place of children in his purposes.

Children are important in God's order

In Roman times, children had no rights. They did not count. The father had absolute rights over the children. He could punish them at will both with corporal and capital punishment without any interference from the state. The practice of infanticide was commonplace.

What we can easily take for granted is often actually very precious. What we understand as 'childhood' today is a recent and a very precious concept and came to our society through Christian influence.

But, we are in danger of losing childhood completely. Society is increasingly forcing adult lifestyles and outlook onto children. They are being forced to grow up and deal with adult issues earlier and earlier in life.

All this is part of the liberalisation of the family. Increasingly the state, and society in general, is encroaching on the family. Then there is the politicisation of the family. Politicians often speak fine-sounding words but care little and do little to protect childhood and innocence.

Bible facts about children

1. Children are the heritage of the Lord

Genesis 1:28
Psalm 127:3
Deuteronomy 7:13

2. This means children count. They matter. Jesus introduced a revolutionary attitude to children

Matthew 19:13-14
Luke 18:15-17
Matthew 18:1-5

3. Children are on loan from the Lord

Read *Genesis 2:24*

In a real sense, God gives us our children on loan. Although our children will always be our sons and daughters, they will grow into adults with their own responsibilities before God and society as a whole. Failure to recognise this can undermine the lives both of the children and their parents. The marriage relationship is the permanent one. A large proportion of divorces that take place happen when the children leave home because parents have been relating to each other through the children. The parent-child relationship has taken precedence over the husband-wife relationship.

A failure to recognise this damages children. When parents hold on to their children and do not allow them freedom to develop and independence in later life, they forget God's order for family.

4. Children are a sacred trust of the Lord

Children are given by God as a sacred trust. Parents are given a holy charge, a godly responsibility.

The responsibility of parents is to provide their children with:

Dignity
- Your child is an image bearer 'made in the image of God'
- Your child is an individual, not a clone – children vary
- Let them find, discover, become and be themselves.

Discipline
- Create an environment where a child can learn and develop the skills and disciplines of life
- Remember the goal is self-discipline. That is for your child to learn how to make the right choices and maintain them for life.

Destiny

Proverbs 22:6 *Train up a child in the way he should go, and when he is old he will not depart from it.*

- Every child has their own potential and their own destiny to fulfil. They will have their own talents to discover and develop, and their own dreams to fulfil. They are called to live their own lives and not their parents' lives.
- All this takes great care and skill and parental guidance in recognising and nurturing gifts, interests and abilities, and providing the right balance of freedom and intervention.
- Parents are called to excite their children with the possibilities of life on the earth, and beyond that to find God's destiny for their lives.

Development

Parents are called by God to provide for their children's total and balanced development – at every level:

- PHYSICAL – food, clothing, home
- EMOTIONAL – a secure, loving, accepting and affirming environment
- INTELLECTUAL – awaken a sense of wonder and develop intellectual faculty to the full of individual capacity
- MORAL – build an environment that reflects moral consequences
- SOCIAL – develop a sense of society and community
- CULTURAL – help the child develop cultural and aesthetic appreciation of their own and others' cultures
- SPIRITUAL – model the Fatherhood of God.

Returning to God's Order in the Home

Read *Ephesians 6:1-3*.

Acknowledging the God-given role of parents

As a child you began life with little or no personal responsibility. But this changed as your responsibilities began to increase until you reached adulthood when you attained to complete adult responsibility. Parents are called to facilitate their child on this path and to prepare them for adulthood.

Obedience of children is a debt to their parents

It is obviously wrong for you to disobey your parents. They brought you into the world, feed you, clothe you and care for you and in many cases sacrifice themselves and do their best for you.

Even if parents have seriously failed you and perhaps have sinned against you, they are still your parents, and for your own wellbeing God calls you to honour them.

Obedience is '...in the Lord'

This instruction is about Christian living. Paul is talking about creation principles, but also there is an added dimension in godly Christian living.

'Honour your father and your mother'

1. This is how you show your love to the Lord.

2. There is a limit to this obedience. Only God has absolute authority, and parents have no right to command their children to disobey the Lord. It is possible to obey someone without really submitting to their authority, and it is also possible (and sometimes necessary) to submit to authority without obeying it in every detail. For example, where there is conflict between the will of God and the will of parents, children should disagree with their parents but in a respectful manner.

3. There is a difference in God's order between children under their parent's authority when they are young and living at home, and when they grow up and set up their own homes. When children grow up they must accept their full responsibility as adults in society and become responsible for their own decisions. Marriage involves the making of a new home and a new, separate decision-making unit.

Read *Genesis 2:24*.

When children dishonour their parents

Perhaps the most common and the most dangerous way of dishonouring parents is when we harbour angry attitudes towards our parents. Bitterness and resentment against parents can run very deep and have disastrous consequences.

Bitterness comes from unforgiveness.

Luke 6:37-38
Matthew 7:1-2

All parents fail their children in some way and often they fail to come through for their children in highly significant ways that leave them hurt and damaged.

Did your parents fail you in any way?

- Parents playing favourites
- Parents refusing to give unconditional love
- Negative criticisms and comparisons
- Harsh discipline or lack of discipline
- Not being there for you

- Overriding your personality
- Controlling you
- Physical or sexual abuse
- Neglecting you
- Not providing secure family environment
- Not providing a good example in all things
- Having a bad marriage.

All these things can hurt and leave marks deep in the child's personality making it hard for the child to recover. Some carry these hurts for the rest of their lives. But this is unnecessary and is actually a damaging response. God wants you to honour your father and mother and that means letting go of your hurt that they have caused you or you perceive that they have caused you. There is healing from this hurt. It comes from forgiveness.

God says, "Honour your father and mother," which is the first commandment with promise: "that it may be well with you and you may live long on the earth."

Resentment, particularly directed against your parents, works against you. It will trap you into a downward cycle of under-achievement and it will hinder you from rising to your full potential as a person and as a Christian.

Often resentment ties you into the same things that caused the resentment in the first place and you become locked into perpetuating that same behaviour. For example, many abused children become abusers themselves.

Rebellion does not break the cycle. It intensifies it. Rebelling against your parent's authority, their habits or their lifestyle only serves to put you into bondage to those very things. Only the blood of Jesus, the forgiveness of God and the power of the Holy Spirit can break this destructive cycle.

This is an important psychological and a spiritual dynamic. In the Old Testament, rebellion against parents was a capital offence in the nation.

The importance of maintaining good parent-child relationships

1 Peter 1:18-19
Exodus 20:5-6
Exodus 20:12

This danger of dishonouring parents through angry resentment is so apparent that Paul mentions it as one of the main things parents are to avoid provoking in their children *(Ephesians 6:4; Colossians 3:21)*.

For parents:

How may you have contributed to a breakdown in communication and relationship with your child(ren)?

What steps are you going to take to put this right?

For children:

How have you allowed bitterness, anger and unforgiveness to spoil your relationship with your parents?

How have you responded to your parents' faults?

What steps are you going to take to put these things right?

LIFE ISSUES 4

FREEDOM FROM OCCULT BONDAGE

Deliverance means being set free from Satan's power and his bondage in our lives. It is found in the redemption that is in Jesus Christ. He has paid the price to set us free from Satan and all his works.

Sinful humanity has turned away from God and has a fallen nature that is now set on evil. Therefore, we have become a slave of:

- Sin
- Devil and demons
- Ruin
- Affliction

But we are delivered from these things through the power of the cross

For the message of the cross is foolishness to those who are perishing, but to us who are being saved it is the power of God. For it is written: "I will destroy the wisdom of the wise, and bring to nothing the understanding of the prudent." Where is the wise? Where is the scribe? Where is the disputer of this age? Has not God made foolish the wisdom of this world? For since, in the wisdom of God, the world through wisdom did not know God, it pleased God through the foolishness of the message preached to save those who believe. For Jews request a sign, and Greeks seek after wisdom; but we preach Christ crucified, to the Jews a stumbling block and to the Greeks foolishness, but to those who are called, both Jews and Greeks, Christ the power of God and the wisdom of God.

1 Corinthians 1:18-24

The word of the cross delivers us from:

- Sin
  Romans 6:23
  1 Corinthians 1:21

- Demonic curses
  Acts 10:38
  Galatians 3:13
  Matthew 8:16

- Ruin
  Psalm 107:20
  2 Corinthians 8:9

- Affliction
  Isaiah 63:9
  Psalm 107:19

How to get prepared to receive deliverance

- Wanting to be free
- Confessing the victory of Christ over your life
- Faith – standing on God's truth for your life
- Seeking God with all your heart

Jesus preached liberty to the captives, set the downtrodden free, and destroyed the devil's work. He now continues this ministry through his Church, and the Great Commission indicates that this should reach to all nations and continue until the end of time.

We have also recognised that 'deliverance' is a broad concept. Everybody needs deliverance. All people need once-for-all deliverance from sin, guilt and death. All believers need daily deliverance from faults, blunders and temptations. And some people need deliverance from evil spirits. We should emphasise the first two aspects of deliverance ministry, without ignoring or downplaying the third.

Warnings

As part of the ministry of deliverance, we have a responsibility to warn people about those supernatural activities, which claim to be of God, but which are not carried out in his name and power.

The word 'occult' is often used to describe these practices. It comes from the Latin word for 'secret', *occultus*, which also implies something that is forbidden. However, these things are no longer hidden or secretive, so 'occult' is not a totally accurate word today. The practices are supernatural, but they are evil in origin and nature rather than holy, and that is why they are forbidden by God.

The Bible expressly prohibits human involvement with evil supernatural practices and shows that God hates and opposes them[7]. It is important we note that the Scriptures state that any involvement with these practices leads to divine punishment. We see this, for example, in *Exodus 22:18; Leviticus 19:26, 31; Deuteronomy 18:9-12; 32:16-17; 2 Kings 21; 1 Chronicles 10:13; Psalm 106; Acts 16:16-18; 19:18-19; 1 Corinthians 10:20-22; Revelation 9:21; 21:8 & 22:15*.

Evil occultic practices can be divided into three areas

1. False miracles
God's reality is any miracle which is worked in the name of Jesus. An evil miracle is any wonder not worked in the power and authority of his Holy Name. This includes black or white magic (not conjuring tricks or illusions), divination, levitation, acts of strength, astral projection and the many forms of so-called spiritual healing.

2. Lying communication
We communicate through prayer to the Father, in the Spirit, through the Son. The satanic version of this is any attempt at spirit communication – innocent or deliberate which is not genuine prayer to God. This includes ouija, seances, spiritism, spiritualism and so on.

3. Counterfeit knowledge of the future
God's revelation can be found in the Bible and through the gift of prophecy. Demons communicate through evil practices like palmistry, astrology, tarot, mirror mantic, psychometry, divination and the teaching in demonic textbooks.

The Bible gives five reasons why these evil practices are forbidden

1. *Genesis chapter 3* shows that God has placed boundaries on knowledge, and the desire for knowledge not normally available to humanity is the motivating force in many evil practices. As in Eden, the devil traps many in bondage and death through this lust for knowledge.

---

[7] See the Breaking Strongholds list on page 286

2. A desire to dominate and control people, objects, events and the future is normally either the reason for, or the result of, involvement in evil practices. This desire is the opposite of humanity's right nature and is condemned in *Isaiah 47:12-15* and *Ezekiel 13:17-23*.

3. Involvement is dangerous and frequently leads to demonic control and to some element of psychological disintegration or physical destruction. There are many scriptural examples, such as the story of King Saul.

4. It is an attempt to make contact with forces which are at war with God. As we will see later, this is why the Bible teaches that God punishes believers who turn from following him to being involved with any evil practice.

5. God has said, 'No!' Such practices are expressly forbidden in the New Testament – though it must be remembered that they are normally mentioned in association with other sins that God finds equally repugnant. *Galatians 5:19-21*, for example, condemns sorcery (witchcraft) alongside jealousy, bad temper and quarrels. It is wrong to suggest that some sins are more sinful than others, and to infer that people are spiritually safe as long as they avoid practices that are specifically demonic.

Receiving God's thoughts about evil practices is one element of our deliverance, but we also need to be confronted by persuasive and powerful ministry in the Holy Spirit. The following teaching shows how to give and receive that kind of ministry.

Diagnosis

In the Scriptures, the commonest symptoms of demon affliction or 'demonisation', are:

- A permanent loss of self-control
- A temporary loss of control when confronted by Christ
- A severe physical disability.

Any loss of control is demonstrated, for example, by some of these:

- Suicidal tendencies
- Unusual strength
- Violence
- A vocal outburst involving supernatural knowledge
- A complete change in voice.

Although at least one of these signs of demonisation is present in most New Testament examples, we cannot assume they always prove someone is demonised. We depend on the Spirit's insight in every instance. We need him to reveal to us if there really is a demon at work and how we should respond if there is.

In the Bible, most people with severe physical disabilities, mental illness or epilepsy, did not need to have a demon cast out. But some did, and we will only know who needs deliverance by listening to the Holy Spirit, and by testing what we understand him to be suggesting by the Scriptures and the spiritual gift of discernment of spirits.

As servants of Christ and fellow-servants with him, we are called to destroy the works of Satan. This means that we should be ready to receive or minister deliverance whenever God shows us that a demon is present.

Helping someone who is demonised

In many cases, as in the New Testament examples, it is obvious when somebody needs this help, and then there should be no hesitation. We need to ask God only two simple questions. 'Who should be my partner in ministry?' and, 'What exactly, should we say and do?'

At other times, we will need the Spirit's insight – especially when identifying anyone with a severe disability as 'demonised'. In such cases, the Spirit often gives a growing conviction or prophetic 'burden' that deliverance ministry is the appropriate help. This should be shared with the leaders in the local church, and guidance should be sought from God as to when and how such ministry should be given.

Medical help

We should not overlook the fact that a doctor was present at the only detailed example of casting out ministry in Acts, and must recognise that professional medical help benefits many people today.

It is a mistake, however, to think that deliverance ministry is appropriate only for people who remain unhelped after a lengthy programme of medical treatment.

In a modern situation like *Mark 1:21-26*, it would be crazy to ask the man to sit down and wait while we arranged for him to see a psychiatrist. But it would be equally ridiculous not to refer a sufferer to a doctor if they remained unchanged after several sessions of ministry.

The Ministry of Deliverance

The following are simple guidelines to help believers faced with a demon to be cast out.

Do not be fearful

In the face of a violent loss of self-control there will always be some apprehension and distress. We have no need to fear the demon – the promise of *Luke 10:19* is absolute – but the demonic reaction to Christ can be distressing so be prepared. If we are fearful, we should ask Christ to remove our fears and fill us with his self-confidence. Passages like *Psalm 124 and 125* are helpful.

Be well prepared

We should ensure that our total dependence is upon Christ and not on any technique, form of words or pattern of ministry, and that we have no bitterness, broken relationship or sin which has not been dealt with.

You should come for deliverance ministry prepared by prayer, fasting, and in dependence on the Spirit's help. Make sure that you have prayer partners. We need to do everything necessary to prevent interruptions, and to remind ourselves that confession, repentance and receiving God's forgiveness may be all that is needed.

Resist the demon's attempts to manifest

Be ready to resist the devil yourself and to claim God's promises of freedom. Resist the temptation to surrender to any unnecessary responses – such as shouting and extreme or repetitious bodily movements.

Bringing your sins to the light of the cross

Begin by acknowledging and renouncing the sins which the Holy Spirit brings to mind and embrace the power and freedom of God's forgiveness. Remember the blood of Jesus Christ cleanses, and keeps on cleansing you from every sin.

Books, objects or clothes that relate to the demonic practices confessed and forgiven should be destroyed. You must deal with every demonic contact or point of entry into your life.

The Path to Freedom

See the teaching found on page 97.

1. Renounce any contact with evil spirits

2. Forsake your sin and confess your righteousness in Christ

3. Forgive all those who have sinned against you

4. Confess your freedom and liberty in Christ

5. Expel every evil presence in your life

6. Praise and magnify the Lord

7. Seek a fresh infilling of the Holy Spirit

Living Free

>   DELIVERANCE + DISCIPLINE = FREEDOM
>   TRUTH + ANOINTING = FREEDOM
>   REVELATION + ACTION = FREEDOM

Galatians 5:1 shows that freedom is a lifestyle that you must maintain by looking in faith to the Lord, not by trusting in your own efforts.

Freedom is the lifestyle of those who walk with the Lord. It comes as you continually yield yourself to the Lord and live out your new life in Christ, as the following verses show: *Romans 6:13; Romans 12:1-2; Ephesians 4:17-24*.

How to live out your freedom in Christ

You can only effectively do this and follow the principles below as you are in committed relationships of fellowship and accountability within the body of Christ. How can you fight a spirit whose influence has its origin in the rejection of God's order while you are refusing to come under that very order in your home, your marriage, your church or your life in society?

1. PURSUE GOD WITH ALL YOUR HEART
   Psalm 27:4
   Psalm 42:1-2

2. FILL YOUR LIFE WITH PRAYER AND INTERCESSION
   1 Thessalonians 5:17
   Philippians 4:6-7

3. LIVE IN THE WORD OF GOD
   John 8:31

4. WALK IN OBEDIENCE TO THE LORD
   James 1:22

5. DEVELOP A LIFESTYLE OF WORSHIP, PRAISE AND THANKSGIVING
   1 Thessalonians 5:18
   2 Corinthians 6:10
   Ephesians 5:20

6. MAINTAIN GOOD WORKS AND ACTIVE SERVICE
   1 Corinthians 15:58

7. KEEP A GOOD CONSCIENCE BEFORE GOD AND PEOPLE
   1 Timothy 1:19

Your Call to Holiness

Once you have been released from a demonic influence, it is important to fill the 'vacuum' through holiness and Spirit-filled living. You turn away from your sins by turning your eyes back on the Lord. Seek him above all things. Revel in his righteousness. Meditate on the glory and perfection of Christ. And the Holy Spirit will work in your heart drawing you out of your sin and into the holiness you have in Christ.

LIFE ISSUES 5

DEVELOPING A HEALTHY SELF-IMAGE

One of the main reasons for the growing problems of self-image is the breakdown of the family. Far from strong and healthy family units where children growing up can receive affirmation in their identity, worth and value, we now have dysfunctional families, 'non-traditional' families and broken families. The ravages of divorce, marital breakdown and the whole range of social and economic problems in our society have left us wondering who we are and whether we even count at all.

One of the main causes is the 'absentee father syndrome'. The father figure in the home is largely responsible for bestowing the sense of worth and value, providing, according to the plan of God, the unconditional love and acceptance that should be a model of our heavenly Father's love.

Society has tried to compensate for this loss of value, identity and worth by filling the void with all the 'cults of the self'. Society is heavily influenced by humanistic psychology in which the self is worshipped, but to no avail. Still we feel bad about ourselves.

The State has been complicit in the breakdown of the family. Political correctness now makes it almost impossible for people to speak up for the family. Perhaps one of the main reasons why public policy has become so anti-family is that those who shape it are themselves the hurting victims of its breakdown. It is a vicious circle.

It is time to break that cycle and build strong families, which reflect the heart of God. We need a new generation of people who walk in the restoration of the Father, who know how to build strong and healthy families which affirm God's love and help re-build God's image in others.

God's way to a healthy self-image

It is said that we gain our self-image from what we think others think of us. This principle is put like this:

I am not what I think I am, nor am I what you think I am; but I am what I think you think I am.

Now, that is not as complicated as you might imagine. It is obvious that we are influenced by what others think about us. We long to be accepted and judge ourselves to be people of worth or value if people like us, enjoy our company, value our opinion and so on. But what truly forms the image we have of ourselves is our perception of what other people think of us. And all of this happens despite the humorous comment I once heard, "People would pay less attention to what other people thought about them if they knew how seldom they did!"

But there is someone who is thinking about us all the time, and his thoughts are always good. He sees us as people of infinite worth and value. God sent Jesus to pay the highest price imaginable – the precious blood of the Son of God to redeem us. Clearly, he thought we were worth it.

Look at what God thinks about you:

- You are created in the image of God *(Genesis 1:27)*
- You are loved with an everlasting love *(Jeremiah 31:3)*
- You are bought at a price *(1 Corinthians 6:20)*
- You were chosen from before the foundation of the world *(Ephesians 1:4)*
- You are worth redeeming *(Galatians 4:4-6)*
- God thinks so highly of you that he lives in you *(Galatians 2:20)*
- God will never leave you nor forsake you *(Hebrews 13:5)*
- God will not allow anything (including yourself) at any time (past, present or future) to separate you from his love *(Romans 8:38-39)*

If you can only begin to see yourself as God sees you, you will never have to fight a negative self-image again. But why is it that people develop a negative self-image in the first place?

Often this comes through childhood experiences, which affect the person and the formation of their personality as they grow up. These false beliefs become part of our us, shaping how we view ourselves, others and even God himself. We remain in bondage to them until we can experience the pure unconditional love of God in Christ.

The roots of a negative self-image

A poor self-image can develop through:

- Parents linking your sense of worth with your achievement, leading you to believe you are not a person of worth unless you fulfil their expectations
- Harsh, negative and judgemental treatment in the home
- Authority figures telling you that you are no good and that you will never amount to anything
- Physical, emotional and sexual abuse can leave you with a sense of total worthlessness
- Being ridiculed for some physical feature such as being overweight, or having some blemish, or being of a different race or religion
- A sense of guilt through the false belief that you are responsible for the happiness of others, especially key family members
- Being the victim of domination or manipulation which demean the individuality of your personality
- Other forms of neglect or deprivation such as being negatively compared to your siblings or step-siblings
- Religious teaching that focuses on what you have to do for God, rather than what he has done for you.

These experiences can leave you burdened under the many curse-like pronouncements continually being made over your life. These must be broken and the roots of negative self-image must be removed from your heart.

'Worm theology'

This is the mistaken belief that God wants us to feel unworthy in his presence and to rise above our sin and shame is rank arrogance. But this is the opposite of God's will. God lifts up the poor and needy. He heals the broken-hearted and comforts those that mourn. He gives beauty for ashes, the oil of joy for mourning and a garment of praise in exchange for a spirit of heaviness.

God doesn't want you to constantly repeat in his presence, 'I'm so unworthy, I'm so unworthy!' He has taught you a new song, "You are worthy, You are worthy, O Lord!" Remember, your unworthiness has been lost in the infinite ocean of the worthiness of Jesus Christ!

Look at these truths from *Psalm 139* in the NIV:

Go through this Psalm taking in every phrase and word that speaks about the infinite value God places on you:

1. O LORD, you have searched me and you know me.
2. You know when I sit and when I rise; you perceive my thoughts from afar.
3. You discern my going out and my lying down; you are familiar with all my ways.
4. Before a word is on my tongue you know it completely, O LORD.
5. You hem me in – behind and before; you have laid your hand upon me.
6. Such knowledge is too wonderful for me, too lofty for me to attain.
7. Where can I go from your Spirit? Where can I flee from your presence?
8. If I go up to the heavens, you are there; if I make my bed in the depths, you are there.
9. If I rise on the wings of the dawn, if I settle on the far side of the sea,
10. Even there your hand will guide me, your right hand will hold me fast.
11. If I say, "Surely the darkness will hide me and the light become night around me,"
12. Even the darkness will not be dark to you; the night will shine like the day, for darkness is as light to you.
13. For you created my inmost being; you knit me together in my mother's womb.
14. I praise you because I am fearfully and wonderfully made; your works are wonderful, I know that full well.
15. My frame was not hidden from you when I was made in the secret place. When I was woven together in the depths of the earth,
16. Your eyes saw my unformed body. All the days ordained for me were written in your book before one of them came to be.
17. How precious to me are your thoughts, O God! How vast is the sum of them!
18. Were I to count them, they would outnumber the grains of sand. When I awake, I am still with you.

Look at some of these powerful truths:

- God knows you through and through – and loves you as you are
- He is always with you guiding you and keeping you safe and close to him

- He created your inmost being, that is, the person who is you, uniquely and authentically you, that person is the person God created you to be
- God is always thinking wonderful, precious thoughts about you!

Make a list of the people, situations and words which have had a negative influence over you in your past:

Now forgive from your heart all those who have sinned against you in word and actions:

"Father I forgive, wholeheartedly, totally and unreservedly, every person who sinned against me in this way (name them all here). Father, I ask you to bless them as I release them to you now."

Then pray a prayer revoking the negative words spoken against you:

"Father, I revoke every negative word spoken against me and release myself from every negative action done against me. I declare that I am now free from every effect of these things in the name of Jesus. And Father, I ask you to release me now from anything that I have said, thought or done to that is negative or harmful against those who hurt me."

Having done this you will probably feel great relief, but remember you must still learn to put off the negative thoughts and words you have been repeating to yourself and others which reflect your negative self-image.

And you must also learn new ways of seeing yourself so that you reflect accurately how God thinks and feels about you.

Make a list of Bible verses that speak to you about who you are in Christ and how God sees you. Learn these verses by heart and repeat them often, reminding yourself who you really are.

Make a list of the things you constantly find yourself saying or thinking that are negative or unworthy of who God has made you and how he loves you. Then write out what you will learn to say and to think in place of these negative things.

The negative things I will stop thinking and saying about myself:

The positive things I now believe to be true of me and which counter the negative things on my previous list:

LIVING FREE! LIFE ISSUES

LIFE ISSUES 6
....

FORGIVENESS AND INNER HEALING

This topic is covered fully on pages 67 to 81. Please refer to that material as you approach these issues. Here we look at two issues that are related to inner healing: rejection and judgementalism.

REJECTION

God created us as relational beings. We need relationship with both God and fellow human beings and the fullness this brings in order to function as human beings according to God's plan.

Our family relationships are the most important ones that God has given us. But where there is a breakdown of relationships in the family there can be serious problems of emotional pain and rejection.

The hurt coming from rejection is one of the most painful of all negative human experiences. The pain of rejection by a parent, or a spouse, a sibling, or by any other significant person can be so intense that it can seriously affect a person's functioning throughout the course of their lives.

Rejection can lead to:

- Fear
- Shame
- Anger
- Vengeance

- Judgementalism born out of a sense of injustice
- Negative self-image
- Sense of failure
- Loneliness, isolation and alienation
- Lack of trust
- Negatively comparing yourself to others
- Wounded or grieving spirit
- Inability to give or receive love
- Pattern of broken relationships
- Despair
- Despising others or yourself
- Bitterness
- Resistance (not accepting reality).

Rejection can come from:

- The womb – when a parent rejects the pregnancy, attempts abortion or simply reacts negatively to being pregnant
- Being rejected at birth – this can be caused by the lack of mother-child bonding, absentee father, medical complications resulting in lack of physical contact, giving up of the child for adoption or the parents rejecting the child because it is the 'wrong' sex or has some physical abnormality
- Rejection in early childhood when parents do not bother about their children, communicate badly with each other and their children, do not respect their children, preferring one child above the other(s) or fail to balance discipline with love or fail to provide emotionally or physically for their children
- Physical or sexual abuse
- Divorce – either being rejected by your spouse or the pain caused to children of divorced parents
- Other broken relationships – broken friendships, engagements, immoral affairs.

The healing of rejection

We are not the result of chance or an accident. God has loved us, chosen us for himself and has accepted us in Christ. Jesus Christ also took our rejection on the cross so that we might receive the total acceptance of the Father. Read through these verses and write down what they say to you about your problem with rejection:

LIFE ISSUES 6   FORGIVENESS AND INNER HEALING

Ephesians 1:4-6

Psalm 139:15-16

Ezekiel 16:4-6

Jeremiah 1:5

Job 10:12

Psalm 34:4

Philippians 4:13

1 Corinthians 1:27-29

LIVING FREE! LIFE ISSUES

Malachi 4:6

Malachi 2:15-16

Isaiah 54:4-7

Christ healed us from rejection

According to *Isaiah 53:3*, Jesus was despised and rejected by men. He is the only one capable of understanding all circumstances in our lives. He was betrayed by one of his disciples and another one denied him. His own people asked their governors to crucify him. They mocked him and God abandoned him for a moment.

But Jesus did all of this for us. He was rejected that we might be accepted. When he cried out on the cross, "My God, My God, why have you forsaken me?" it was because at that moment he was carrying your rejection on the cross. Because Jesus Christ received our punishment, we do not have to be punished now.

The greatest pain of rejection is the pain of being rejected by God, and the greatest healing from rejection is the healing that comes from being totally, unconditionally and eternally accepted by God.

PRAYER FOR HEALING FROM REJECTION

"Father, I bring my rejection to you now. I forgive all those who have rejected me. I ask you to take away my rejection now and forever. I thank you that I am accepted fully and forever by you through the cross of Jesus Christ. I am not abandoned, rejected or forsaken. Rather, I am accepted in the well-beloved Son of God! Amen."

LIFE ISSUES 6   FORGIVENESS AND INNER HEALING

Now, begin to write down the changes in the patterns of your thoughts, intentions and actions you must begin to develop in your life:

Thoughts, intentions and actions based of rejection I must put off:

Thoughts, intentions and actions based on acceptance I must put on:

Judgementalism

Judgementalism has its source in bitterness

See *Matthew 7:1-2* & *Luke 6:37-38*. Jesus said, "Do not judge lest you be judged... the measure you use on others will be used on you."

What is judgementalism?

- Negative or critical judgements made against others
- Self-righteous judging
- Unmerciful attitudes
- Biased or prejudiced attitudes
- Judgements made without all the facts
- Judgements made behind the person's back
- Judgement according to human standards
- Judgements made about people's motives
- Judgements given as if our opinion was the final one
- Judgements made without deferring to God, the Judge.

The consequences of judgementalism

Judgementalism brings many negative and harmful consequences. Every negative judgement you make against others rebounds back on you. You become trapped by the negative judgments you made against others.

Proverbs 26:27

Whoever digs a pit will fall into it, and he who rolls a stone will have it roll back on him.

Psalm 109:17-19

As he loved cursing, so let it come to him; as he did not delight in blessing, so let it be far from him. As he clothed himself with cursing as with his garment, so let it enter his body like water, and like oil into his bones. Let it be to him like the garment which covers him, and for a belt with which he girds himself continually.

1. Inner vows or 'bitter root judgements.'

Harsh and negative judgements become inner curse-like vows, or open pronouncements against others.

- 'I will never trust you again.' This can lead to fear, isolation and emotional closedness.
- 'I will never love you again.' This can lead to impotency, frigidity, sterility, infertility and miscarriage.

- 'I will never forgive you for what you have done to me.' This is a curse of condemnation.

These pronouncements set a powerful process in motion which causes much damage physically, emotionally and spiritually. The Bible speaks of these bitter roots bringing much defilement.

Pursue peace with all people, and holiness, without which no one will see the Lord: looking diligently lest anyone fall short of the grace of God; lest any root of bitterness springing up cause trouble, and by this many become defiled. — Hebrews 12:14-15

2. Ask God to release you from bitter root judgements as you reject and renounce them in the name of Jesus.

This is an important part of your own healing. It is not enough to forgive people of their offences against you, but you must also renounce and revoke all 'curse-like' pronouncements you have made against anyone else as a result of resentment or bitterness that springs from the hurt they have caused you.

Write down the name of the person and what they did against you.

Describe your feelings connected with the situation of hurt.

Describe your reaction. What did you do?

Write down any curse-like pronouncement, or attitude you have against the person.

Now turn to the Father for healing from your inner pain as you forgive the person who has hurt you. Revoke any bitter-root judgments you have made and pray a prayer of blessing over the one who has sinned against you.

PRAYER FOR INNER HEALING

"Father, thank you that you are the God of all healing and comfort. I acknowledge that I have been hurt by (name the person and/or the specific circumstances involved). I ask you to come and heal me of this inner pain. Bring the comfort and deliverance of the Holy Spirit, in Jesus' name. Amen."

"Father, I now forgive _____ for his/her part in this pain. I release him/her from any resentment, any bitter attitudes, thoughts and judgments I have made against him/her. I revoke any curses that I have spoken, either verbally or in my heart, against (name and verbally renounce curses or bitter judgments) I now ask you Father, to bless and prosper _____ in everything that he/she does.

Forgive me for my bitterness that I have sinfully held against her/him. Cleanse me from this defilement; heal me from its effects on me physically, mentally, emotionally, and spiritually; deliver me from every bondage that has come through my bitterness, in Jesus' name. Amen."

LIFE ISSUES 6   FORGIVENESS AND INNER HEALING

INNER HEALING DECLARATION

"Dear Lord, I thank you for healing me from all my hurt and pain, and for giving me the grace to forgive all those who have sinned against me. I now declare that I have been healed from every negative effect of what has happened to me. I am being made whole by the power of the Holy Spirit, and by the Father's love, in the name of Jesus. I am free now to prosper and flourish as a human being, spirit, soul and body. I am free to learn new patterns of thinking, feeling and behaving. I renounce the notion of being a victim because I am more than a conqueror through Jesus Christ my Lord. Amen!"

Now begin the write down the changes in the patterns of your thoughts, intentions and actions you must begin to develop in your life:

Thoughts, intentions and actions based of bitter root judgements I must put off:

Thoughts, intentions and actions based on forgiveness and blessing I must put on:

LIFE ISSUES 7

DEALING WITH DRUG AND ALCOHOL PROBLEMS

Therefore if the Son makes you free, you shall be free indeed — John 8:36

Many people in society today struggle with substance abuse, and some situations are more extreme than others. It is not unusual, therefore, to find people coming to Christ today who have this problem.

In this section we seek to explore and identify the problems that surround this important issue. We will be outlining some principles, examples and steps now you're a Christian, that will help you to begin the journey to recovery.

What does the Bible say about abuse?

The Bible condemns drunkenness and alcohol abuse but makes no specific references to other drug abuse, eating disorders, workaholism, or most other addictions that concern us today. Nevertheless, biblical principles such as the following can apply to every problem of addiction or abuse.

DON'T be mastered by anything

Paul mentions food and sex both of which are good in themselves but can be abused. In addition, the apostle warns people who are sexually immoral, greedy, idolaters, drunkards, and in other ways mastered by behaviour that they fail to control.

DON'T expect to come to God through drugs

We come to God only by way of Jesus Christ, and we are to come with clear minds rather than brains that are drugged by addictive substances. Drugs are no pathway to the divine.

DO keep the body pure

The Holy Spirit dwells in the body of each Christian, and for this reason we must do whatever we can to keep our bodies free of pollutants, such as those produced by drugs and alcohol abuse. Every human body was made by God, and the Christian's body belongs to him both because of divine creation and because of divine redemption. Scripture and common sense tell us, therefore, that we should take care of ourselves so that we can glorify God with our bodies.

DO practice temperance, self-discipline, and self-control

The fruit of the Spirit is 'self-control'. All believers are expected to say, 'No' to ungodliness and worldly passions, 'and to live self-controlled, upright, and godly lives.' Self-indulgence and selfish ambition are condemned. Gluttony however might involve addiction to eating, greed might involve addiction to possessions and material things, and lust could lead to sexual addiction, which we are all warned against and are also to be rejected by all those living under the grace of God.

DO be filled with the Spirit

Ephesians 5:18 instructs us to avoid drunkenness and be filled instead with the Holy Spirit. A life controlled by the Spirit is presented in the Bible as superior to any alternative, including a life filled with chemical or other substances.

Why do people use drugs & alcohol?

In everyday language, the term 'drug' is most often used to describe those substances that are defined as illegal in the UK. The users of such substances are often described in very negative and stereotypical terms such as 'junkie', 'alkie,' or 'addict'. However, the reality is that all sorts of people use drugs for all sorts of reasons: to cope with life, to relax, to forget problems, to give them a 'high', because of peer pressure, or to try a new experience. And it is also important to remember that not all people who try drugs become dependent on them.

It is important to remember why a person feels the need to use drugs or alcohol. There are in fact two kinds of dependence: physical and psychological. Physical dependence means the body has become dependent on the drug and therefore 'needs' it in order to function and to avoid unpleasant withdrawal symptoms. Psychological dependence indicates that the user 'needs' the drug for the stimulation, pleasure or escape from reality it provides.

These dependencies often stem from a lack of spiritual identity and the spiritual conflicts that lie deep within the person, such as wrong self-image, unforgiveness, guilt and physical as well as psychological abuse from an early stage of life.

Regardless of why you chose to drink or take drugs, each person with an addiction has at least two of the following three conditions.

- First, your basic needs are not being met in legitimate ways
- Second, you have not learned how to cope with life's problems
- Third, you can't seem to resolve your personal or spiritual conflicts in responsible ways.

The chemicals you become addicted to will not meet your needs. Neither will they enable you to cope or resolve your conflicts. Your addictions only make matters worse. Nobody plans to become addicted. Nobody likes being addicted. And everyone is sure it will never happen to them. So how does it happen?

Identifying the cycles of addiction

You are mentally, emotionally and relationally at the 'baseline experience' when you first begin to use drugs or alcohol. Most 'party people' probably have a pretty good baseline experience. They are merely looking for a good time, and want to join in the celebration. The first drink, puff or snort causes an immediate onset of chemical reaction in your body. You feel a certain rush. Alcohol and drugs don't step on the accelerator, they release the brake. Inhibitions are overcome, and feelings of euphoria flood the mind. Getting high can be momentarily fun.

The baseline experience is different for those who are searching for a temporary reprieve from the pressures of life. They are usually a bundle of nerves or depressed about their circumstances and are looking for a high to lift their spirit or calm their nerves. Melancholic people just want to drown their sorrows. Drinking helps you mellow out. It works! Within a matter of minutes you feel better. The same is true for those of who want to stop the pain. They can't wait for the rush to take effect, to make them feel better.

When you are on a high, you feel like the king of the castle. You are filled with grandiose ideas, and can even become aggressive in your behaviour. But when the pattern of abuse sets in you begin to experience memory blackouts, and you repeatedly fail when you try to regain control of your life. You think: 'How did I get home last night?' 'What happened? I better get a grip on myself, I'm starting to lose control!'

How can you know when you are addicted?

Do you lose time from work due to drinking?	Yes / No
Is usage making your home life unhappy?	Yes / No
Do you use because you are shy with other people?	Yes / No
Is it affecting your reputation?	Yes / No
Have you ever felt remorse afterwards?	Yes / No
Have you gotten into financial difficulties because of it?	Yes / No
Do you seek out an inferior environment when drinking or using?	Yes / No
Does it make you careless of your family's welfare?	Yes / No
Has your ambition decreased since?	Yes / No
Do you crave it at a definite time each day?	Yes / No
Do you want to use the next morning?	Yes / No
Do you often use drink or drugs to alter your mood?	Yes / No
Do drugs or drink cause you to have difficulty in sleeping?	Yes / No

If you have answered yes to any one of the questions, it is a definite warning that you may be on your way. If you have answered yes to any two, you probably are. If you have answered yes to three or more, you are definitely on the addiction path.

Honestly state where you are on this path right now:

1. "Yes, I see the warning signs that I am on the way to addiction – and I recognise I must do something about it."
2. "Yes, I am on the path to addiction – and I recognise I must do something about it."
3. "Yes, I am definitely addicted – and I recognise I must do something about it."

Choose one of the above options and sign your name and put the date below:

Signed   Date

LIFE ISSUES 7   DEALING WITH DRUG AND ALCOHOL PROBLEMS

How you can find the road to recovery

The first step a person who has a problem with drug or alcohol abuse must take in recovery is to admit he or she has a problem. You must start by speaking the truth. As long as you believe you can hide your addictions, or live with your addictions, you will continue in your addictions.

A widely held belief used to be that you could not be helped until you hit rock bottom. Professional groups now practice something called 'intervention.' This approach requires experienced help, because family members are often too judgmental and condemning, or too busy covering up and pretending, to employ it themselves. This means coming for help and being willing to face your problem God's way. There is hope for your problem. You can change.

The recovery cycle

How do you recover from this cycle of addiction? First, you need to understand that you do not have drug or alcohol problems. You have life problems. Simply getting you to abstain would probably leave you miserable. Your images of yourself are down in the mud. When addictive substances are withheld from you, you no longer have a way to cope. That is why many traditional secular treatment programs have such dismal lasting results.

Second, you don't just have personal problems. You have family and community problems. Your addictions have affected every person who has had any meaningful relationship with you. Relationships need to be restored, and wrongs need to be made right.

This is the point where your pastor or cell leader can help you understand your freedom in Christ and show you how Christ can meet your most critical and personal needs. Jesus is not just some higher power whom we acknowledge while working a program. Programs don't save people, nor can they set people free – only Jesus can do that. Finding a good Christian rehabilitation or counselling centre is recommended if you are an addict, so that these issues of addiction are uprooted and destroyed in your life.

Why do you drink and how did you become chemically addicted?

There are many reasons why people turn to alcohol or drugs, but they fall into one of three general categories.

1. To appease peer pressure

You may have begun to abuse drugs by simply responding to peer pressure. In some settings you may feel intimidated into doing what everyone else is doing. You might ask yourself, 'If I don't want to do it, why am I doing it?' Probably because each of us has a need to be accepted and to have some sense of belonging. Your ability to stand against peer pressure and to resist the temptation and to throw off your inhibitions is dependent on how secure you are and how your basic needs are being met. This is probably the primary reason you may drink or take drugs. You don't want to be the odd one out, or the nerd, or the party pooper! Not many addicts are secure enough in their identities to stand alone.

Does the paragraph above describe you? If so, how?

2. To escape life's pressures
Drugs and alcohol seem to offer an escape from pressures such as:

- "My work is unbearable."
- "Nobody understands me."
- "My boss is an unreasonable jerk."
- "I don't have any money, and my bills are piling up."
- "Maybe I could get my work done if they would just get off my back."

The pressures of life can feel overwhelming. However, running away from them or abdicating your responsibilities will only make your problems worse. Paul said,

Romans 5:3-5

"We also exult in our tribulations, knowing that tribulation brings about perseverance; and perseverance, proven character; and proven character, hope; and hope does not disappoint, because the love of God has been poured out within our hearts through the Holy Spirit who was given to us"

LIFE ISSUES 7   DEALING WITH DRUG AND ALCOHOL PROBLEMS

You need to establish this hope for yourself, because many times you'll find yourself facing choices between dealing with your problems and accepting wrong solutions:

- "My job is hopeless!" Solution? Change jobs!
- "My marriage is hopeless!" Solution? Change spouses!
- "My situation is hopeless!" Solution? Change the situation!

Your hope lies in your proven character, not in changing the circumstances of your life or drowning out the consequences with drugs and alcohol (see Paul's example in *Philippians 4:11-13*). Christ has your best interests at heart. Drug dealers and bartenders could not care less about you. Their businesses are better served if you keep using and drinking.

Does the section above describe you? If so, how?

3. To stop the pain

If you have experienced a bad toothache, you know the only thought in your mind is to stop the pain. The third reason people turn to chemicals and become addicted to prescription or illegal drugs is because their pain is unbearable. Everyone has to live with a certain amount of pain. No pain, no gain! Learning to cope with pain is a critical part of growing up. But some pain seems unbearable, so you turn to drugs or alcohol to stop it.

Does the paragraph above describe you? If so, how?

What about the family?

The primary victims are the family members. The spouse is often the first to be affected, and when they request prayer, it is a cry for help, but the person rarely, if ever, shares the entire family secrets.

Many family members live under the constant threat of abuse, if they don't play along with the abuser. And even if they do, they may still suffer mental, emotional and physical abuse. The shame you bear keeps you locked in silence.

You refuse to lose your last shreds of dignity by blowing the whistle. You fear people will blame you for breaking up the family, and this actually happens in some abuse cases. The biblical mandates of "speaking the truth in love" *(Ephesians 4:15)*, and "walking in the light" *(1 John 1:7)* are abandoned for self-preservation. Instead, the opposite happens — self-destruction.

So what should you do?

Tell your addicted loved one that you will no longer lie or cover up for him or her. Let the person know that you are going to seek help for yourself. Next make an appointment with your pastor/leader. You need moral support and spiritual advice. Find a Christian-based ministry that supports spouses and children of addicts. Seek professional help to schedule an intervention. You must do something constructive for yourself.

A word of caution

Every Christian is co-dependent in a positive sense. We are commanded to love one another, which means we are subject to one another's needs. This is not wrong, it is Christ-like. However, Christ-like love must be tough when the situation calls for it. When others dictate how and when we are to love them, it is wrong. They are controlling us through their problems.

We are not subject to another person's wants or addictions. When we cover up their addictions, their bondage becomes your bondage. The Spirit of God enables us to have self-control. That same Holy Spirit will lead us into all truth, and the truth will set us free. Nobody on planet Earth can keep us from being the person God wants us to be. Both the addict and the co-addict need to find freedom in Christ.

LIFE ISSUES 7   DEALING WITH DRUG AND ALCOHOL PROBLEMS

How to overcome your addiction

Deal with the battlefield of the mind

The major battlefield is the mind. *Proverbs 23:7* says, "As a man thinks within himself, so he is." In other words, you don't do anything without first thinking it. All behaviour is a product of what we choose to think or believe. We can't see what people think. We can only observe what they do. Trying to change behaviour, without changing what we believe and therefore think, will never produce any lasting results.

Four main addictive thoughts:

1. Hopelessness
It doesn't matter what behaviour or addiction enslaves you, if you feel helpless, and believe that your situation is hopeless, you will never change. Your beliefs determine the difference between victory and defeat in your life – whether you accept the lying schemes of Satan or the truth of God. Also, inherent in the stronghold of hopelessness, is the wrong belief that, 'I'm different and my problem is different. Therefore I need a different answer.'

Do you feel hopeless? Identify the thoughts which steal your hope and write down the positive truths which counteract these negative beliefs.

Negative beliefs:

i.

ii.

iii.

iv.

Positive truths:

i.

ii.

iii.

iv.

2. Guilt

No one can experience peace, freedom or joy when consumed with guilt. Satan uses this scheme to rob Christians of their freedom. One of the first major barriers for the alcoholic/addict is the admission of a problem. Most of us fear exposure. We'll go to great lengths to create the impression that we are OK, but we won't ask for help until the great wall of denial is broken.

Do you feel guilty? Identify the thoughts connected with your feelings of guilt and write down the positive truths which counteract these negative beliefs.

Negative beliefs:

i.

ii.

iii.

iv.

Positive truths:

i.

ii.

iii.

iv.

3. Self-help

Inherent in the stronghold of self-help is the wrong belief that I can change myself. It's just another version of 'God helps those who help themselves'. For some strange reason, most people believe that if they can change their behaviour, they will be able to change as a person. This is simply untrue.

Examine your life and honestly describe how you think you can deal with your addiction problem.

What part does Christ play in your desire and plan to change? Is he central? If not, what are you going to do practically to change that?

4. Insecurity

We were created for a relationship with our Creator. Those without friends or comfort and those without meaningful relationships are destitute and poverty-stricken. The largest group of insecure people are people who lack relationships, roots or connections in their life. What is your greatest need? It is to be loved by God and accepted by God.

How will the truth contained in the above paragraph affect you from now on? How will you outwork this revelation in your life?

Dealing with the physical battle

As Christians we believe in the infinite value of every person to God and in the power of God to bring about change in an individual's life. Thus many drug users have been radically changed through spiritual conversion, and their personal Christian faith can bring about a new purpose for life as an overcomer.

Becoming a Christian does not guarantee immunity from problems or danger. However it does provide a means of coping with the stresses and problems of life without the need to resort to mood-altering drugs.

Romans 6:12 — *Therefore do not let sin reign in your mortal body so that you obey its evil desires.*

We can fully trust him to be our life, the only infallible resource who will meet all our needs.

But we also need to understand that a physical dependence on drugs and alcohol means a detoxification process will be necessary. This will mean spending some time in a medically-supervised environment, followed by a process of recovery in a similar structured environment such as a rehabilitation centre.

Once detoxification is complete, the work on the psychological aspects of dependence can begin.

And throughout this whole process the goal is to transfer your dependence on drugs and alcohol to an 'addiction' to the Spirit-filled life in Jesus. Then, you become dependent on him and submit to his loving and life-giving control.

Read *Ephesians 5:18* and describe what this means for you practically in your life as you deal with the issue of drug or alcohol abuse.

A word to leaders

Many leaders will come across the problem of drug and alcohol dependency in their cells and in their work of evangelism. What can leaders do to help?

1. The leader can help by listening and treating the person with dignity and in finding out which local services can be of assistance. Often the situation is complex with legal issues, housing and benefits which need to be sorted out.

2. Christian counselling can help and much support can be given by the cell if the person is determined to be drug free, especially on hard days.

3. The cell group can help with practical care during the initial withdrawal period. In the case of people withdrawing from tranquillisers friendship and a listening ear by sympathetic members is of great help.

4. Confidentiality is of importance, the person may not wish their drug habit to be common knowledge to all the members of your cell. Always keep your primary leader informed of any advice you give to the person seeking help.

5. Leaders need to know how to identify drug and alcohol problems in their members. The following are some signs that could lead to further questions to determine if there is a problem:

- Social/business life centred on substance
- Unexplained financial problems
- Unexplained and frequent mood swings
- Loss of family/social priorities
- Family rows and tension
- Stomach trouble, headaches
- Establishment of patterns or cycles of negative behaviour
- Aggression, depression and loss of motivation
- Withdrawal from social life or fellowship of the cell
- Criminal activity.

Where to find further help and support

We would recommend you always start with your cell leader or church pastor who may refer you an organisation such as listed below for further help.

Alcohol Advice

Alcoholics Anonymous
London Tel: 020 7833 0022
National Tel: 0845 769 7555

Alcohol Concern
Tel: 020 7928 7377

Drug Advice

City Road Crisis Intervention
A 24-hour crack cocaine and Opiates helpline
Tel: 020 7278 8671/2

The Arbour
16 The Chase, Clapham
London SW4 0NH
Tel: 020 7498 2423

National Drugs Helpline
Tel: 0800 77 66 00

Young People

Childline
24hr help for children and young people in trouble or danger.
Tel: 0800 1111

Life For The World Trust
Wakefield Building
Gomm Road, High Wycombe
HP13 7DJ
01494 462 008

Drinkline
Tel: 0800 917 82 82

Teen Challenge UK
52 Penygroes Road
Gorslas, Llanelli, SA14 7LA
01269 842718

Drug Scope
Tel: 020 7928 1211

Victory Outreach UK
High Street,
Abertillery, Gwent, NP13 1DD
Tel: 0845 409 2449
Email: office@vouk.org.uk

LIFE ISSUES 8
....

FINANCIAL PROBLEMS

Jesus spoke more about money than any other subject except the kingdom of God. This shows how important finance is in our lives. Submitting your financial life to the principles of God's word and allowing the Holy Spirit to direct you in this area is perhaps one of the most important aspects of life and living.

God's attitude towards finance

Finance is one of the many resources with which God blesses our lives. God wants us to know that he is the source of all things, including the finance that flows through our lives, and in response, he wants us to continue to look to him as our loving heavenly Father who provides for our needs. The apostle Paul wrote, "But my God shall supply all your needs according to his riches in glory by Christ Jesus" *(Philippians 4:19)*. Earlier in the chapter Paul said, "Be careful for nothing; but in everything by prayer and supplication with thanksgiving let your requests be made to God" *(Philippians 4:6)* and the apostle Peter wrote "cast all your care on him because he cares for you" *(1 Peter 5:7)*.

But God's giving of financial provision does not stop with us. He wants to go beyond meeting just our needs and those of our immediate family and loved ones to meet the needs of everyone. In order for us to partner with him in this, he wants us, in turn, to go beyond the point of our own blessing into the area of meeting the needs of others.

But how do we begin to do this? We must recognise that we are stewards of the financial resources that God entrusts to us and that we must honour God with our finance and not spend it all on ourselves. We honour God with our finance in the giving of tithes and offerings and, as he leads us, in giving to our neighbours, particularly the poor and the needy.

As we humbly give in this way with the right attitude before God and with an ever conscious dependency on him as the source of the very finance with which we are able to give, so we will find that he transforms us more and more into givers. We grow more and more into the image of himself who gave not just everything that we see and enjoy but everything that he had in the giving of his Son Jesus Christ for us.

Exercise
Using a simple scale of 1 to 10 (with 10 as the highest) and taking the three areas mentioned above (the meeting of your own needs, the giving of tithes and offerings, and the giving to the needs of others) make an honest assessment of how much you trust in God to supply finances to you in these three areas is evidenced in your life and write down what practical steps you can begin to take to increase your trust in God's provision for each one.

Trusting God

Rate on a scale of 1-10 how far you are trusting God in the following areas:

Your own needs	1 2 3 4 5 6 7 8 9 10
Giving of tithes and offerings	1 2 3 4 5 6 7 8 9 10
Giving to the needs of others	1 2 3 4 5 6 7 8 9 10

Financial management

Many of us will have been, at some point in our lives, in the position where we seem to have run out of money and do not have enough to make ends meet. We will often be left with such questions as 'How did I get in to this situation?' and, 'How can I prevent it happening to me again?' In short, either we must manage our finances or our finances will begin to manage us!

At the heart of good financial management must be a desire to live within our means. It hardly needs mentioning that we cannot buy what we cannot pay for and we certainly cannot give to others what we first do not have, no matter how genuine our intentions and desires might be.

In practice, good financial management involves planning, forward thinking, honest evaluation, patience and making the right choices. It can be reduced to the following steps:

1. Listing out current monthly income and expenditure – where these fluctuate significantly you might like to take the average in the recent quarter or suitable longer period

2. Making an honest assessment of these and identifying areas where either income could be increased or our expenditure could be reduced, especially where expenditure exceeds or is close to exceeding income

3. Setting realistic goals for future income and expenditure over the next 1-2 years

4. Keeping simple records and personal accounts to see how you are doing against these goals and identifying any areas for concern as early as possible

5. Taking the necessary corrective action to reduce expenditure where necessary

6. Seeking the early advice of a trusted friend or financial advisor where you cannot seem to find the solution to your financial difficulties yourself or where you cannot seem to keep on track and live within your means

7. Avoiding unnecessary debt and payments on credit.

Exercise
From memory, list all of the sources of your income and all of the types of expenditure that you made in the last month and estimate how much you think you received/spent on each. Calculate the 'profit' or 'loss' that you think you made.

FROM YOUR MEMORY:
Period:

Income:

Expenditure:

Balance ('profit' or 'loss'):

Now go through your financial records and repeat the exercise with accurate information and highlight the areas of significant difference.

FROM YOUR RECORDS
Period:

Income:

Expenditure:

Balance ('profit' or 'loss'):

Using a scale of 1 to 10 (with 10 as the best score) grade your awareness of your personal finances and then rank the seven steps listed above in order of the priority with which you need to get to grips with each one in order to bring your personal financial management to where you want it to be.

My awareness of my personal finances (on a scale of 1–10)

1 2 3 4 5 6 7 8 9 10

Steps I must take in order of priority:

1.

2.

3.

4.

5.

6.

Dealing with debt and financial difficulties

Most people would agree that the rising level of personal debt in the UK in recent years is a cause for concern and that it is far better to be debt-free than to be in a position where a large part of your monthly income is being used to repay loans and other debts. Whilst it is clear that some borrowing may be a wise decision (for example to enable you to buy rather than rent your own house or to enable you to launch a sound and well-planned business venture) and other types of borrowing may be classified as necessary in the short term or as a one-off (for example to be able to buy a car or to set up or improve your home) it is also clear that excessive or unnecessary borrowing is one of the largest causes of financial difficulties in peoples' lives.

In managing debt it is perhaps helpful to firstly avoid it where possible, secondly to only allow it to finance essential items or those that will generate value (such as the examples listed above) rather than those purchases that arise out of a 'don't want to save up for it but want to buy now and pay later' attitude and thirdly to seek and accept proper advice from a reputable financial advisor in advance of the decision to borrow (and to follow this up with on-going advice from time to time).

But financial difficulties are not just a result of excessive debt obligations. They can be the result of any number of ill-advised expenditure decisions or missed income opportunities as well as the result of circumstances, often tragic, that are outside the control and beyond the means of the individual involved. While great care and sensitivity must be exercised when approaching the latter, there is often something that can be done about easing the financial strain by addressing what can be done to improve income and expenditure flows.

Exercise
Consider your current financial situation and any financial difficulties that you may have recently encountered (or come close to encountering) in recent years (where you cannot think of any obvious financial difficulties then consider where you should be financially compared to where your are) and describe to what extent these difficulties are the result of:

1. The burden of excessive debt
2. Missed income opportunities
3. Bad expenditure decisions
4. Circumstances outside your control

What practical steps do you need to take to ensure that you never fall in to financial difficulty again as a result of your own actions?

1.   6.

2.   7.

3.   8.

4.   9.

5.   10.

What do you need to do now in order to reasonably protect yourself against circumstances outside your control?

1.	6.
2.	7.
3.	8.
4.	9.
5.	10.

Increasing income and decreasing expenditure

Whilst it might seem more obvious to think of ways of better managing our expenditure, there is often something that can be done to improve our income as well. For example we might be able to secure better employment, take a second job, start a business, obtain grants, claim benefits to which we are entitled or maximise the interest that we earn on money that passes through our bank accounts. Of course, God is able to do much more than this and he might be calling you right now to believe him for an abundant increase in your income in the year to come.

One of the first places to start in reducing expenditure is debt repayment. Consolidating your debts in to one loan that charges the lowest available rate of interest may significantly reduce your monthly cash outlay. If you are paying the standard variable interest rate on your mortgage to your mortgage provider then you could almost certainly save money by moving it to a mortgage that has a discounted rate for the first 2-3 years, especially if:

- Your financial advisor is 'whole of market' (i.e. has access to all mortgages available on the market and is not tied to one or a group of lenders)
- Your financial advisor does not charge you a fee for their services
- There are no penalties for you moving your mortgage.

A person with a mortgage of £100,000 can save £1,000 per annum simply by securing a discount below their existing mortgage rate of 1%. Another way of approaching it is to take a long-term view and try to cut expenditure in the long-run by prepaying your mortgage (paying an additional sum each month over and above the normal amount) which can significantly reduce the length of your mortgage and hence the interest that you will pay overall on the amount borrowed, although this assumes that you have the spare funds to enable you to do this.

Finally, there are lots of ways of reducing the amount we spend on goods and services although we have to balance this with the time and effort of taking the necessary action. The range of opportunities to cut expenditure includes the cutting out of obvious unnecessary items, to buying during sale times, bulk purchasing of certain items, delayed purchasing of items that are premium priced in their early market life, cutting utility bills, cheaper insurance, bargain holidays, buying nearly-new/used, taking advantage of introductory offers, coupons and vouchers normally discarded, even reduction in car roadside assistance! There are lots of sources of information available (such as the website www.moneysavingexpert.com) as well as the advice of a trusted friend or financial advisor.

Exercise

List the ways in which you could practically increase your monthly income and the ways in which you could reduce your monthly expenditure. Try and estimate the percentage change in each that you think you will be able to achieve within 12 months.

Action I could take to *increase* my income:

1.
2.
3.
4.
5.
6.
7.
8.
9.
10.

Estimated percentage increase over next 12 months: _____

Action I could take to *decrease* my expenditure:

1.
2.
3.
4.
5.
6.
7.
8.
9.
10.

Estimated percentage decrease over next 12 months: _____

APPENDIX I

BREAKING STRONGHOLDS OF THE MIND

Have you been struggling with bondages, habits or emotions seeking to control your life? Jesus is more powerful than these strongholds and you have the absolute right, as a child of God, to know that you are set free from them.

The Word of God speaks to us about these strongholds in our lives. They are like prisons that, for some reason in our past, hold us captive and bound. These areas of bondage hold us back and prevent us from moving forward in our lives as disciples of Jesus. Such strongholds of the mind can totally defeat us spiritually.

How do these strongholds develop in us? Consider carefully the following Scripture passage:

For though we walk in the flesh, we do not war according to the flesh. For the weapons of our warfare are not carnal but mighty in God for pulling down strongholds, casting down arguments and every high thing that exalts itself against the knowledge of God, bringing every thought into captivity to the obedience of Christ, and being ready to punish all disobedience when your obedience is fulfilled.

2 Corinthians 10:3-6

Here, the apostle Paul is dealing with the false teaching that had entered the Corinthian church. False teachers were asserting human wisdom and ideas above Christ. Paul corrects this thinking in the very first chapter of his first letter to the church. He directs their attention to the provisions of God grace:

1 Corinthians 1:30-31

But of him you are in Christ Jesus, who became for us wisdom from God - and righteousness and sanctification and redemption - that, as it is written, "He who glories, let him glory in the LORD."

Unfortunately, the Corinthians had been influenced by teaching that drew them away from this simplicity and sufficiency of pure grace and simple faith in Christ. They were being drawn away to 'another gospel', which was not the true gospel of Jesus *(2 Corinthians 11:2-4)*.

Paul says this teaching had built strongholds in the minds of the people. They had been drawn back into the bondage of the devil. Paul wages war on the devil using spiritual weapons to tear down these strongholds of false teaching that exalted itself above the knowledge of God. He calls them back into their liberty in Christ.

They had succumbed to a 'super spirituality', which took them away from the pure grace of Christ. They had begun to believe that their spiritual achievements, their gifts and abilities made them something special. By means of these things, they could attain to a new level of spiritual victory, a higher status of freedom in the Spirit even than Paul himself had attained. The 'super apostles' of the church criticised Paul and despised his ministry. This teaching had set up strongholds of human pride, self-sufficiency and self-promoting spirituality. They thought they were free, but in fact they were in bondage.

Similar ideas are current in today's church. Rather than pointing people to Christ and the victory he has won for us, some teachers hold out a 'superior lifestyle' that promises a false freedom. The teaching goes something like this. "You are saved, but that is not enough. You need something else. You need to do more than just believe and rest in who you are if you are going to be really free."

Instead of leading you back to the cross, they give you endless tasks to perform so that you can get into victory – you have to pray more, fast more, repent more and receive more prayer before you can be free. You have to attain to a high state of spirituality before you can live in victory. Nothing could be further from the truth. We never move on from the blood of Jesus – God always calls us back to the cross and the riches we have in Christ. True freedom comes from knowing the truth that is in Christ. Jesus said that through faith in his word we would know the truth and the truth shall set us free.

John 8:31-32

Then Jesus said to those Jews who believed him, "If you abide in my word, you are my disciples indeed. And you shall know the truth, and the truth shall make you free."

And, the truth is, in Christ you are free, absolutely free. All we have to do is believe the gospel truth, and the strongholds of the mind come tumbling down!

Let's see what happens when we look elsewhere than the cross for freedom. Whenever we look to our own efforts, to 'additional' spiritual experiences, to constant 'ministry sessions', to the touch from some famous, anointed man or woman of God – rather than to Christ alone, we put ourselves back under bondage. In effect, we put ourselves back under the bondage of the law, and we find ourselves trapped once again in the negative patterns of sin and failure.

Sadly, even this does not cause people to turn back to the grace and forgiveness of the cross. They go on seeking victory through the latest gimmick or teaching of those who draw them still further away from the only true and lasting secret of success – to live under the grace and favour they already have in Christ. Read these verses from Ephesians one more time:

Blessed be the God and Father of our Lord Jesus Christ, who has blessed us with every spiritual blessing in the heavenly places in Christ, just as he chose us in him before the foundation of the world, that we should be holy and without blame before him in love, having predestined us to adoption as sons by Jesus Christ to himself, according to the good pleasure of his will, to the praise of the glory of his grace, by which he made us accepted in the Beloved.

Ephesians 1:3-6

Can you see it now? You are *already* blessed with *every* spiritual blessing in heavenly places in Christ. You do not have to do anything to qualify for these things – they are already yours in Christ. In fact, you could never do enough to earn them or to qualify for them in your own strength. Jesus has paid the price and gives you every blessing free – absolutely free! All you have to do is accept the fact that the grace of God has made you accepted and highly-favoured in the Beloved.

Strongholds begin to develop in the mind when you move from this position. When you stop seeing yourself as complete in Christ. When you try to earn your blessings thinking that you must somehow qualify yourself for the blessing of God, Satan moves right in and begins to accuse you. He points out your failures and your sins, telling you that you do not deserve to be blessed. Of course, you could never deserve God's blessing – but that's just the point. Jesus has not blessed us according to what we deserve – he blesses us by grace, he bestows unmerited favour on us.

A major strategy of the devil is to keep you focussed on yourself making sure that you keep on feeling guilty. He tells you that you have to confess your endless list of sins and failures again and again. That is not freedom in Christ!

The Bible says that once you have accepted that you are a sinner and have confessed Christ, the blood of Jesus keeps on cleansing you from every sin. The secret is to become Christ-conscious and not sin-conscious. God never reminds you of your sins or uses them against you. He has forgiven all and has forgotten all.

Whenever God reminds you of what you were, he does so to show you his grace in putting you where you are – seated with Christ in heavenly places!

Ephesians 2:4-7

But God, who is rich in mercy, because of his great love with which he loved us, even when we were dead in trespasses, made us alive together with Christ (by grace you have been saved), and raised us up together, and made us sit together in the heavenly places in Christ Jesus,

When you see that you are free in Christ, and that all your sins are nailed to the cross, the strongholds of sin come crashing down!

Below is a list of strongholds that experience tells us the devil loves to plant in people's minds. Read carefully through the list and tick all that you think apply to you, or you are troubled about. Some of these things may not relate to your cultural experience, so ignore them for the sake of this exercise.

Breaking Strongholds List

- I have a poor relationship with my mother/father. This could be the reason why I find it difficult to believe that God loves me.
- It's hard for me to forgive myself for what I've done in the past.
- I was hurt in the past and I suffered. I find it hard to be free from the anger that I feel inside when I remember these things.
- I find it hard to build relationships. I don't trust people.
- I am prone to depression and sometimes the feeling of self-pity dominates me.
- I have a sin or bad habit that controls me. I try to stop but I haven't succeeded.
- I have problems in my sexual life. I haven't been able to break habits in this area.
- I have a behavioural disorder, for example: eating too much, gambling, exaggerating, oversleeping, smoking, drinking, drugs, and so on.
- Sometimes I feel like the desire for money or material possessions controls me.
- Sometimes I can't control my anger. It seems to boil up inside of me and explodes before I can stop it.
- I have a problem with anxiety. Sometimes I even do not know why I am anxious.
- I have many fears in my life, for example: fear of the dark, of being alone, of illness, death and phobias.

- I have thought of committing suicide.
- It's very difficult to concentrate when praying or reading the Bible. I find myself getting tired too easily.
- In the past I have been involved in certain practices of the occult.
- In the past I have been dedicated to idols.
- I still have objects of idolatry and of the occult in my home.
- My parents dedicated me to false gods.
- My parents and/or grandparents are (or have been) involved in the occult or freemasonry.
- There has been involvement with idolatry by my parents and/or my grandparents
- My parents are divorced.
- There is history of adultery in the life of my mother/my father/one of my grandparents.
- One of my parents, grandparents or great-grandparents has committed a crime.
- There has been prejudice against the Jews in my life or in my family.
- There have been racist attitudes in my life or in my family.
- I have had incisions and tribal markings done to my body.
- I have been named after a local god or idol.
- I often have sex with someone other than my spouse in my dreams.

Traumatic Experiences

At which phase of your life?
- Birth
- Infancy
- Adolescence
- Youth
- Adulthood

In which category?
- Death of a loved one
- Sexual abuse
- Divorce
- Severe physical shock
- Traumatic accident
- Excessive punishment
- Injustice
- Parents rejected pregnancy
- My parent tried to abort me
- Traumatic birth
- Birth complication
- My parents wanted a child of the opposite sex

Attitudes and Feelings
- Abandonment
- Accusation
- Affliction
- Aggressiveness
- Bitterness
- Anxiety
- Self-pity
- Denial
- Self-rejection
- Jealousy
- Envy
- Competition
- Confusion
- Control
- Guilt
- Depression
- Defeat
- Bewilderment
- Desire to kill
- Desire to die
- Disobedience
- Destruction
- Lack of confidence
- Selfishness
- Infirmity
- Mental infirmity
- Phobias
- Obstinacy
- Fatigue
- Irresponsibility
- Frustration
- Ambition
- Greed
- Hyperactivity
- Mental idolatry
- Religious superstitions
- Negative thoughts
- Fascination with the demonic
- Impatience
- Human-based thinking
- Indecisiveness
- Indifference
- Inferiority
- Insecurity
- Insomnia
- Intellectualism
- Irritation
- Mental health problems
- Cursing
- Fear
- Fear of death
- Nervousness
- Hatred
- Oppression
- Pride
- Passiveness
- Persecution
- Worry
- Rejection
- Religiousness
- Hypersensitivity
- Loneliness
- Superstitions
- Sleepiness
- Sadness
- Vengeance
- Violence
- Own will
- Others

Destructive Habits
- Alcohol abuse
- Drugs
- Drunkenness
- Smoking
- Gluttony
- Gambling
- Lottery
- Bad temper
- Lies
- Swearing
- Not tithing
- Stealing
- Tendency to criticise
- Eating disorders
- Self-mutilation

False Philosophical Beliefs
- 'Christian' cults
- Liberalism
- Religious formalism
- Materialism
- Humanism
- New Age
- Non-Christian philosophy
- Non-Christian psychology

Sexual Areas
- Abortion
- Perversion
- Adultery
- Obsessive fantasies
- Fornication
- Pornography
- Others

False Religious Beliefs
- Atheism
- Buddhism
- Christian Science
- Hare Krishna
- Hinduism
- Islam
- Kardecism
- New Age
- Jehovah Witness
- Lodge or Freemasonry
- Voodoo

- Any type of pact or dedication
- All White Garment Churches, Celestial Church of Christ, Cherubim and Seraphim, Brotherhood of the Cross and Star, Eckankar, Grail Movement & others
- Other cults

The Occult
- Astrology
- Tarot cards
- Consulting mediums
- Palm-reading
- Divination
- Enchantments
- Spirits associated with horror films
- Witchcraft
- Some type of pact or consecration
- Mystical experiences
- Graphology
- Hypnotism
- Faith healing
- Acupuncture
- Other forms of alternative healing involving energy or forces
- Crystals
- Channelling
- Horoscopes
- Video or any other games involving occult characters
- Telepathy
- Reading books about the occult
- Magic
- Transcendental Meditation
- Pendulum
- Satanism
- Spiritualism sessions
- Use or possession of an amulet
- Spiritual marriages to deities and family idols
- Describe any other

Participation in False Religious Festivals
- Attending and participating in African spirit festivals
- Hindu festivals
- Buddhist festivals
- Rituals for the dead
- Satanic rites
- Pagan festivals
- Necromancy
- Others

Supernatural Capacities Developed
- Divination
- Hypnotism
- Ability to stop or move objects
- Levitation
- Vision of spirits
- Magic
- Out of body experiences
- Other

Other Areas
- Are there any ghosts, demons or familiar spirits attached to you or your family?
- Have you been named after a false god, demon, or ancestral spirit?
- Have you ever had any demonic manifestations?
- Have you participated in any blood pact or bloodletting ceremony?
- Are there any curses operating through your family bloodline?
- Are there any traditions relating to non-Christian beliefs or practices in your family?
- Do you have any demonic symbols in your family tradition? (e.g. crests, mottoes etc.)
- Have you ever received or given a false prophecy?
- Have you ever been involved in false doctrine or heresy?

Please write below any other difficulties that have not been mentioned in the previous pages.

What a long list! Did you tick any of the things above? Most people's list is very long! But that just shows us how deceptive the devil is. Because the truth is – Jesus has taken all these things and nailed them to the cross – they no longer have any power over you. Take this list and destroy it – it no longer describes you – that's the old you! The new you is perfectly righteous and complete in Christ!

2 Corinthians 5:17-18

Therefore, if anyone is in Christ, he is a new creation; old things have passed away; behold, all things have become new.

Prayer of Release

"By the power of the blood of Jesus, I reject all the things in the Strongholds list! I am a New Creation and I am completely free in Christ! All arguments that the devil and the world had against my life are broken and cancelled in the name of Jesus! I now take every thought captive to the obedience of Christ."

APPENDIX 2

EMOTIONAL PROBLEMS AND MENTAL HEALTH

In cell life and ministry we have to recognise and accept that some of the challenges people face are very serious ones.

In many situations individuals who come for counselling (and indeed we may recognise this in ourselves) may be suffering from mental health problems and need medical attention. Prayer and scriptural verses alone will not be enough. If they are suffering from acute anxiety or depression, usually they are unable to concentrate sufficiently to read the Bible or pray and they need to be referred to a doctor or hospital.

As cell members, leaders or counsellors, we should not feel we have failed them if we refer people with such needs to medical professionals. We can go on supporting them and praying for them alongside their medical care or treatment.

Some of these challenges, which come up in counselling, could be extreme fear or anxiety, which usually go hand in hand. Fear produces worry and worry and lead to serious anxiety which can also develop into acute depression.

Anxiety

Anxiety is a symptom, a response to a potentially challenging or threatening experience. Even when the threat is not acute or sudden, worry and nervousness can produce anxiety. Anxiety is closely linked to fear which is a primary emotion that helps us deal with danger.

Therefore, not all anxiety is negative. It can sometimes be very positive. Living in our present hectic society some form of anxiety is unavoidable. It is the body's way of telling us to pay attention, especially in dangerous situations, otherwise the consequences could be disastrous. But sometimes, anxiety seems to spiral out of control and it becomes a serious issue which begins to take over a person's life. Desperate feelings of anxiety, which are not related to obvious external circumstances, seem to dominate a person's thoughts. They are filled with a sense of dread and negative foreboding. Severe problems of anxiety like this, which can often be linked to depression, need medical input.

Depression

There are many different forms of depression – from discouragement to severe depression and everything in between.

Life issues often get people down and usually ministry and support will bring the individuals back to a place of trust and confidence in God to bring them through. But a person, who has prolonged sadness with unrelenting symptoms, becomes unable to enjoy life and loses interest in everything. This results in a pervading sense of hopelessness, feelings of dread and a general lack of ability to concentrate or to control thoughts. This is a disabling condition and needs urgent medical help.

People suffering from severe depression will usually have a chemical imbalance in their body, which is why they are prescribed some form of medication. When that is corrected they can enter fully into the counselling process.

For a Christian to accept he/she is depressed can be very difficult. And so they need a lot of encouragement and support to seek medical attention and indeed to take the medication prescribed (if there is a prescription).

In *John 5:2-9*, we read the story of the man by the pool with no one to put him in when the waters were troubled. When Jesus came along he was totally healed. There is emotional healing as well as physical healing in the cross. Healing is available for fear, rejection, poor self-image, past hurts and every other symptom of damaged emotions. When we release forgiveness to the individuals who have hurt us we step into the pool. And that pool is big enough for all of us.

www.ingramcontent.com/pod-product-compliance
Lightning Source LLC
Chambersburg PA
CBHW051253110526
44588CB00026B/2982